WAKING UP,
ALIVE

WAKING UP, ALIVE

ALIVE

The Descent,
The Suicide Attempt,
and the Return to Life

RICHARD A. HECKLER, PH.D.

A GROSSET / PUTNAM BOOK
PUBLISHED BY G. P. PUTNAM'S SONS
NEW YORK

A Grosset/Putnam Book
Published by G. P. Putnam's Sons
Publishers Since 1838
200 Madison Avenue
New York, NY 10016

Library of Congress Cataloging-in-Publication Data

Heckler, Richard A.
Waking up, alive: the descent, the suicide attempt,
and the return to life
Richard A. Heckler
p.   cm.
"A Grosset/Putnam book."
Includes index.
ISBN 0-399-13945-1 (acid-free paper)
1. Suicidal behavior.   2. Suicidal behavior—Case studies.
3. Despair.   4. Hope.   I. Title.
RC569.H43   1994
616.85′844509—dc20   93-50873
CIP

Book design and composition by The Sarabande Press

Printed in the United States of America
1 2 3 4 5 6 7 8 9 10

This book is printed on acid-free paper.

*To all those who have attempted or contemplated suicide,
and to those courageous enough to respond to my inquiries.
I'm sorry I wasn't able to interview all of you.*

and

*To Lucinda Stockdale, my wife, a truly elegant woman,
a gifted therapist, for her quiet confidence in me,
the contribution of her intelligence,
her love, her zany sense of humor, and
her commitment to the truth.*

*When the bond between heaven and earth is broken,
even prayer is not enough; only a story can mend it.*
—BA'AL SHEM TOV

Contents

Preface

The field of psychology was graced in the 1960s with the intellectual innovations of Abraham Maslow. The father of Humanistic Psychology, he helped wrest social and psychological research away from its emphasis on psychopathology as the primary model for understanding people, challenging investigators to study instead the upper limits of human potential: optimal states of well-being. His work not only affected psychotherapists and researchers seeking new ways to understand psychological and spiritual experience, but had a profound effect on many younger students, myself being one.

It is unjust to reduce the work of a lifetime to one concept or theory, and yet Maslow's work profoundly affected my very impressionable intellect because of one iconoclastic proposal. He asked, How can we help people regain their health and happiness unless we truly understand what health and happiness look and feel like? He suggested that we can best encourage psychological healing by studying those who are healthy and are leading extraordinary lives. This would provide a vision and a goal to which all therapeutic methods could aspire.

This book shares this sentiment. In a sense, *Waking Up, Alive* represents the application of wellness research "in the trenches." I have attempted to discover how one recovers from the horrific circumstance of being moments away from dying by one's own hand, and eventually goes on to lead a full and meaningful life. For as I studied the voluminous research concerning suicide—the tremendous carefulness and artfulness of the social and biological analyses; the complex demographics; the pooling of some of the brightest and most committed minds in psychological investigation—I was puzzled. Why was there so much literature about suicide, and virtually nothing written about how people recover from suicide attempts and move on in their lives? Why was so much attention paid to the precursors of suicide, and so little to whether and how it is possible to regain one's balance and lead a life that is rich, satisfying, and, for many, unusually creative? We now have many models to describe why someone attempts suicide, but none for how someone emerges from the attempt and learns to thrive. I felt that such information, in the words of those who have traveled the perilous waters of suicide, is crucial, primarily for those in emotional pain but for researchers as well.

In almost two decades of clinical work and in my career as a teacher and supervisor of students of psychotherapy, I've found that the greatest teachers are the stories themselves. They give life to statistical research and provide criteria of accuracy for theoretical constructs. These stories not only offer entry into the intimate details of individual lives, but serve to mirror the collective. Regardless of the tale, we can always find pieces of ourselves in the stories of others.

For this book, I have made some unusual decisions as regards methodology. What I do as a social scientist is called "participatory research." I attempt to enter another person's world as completely and nonjudgmentally as I can during our time together, not only to "get the story" but to learn intimately about the storyteller. My task is to intuit the intangibles: What made this person's descent into suicide so vexing and painful, and what specific qualities of heart and mind enabled this person to recover so successfully. I have interviewed a small number of people, about fifty, for this study, deciding to spend more time with

each person rather than covering a larger number with shorter interviews. (I also spoke less formally with a much larger group during the
course of this research, and the fifty were a subset of the larger group.)
We have conversed for hours, first in initial interviews and then in
follow-ups. I chose almost exclusively to visit with the people in person,
either meeting them in my office or flying around the country to meet
them in their homes. All of the interviews were rich and moving. We
have cried together, laughed uproariously, and marveled at the myriad
loops and turns a human life can take.

I make no claims of statistical significance here. The merits of this
research must be judged by other criteria. I have endeavored to bring
each person to life on the page, accurately and faithfully. There are no
composite characters in this report, and each incident described has
been set down as it was recounted to me. Only certain names and
places of residence have been changed, at the request of some who were
interviewed. To eliminate the almost irresistible editorializing to which
an author falls prey, I have included portions of the actual tape-
recorded transcripts when describing pivotal events, be they heart-
breaking losses, intimate and disturbing moments of the attempt itself,
or the exhilarating breakthroughs on the road back to life.

Despite my allegiance to accuracy, I do have blind spots, and I most
assuredly have made errors. People's lives are enormously complex and
defy neat categorization. A researcher must accept this fact and then
proceed, respecting the diversity while searching for underlying order. I
apologize for any inaccuracies in detail or story line, and for possibly
missing an important episode in someone's life. I hope that I haven't
caricatured or romanticized those who have been so brave and candid
with me.

One final note about recovery from a suicide attempt. Scarcely a
bookstore in our country carries fewer than twenty or thirty books on
recoveries from various afflictions. Many of the books have been
helpful to both professionals and nonprofessionals. Some books, unfortunately, are overgeneralized and inaccurate, capitalizing on current
popular interest. Attempting suicide is not a disease. It is, however, a

deeply wounding experience, both before and during the act, and it is from those years of pain and turmoil and from the person's belief that suicide was his or her only alternative, that those interviewed here have recovered.

It is not my intention to create another trend or another series of identities through which people can define themselves. In fact, it is my fervent hope that as we move toward the end of this century, people will define themselves in terms of their strengths and their potential rather than their wounds. I have undertaken this work in order to break the silence to which so many—be they survivors of suicide attempts or the enormous number of people who secretly contemplate the act—have been sentenced, and to open communication between those who have attempted and those who haven't. Ultimately, this is a book for everyone, for each person bears his or her share of pain, and everyone has felt stuck at one point or another in his or her life.

I have also chosen to write this book so that we may remember that there often exists a "yes" after what seems to be the final "no." I hope that in some small measure this work may alleviate suffering in the mysterious world in which we live.

RICHARD A. HECKLER, PH.D.

SAN FRANCISCO

Acknowledgments

On a lovely September morning, between helpings of scones and coffee, overlooking the beautiful city of San Francisco, this project had its unlikely birth. It was there I met Loretta Barrett, now my agent and friend. Loretta was visiting the Bay Area to say goodbye to an old friend, who was dying. We talked about the book, and inspired each other with its possibilities, but for the most part, we simply sat together, exchanging bits of wisdom we had been able to assemble over the years; common experiences and insights gleaned through the passing of loved ones. It was a time for two strangers to come together for healing and understanding. Neither one of us realized what a powerful and blessed beginning that would turn out to be. Loretta has steadfastly applied encouragement, vision, and sheer enthusiasm to my work. I am ever indebted to her for the clarity and the strength of her convictions.

There are, in addition, many dear friends and colleagues who proved invaluable in the completion of this book.

Wendy Heckler, always, for teaching me the language of creativity, and Kathryn Fischer, who encouraged me to write the "first word." Evan and Daria, bright stars of the future, who constantly remind me what potential this next generation carries. My almost inexpressible thanks to the Reverend Wayne Muller, who has accompanied me for so many years and through so many stages, for his indefagitable sense of inclusion, his humor, and his lessons about the horse's tail. My deep gratitude goes to Jane Isay, Publisher of Grosset Books, one of the last, great writer's editors, for her guidance in the body of the work. My thanks also to the folks at GSI, Neal and Jim especially, for their attention to the work of the body.

Projects such as these cannot be done without the collective understanding and support of community. My deepest love and thanks to the Hakomi Institute, for its goodwill and flexibility during the writing; and to my students and colleagues in San Francisco who have exercised exceptional forebearance while I've completed this book; Devi Records and Rosa Glenn, for their invaluable generosity in reading and commenting at different stages of the manuscript, and to Ron Kurtz, mentor and friend, for our walks, and our talks about jazz, food, Peter Sellers, and psychotherapy, and for modeling the spirit of intellectual adventure. To Frank Rubenfeld, for supporting a vision of the possible through these many years.

To Doctors Douglas Anderson, Reuben Weininger, David Dansky, and Jason Mixture, for their brotherhood and encouragement, and to Rachel Anderson, for her friendship and guidance in the world of publishing. To Christopher, Joshua, Aaron, Ethan, Sheera, Max, Alex, Meridith and Camille, for the gifts of their innocence. To Doctors Laurel Milberg, Joe Werlinich, and Peg Becker, who years ago taught a cocky but impressionable graduate student how to listen.

To all those who have helped me locate subjects for this book, I am ever grateful; To Doctors Robert Coles, Gail Sheehy, Maggie Scarf, Robert Jay Lifton, among many others, who have inspired my work through their mastery of craft in the marriage of psychology and literature. And to the thousands of gifted therapists and researchers, who have shown me that the study of life and death is a rich and powerful lens through which to view our society and culture in these last years of the twentieth century.

Introduction

Pain and suffering visit us all. No one is exempt. No one has earned a special status that enables him or her to live without heartache or anxiety, sadness or fear. Sometimes these emotions galvanize our spirit and our will, emboldening us to forge ahead, confident of brighter horizons. At other times, adversity falls hard about us, like a long, cold, dark winter's night, oppressive and impenetrable, sending us scurrying for warmth, or light, or someone with whom to wait until morning.

But for some people, morning fails to arrive. There is no place to run, or no one to turn to. For others, help may be available, but they are unable to reach out, let a loved one in, or even identify their pain.

This is a book about suffering and the relief of suffering. It is also a book about courage, inspiration, and resilience. The people interviewed for this book have overcome years of turmoil. They now experience joy, a deep sense of meaning and purpose, and intimate and nourishing relationships. Despite the thousand natural shocks inherent in life, they are happy to be alive. What caused these dramatic and merciful transformations? What qualities of heart and mind are born from such suffering? What strengthens the spirit and alleviates their despair and isolation so that people can feel happiness and love again?

These pages attempt to answer such questions by recounting personal stories of the return from worlds unbelievably desolate and remote, almost beyond imagining. And yet within these stories are elements that are familiar to everyone. For when we try to determine what type of person would attempt to end his or her life, we can identify no single personality profile. People who attempt suicide share their most basic similarity with everyone else on the planet: their humanity.

This book addresses the penetrating hopelessness—the loss of faith—that leads one to suicide. Those who tell their stories here are people whose anguish was so extreme that suicide seemed their only option. Whether lasting for only a weekend or for decades, their journeys toward self-annihilation began with a frightening loss of their feelings of wholeness, order, and connection. Faith dissolved, and their confidence in a gentle and nourishing world was shattered. An inner chaos unraveled the very fabric of their hearts and minds. Envisioning their future, they all arrived at the same conclusion: that death was preferable to their ongoing pain.

But this investigation does not stop there. *Waking Up, Alive* tells of heroic and seemingly improbable recoveries. Listening to the accounts of those who recovered and are now actively engaged in life, intrigued by its mysteries and strengthened by its difficulties, we can clearly identify the stages of how people re-emerge from such adversity. Ultimately, this is a book about the indefagitable spirit: the desire to rebuild one's life and claim one's right to happiness and fulfillment.

The people from whom we'll hear in these chapters cannot be easily categorized. They weren't simply crazy, or sick, or suffering from some rare psychological malady. It is commonly assumed that depression, if severe enough, leads to suicide. This is often untrue. As Edwin Shneidman, Professor Emeritus at the University of California at Los Angeles and the "father" of the field of suicidology in America, wrote:

Depression is not the same as suicide. For one thing, they have enormously different fatality rates. One can live a long, unhappy life with depression, but many people—too many—have died of suicide. Suicide is not a psychiatric disorder. All persons who commit suicide—100 percent of them—are perturbed, but they are not necessarily clinically depressed (or schizophrenic or alcoholic or addicted or psychiatrically ill). (Journal of Nervous and Mental Disease, *Vol.* 181, *No.* 3, 1993)

Most of the people in this book, but not all, suffered from bouts of severe depression. All experienced extreme hopelessness. This combination is devastating in itself, but when accompanied by a particular image of death as a release from unbearable pain, it becomes deadly. These unique human beings, full of talent and intelligence, humor and modesty, are now full of the wisdom that sometimes comes from extremely difficult experience.

The people in this study range in age from sixteen to seventy-four, and live throughout the United States. Some of them are professionals—physicians, psychotherapists, or teachers. Some are artists—writers or painters—and some are clergy. Some are auto mechanics, day-care workers, or political organizers. Among them are people entering higher education for the first time, and some who have recently completed new fields of study. Many of those interviewed are parents, and there are a number of adolescents as well, just beginning their journey into adulthood.

The success of this work ultimately depended on the willingness of the people I interviewed to be candid. Throughout the project, I was consistently astonished at how honest and forthcoming they were. Their contribution was an exceedingly courageous one.

NUMBERS

Every seventeen minutes, someone in the United States kills himself or herself. Nearly every minute, there is a suicide attempt. Suicide is the eighth leading cause of death in the United States and the third leading killer of our nation's adolescents and young adults. Each year, we lose more than 5,000 of our youth through self-inflicted violence, and the rates are climbing. There has been a more than 200 percent rise in youth suicides since the 1950s. Guns are the preferred method of killing 60 percent of the time. There are approximately 5 million living Americans who have attempted suicide, and it is estimated that the number grows each year by 300,000 to 600,000 people.*

As epidemiologists throughout the world scour the statistics for trends, they find a particularly disturbing one on the horizon. As the "baby boom" generation (which has shown a greater tendency toward suicide than other generations) advances into its later years, it is possible that we may witness a virtual epidemic of suicide as people confront the insults and indignities of aging in this country. Whereas fifteen elderly people now commit suicide each day—an appalling figure—that number may more than double by the first decade of the next century.

THE FOCUS OF THIS BOOK

When we examine the lives of people who have attempted suicide, some significant questions arise: How did that pain translate into the wish to die? Could she have acted differently? Could someone have changed the downward course of his life? What was the ultimate cause here? The questions may strike even closer to home: Might I have acted differently? Could I have helped, if I were there? Could that be me one day?

The attempt to take one's life is such an unequivocal expression of raw suffering, regardless of whether or not the attempt is completed, that we are often overwhelmed just beginning to consider it. We find ourselves at a loss as to how to proceed. Feelings of aversion and fear

---

* National Center for Health Statistics [1993], advance report of final mortality statistics, 1991. *NCHS Monthly Vital Statistics Report* 42[2, Supp.].

are common and understandable—not just for family members or close friends, but for highly trained professionals and care-givers as well.

This difficulty also has cultural roots. Western culture emphasizes that which it can understand rationally and control mechanically—that which is quantifiable and concrete. Science makes only furtive and delicate forays into matters of the human heart, unable to apply its tools to problems that are murky and unquantifiable. These are the provinces of spiritual investigation or of philosophical musings, or maybe of the arts. Even the field of psychiatry, as most psychiatrists will readily admit, focuses more comfortably on the pharmacological control of symptoms than on the labyrinthine inner world of pain and suffering.

Given this cultural setting, we can appreciate the difficulties of analyzing the wish to die. It represents an inexplicable assault on the ideals to which our rational and scientific culture aspire: enabling all people to be strong, self-reliant, successful, and happy. And yet, to the degree we place a premium on these attributes, we become reluctant to explore their absence. Almost imperceptibly, we slide away from considering the complexities inherent in human life— the dialogue between happiness and pain, clarity and confusion, light and dark. That which we can readily understand, what we can fit into familiar models, receives our attention and our personal involvement. However, when we avoid human problems that are elusive or complex, irrational or subterranean, we tend to close our hearts. We begin to fashion dichotomies between those who suffer and those who don't, as if suffering were an affliction that strikes an unfortunate minority. We not only become more distanced from aspects of other people's lives that we don't understand, but reject those parts of our own lives as well. Ultimately, we run the risk of creating one-dimensional models of human suffering and attempting simplistic solutions.

Throughout this book, I've attempted to demystify the experience of suicide, revealing its basic elements at the deepest levels possible. Judged from afar, suicidal thoughts, emotions, and actions seem to be characteristic of damaged minds; but a closer look shows that, most often, suicidal fantasies are the result of extreme and unusual human predicaments. As we come still closer to those interviewed here, we can see that for the most part, they have experienced thoughts and feelings, hopes and fears, that are not substantially different from our own.

Waking Up, Alive employs a shift from a diagnostic perspective to a phenomenological one. Rather than endeavoring to diagnose the "sickness" of those who have attempted suicide, this book identifies and describes the bedrock experiences of those who have felt such despair. By examining the most common precursors to suicide we can better understand the amalgam of pressures that lead to such drastic action.

Most importantly for our purposes, rather than ending the investigation with the suicide attempt, we follow the lives of those interviewed through the stages of their recovery, from the first decision to live, through the rewards of clarity, happiness, and fulfillment. *Waking Up, Alive* attests to the belief that the most direct way to address hopelessness is to offer clear portraits of hope, from those who were once a hair's breadth from ending their lives.

The structure of *Waking Up, Alive* follows the chain of events leading to a suicide attempt, and then through the stages of returning to life. Chapter one describes the most common preludes to suicide. Chapter two chronicles the experience of the "descent." Chapter three takes us into the actual moments of the suicide attempt itself, while chapters four through ten describe the return to life and the stages of recovery. Finally, in chapter eleven and in the epilogue we hear from those interviewed one more time, about their lives at present and their reflections on suicide. In each section, I have tried to strike a balance between enabling the reader to hear the person speaking their own words, and highlighting the themes most crucial to an understanding of suicide.

The writing of this book continually involved my "stepping into the shoes" of another's life and imagining how I might have felt if I were in that person's place. Instead of distancing myself from the person I was studying, I chose to move closer. The result is an intimate portrait of that person's life: the pain, the struggle for emancipation, and ultimately, the victories. An investigation into the complex world of suicide demands nothing less.

And with each reader who also steps into the shoes of those in the book, not only reading the stories and commentary but endeavoring to touch the humanity underneath, we begin to bridge the gap between those who have attempted suicide and those who haven't. We come closer to understanding the complexities of the human heart—theirs and ours—and we may even save lives.

1

Vanishing

All his means were a heap of old coins that would no longer pass for currency.

HERMANN HESSE, *KLEIN AND WAGNER*

One

Loss

When I was two years old, my mother jumped off the bridge. (Julia)

My mother and father were always separating and getting back together, then fighting and separating again. When I was still little, my father lived on the street in the "bad" section of town, walking the streets, mostly drunk and destitute. (Catherine)

The experience of overwhelming loss forms the centerpiece in virtually all the personal histories of people who have attempted suicide. "The pain was simply beyond my capacity to contain." "Life lost all reason and purpose." "There seemed to be no reason to go on." At least one of three kinds of loss appears in every story. They are the most common precursors to suicide, and the most ruinous. They include:

- Traumatic loss
- Extreme family dysfunction, and
- Alienation

This chapter illustrates what happens when emotional trauma occurs and help is slow in coming; when either critical moments or many years pass without the availability of understanding or support; or when one becomes unable to find others who can see through one's coping mechanisms to the deeply wounded person inside.

For some, the losses are concrete: the sudden death of a parent, the unexpected or unwanted dissolution of a family or a relationship, or the loss of one's physical health. Also included here are cases of extreme family dysfunction, such as spousal and child abuse. For others the loss may be less identifiable at the time, resulting from, for instance, parental or spousal neglect and the consequent ruin of deeply cherished hopes and dreams. Loss can also be progressive, leading to a chronic sense of alienation and a lack of belonging to the world.

Some people attempt suicide shortly after a traumatic loss; but I have found a much larger proportion of suicide attempts seem to reflect losses incurred in childhood and adolescence. Most often, current suffering is compounded and rendered more complex by previous sorrow. Like a long string of dominoes falling, the cascading sequence of loss becomes frightening and enervating, and eventually leads to an attempt.

TRAUMATIC LOSS

Perhaps no experience is more confounding to the human mind than sudden loss. Something or someone once ever-present is suddenly gone. A parent drives to work and dies in an accident. A spouse collapses on the tennis court with a heart attack. A brother, walking to school, is felled by a bullet. How does one deal with such inscrutable circumstance? Tim's story describes the journey of a healthy and talented adolescent suffering the wounds of traumatic loss.

Tim _____

Tim bounced into my office early one winter morning, lively and enthusiastic. An internationally renowned folk-dancer with bright red hair and penetrating green eyes, he carried himself with artistic flair. Oddly, he struck me both as a serious and intelligent full-grown adult of forty years and as an ingenuous adolescent boy. A hint of sadness and fatigue haunted his eyes, and his mildly freckled face seemed to suggest all the pain and confusion, wonder and awe of his first four decades. On this, our first morning together, it was difficult for me to reconcile my experience of this vibrant man with the image of someone dazed, emotionally and psychologically exhausted, lying in the emergency room of a northern California hospital, both hands limp, bandaged and useless. Tim gestured passionately as he spoke.

> *I had lived a "Leave It to Beaver" life—played sports, really good at everything I did—and suddenly my world fell apart. First, my mother and father divorced. My father was devastated and my brothers and sisters were just stunned and confused. Then, Mother, who was a heavy smoker, was diagnosed with lung cancer. In two years, my mother was back at home, having reconciled with my father and apparently recovered from the cancer. I was sixteen, I had only my learner's permit, and I was responsible for driving her to her follow-up treatment. The clinic was in West Los Angeles. One day, just as I came home from school to pick her up, she had a stroke—right then. She was talking to me in English coherently and then she broke into an incomprehensible gibberish and began taking her clothes off. I called the neighbors. We had an old pink Rambler and the front seat went back. We laid her down. She had this stricken black coloring and looked drawn and exhausted. One moment she was fine, and the next, she was very ill. I drove her to the medical clinic. It was totally beyond my capacity to deal with. I never went back to see her. She died two weeks later, but I died a lot in that moment.*

Multiple losses such as these prove to be almost incomprehensible. When a child or parent, sibling, or spouse is abruptly torn from our lives, the pain can feel so overwhelming that the only way to survive is not to feel. For a child or adolescent, the magnitude of such losses is immense. It is as if there simply isn't enough room inside their as yet small hearts and psyches to comprehend and host such pain. Child therapists and specialists who study the effects of trauma on children have observed that when children encounter a catastrophic situation, beyond their capacity to understand or respond, they shunt the painful experience away from consciousness. This response is a natural and organic one, whose purpose is to suspend the terror, confusion, and pain until such time as the person has grown and matured and is able to face the tragedy.

> *I went through life in a kind of a daze, numb and shut down. Six months later, one morning, my father told us he was going to the hospital for some tests. Nothing serious, just routine. That afternoon, I got a call in school he was critical. He died later that night from an intestinal disorder. After what happened with my mother, I just couldn't bring myself to see him. I never saw him again.*

Tim was just an adolescent when he lost his parents twice, once through the dissolution of their marriage and then through their deaths. The losses were overwhelming. A cohesive family was buffeted by a divorce, fragmented after the mother's sudden death, and then shattered by the demise of his father. Tim was overcome not only by the loss of both parents but by the dizzying pace with which one trauma followed another. The family was in shock, and its remaining members were incapable of providing the necessary understanding and care. That would come only years later. In the interim, an adjustment had to be made in order for Tim to survive. Somewhere deep within, a primitive but self-preserving mechanism aided Tim by allowing him to become numb.

I was devastated by seeing her stroke. It felt like I'd seen death itself, but I had no ability to talk about it. I was just a kid. Everyone was so blown away. With Dad, it was so sudden, I didn't even have the capacity inside to choose to go to the hospital. I felt nothing for a long time. I cried for about fifteen seconds between sixteen and twenty-seven years old.

In Tim's large family, his pain was rendered even more inaccessible by the confusion of the other family members. When I asked him how the rest of the family dealt with such a sudden catastrophe, he answered quickly, almost before I finished the question:

Denial! We just didn't deal with it. My two older brothers, who were twenty-four and twenty-six, pulled away from the family, emotionally and physically. Phil, who is eight years older than me, became a born-again Christian and began to drink heavily. He was very dogmatic and remote. Michelle, who was twenty-two at the time, was consumed by her pain and just seemed lost. She was the least able to care for the three younger ones, but it fell on her. She also became alcoholic, did lots of drugs, and was pretty abusive to us. My twin sister closed down a lot—became conservative, kind of timid and reclusive, and stayed close to home. Donny, my younger brother, was different. He always had a strong nurturing side to him. We stayed pretty close.

During the next ten years, Tim attempted to paste his life back together. After high school, he moved to the redwoods of northern California. He needed to leave the congestion of the Los Angeles basin and the parochial confines of its suburbs, but mostly he needed to sever contacts with a life that had become too bewildering and painful. He became involved with a number of highly political environmental organizations, and devoted his considerable intelligence to protecting endangered land from logging and development. He studied legal precedents and environmental law, and frequently testified in court. He also began to dance, learning hundreds of intricate folk-dances from eastern Europe and the Americas. Tim learned quickly and excelled in everything he did. He was talented, but there was an additional factor firing his desire to excel. Tim was young and he was not yet strong or stable enough to address what lay beneath consciousness. The pain and grief of the uncontrollable, utter dissolution of his family needed to be kept at bay. He did this through a strong desire for achievement and connection. Tim amassed an impressive number of political victories and was voted Man of the Year at the local university. He also became a central member in a number of performing dance troupes. In a very creative way, Tim fashioned his second "family."

In the lives of people who have attempted suicide, there is frequently a holding period when the person is able to suspend dealing with traumatic loss. These coping mechanisms help to create an almost parallel life, free from the weight of the pain. One's personality develops, skills are learned, relationships are formed, and even new families are created, while at the same time the embers of past trauma lie relatively dormant. The human psyche seems able to monitor both the inner and the outer landscapes—both the strength of one's personality and the substantiality of support in the surrounding world. Psychologists are just beginning to understand that the unconscious is able to judge when the time is right to render the past accessible, allowing the grief to surface and be integrated into one's present life, and when it is not. For many who have experienced devastating loss or trauma in childhood, it is as if an inner alarm clock signals the beginning of a new era—an era which starts with the reliving of the original traumatic events and ends in reconciliation and completion. Often, as with Tim, this process begins with a present loss that mirrors a more painful previous one.

Nine years later, a woman with whom I was involved suddenly died of an aneurysm. We had broken up two years before and were

starting to reconnect. Some days later, I went to see a movie, Terms
of Endearment. *In the middle of the movie, as she dies of cancer, I
started feeling overwhelmed by emotion. There's this scene in the
hospital where they're together and the son, the younger son, is
totally alienated from everyone. That's* exactly *how I'd felt since I
was sixteen—alienated and rebellious, out of touch with what I
felt inside, and deeply hurt. Driving home, I cried my eyes out. It
was the beginning of a grief process that I would go through for
some years. It was a long process, full of peaks and some very scary
valleys.*

Tim began the difficult task of uncovering and then mourning
the losses he had buried. Along the way, he experienced withering
pain, survived terrible depressions, and attempted suicide.

*In '86 I was living with my ex-wife and daughter. There was this
major storm in January or February, and Sebastopol was inun-
dated. Napa flooded, and so did the Russian River, and I fell into a
deep depression. I couldn't function. I was terrified of being alone.
I couldn't sleep. Thoughts raced through my head at a thousand
miles per hour, and my mind seemed totally out of my control. I
felt this claustrophobic closing-in and I was sure I was going to
have a heart attack. Inside was a feeling of deep, ripping chaos.*

These were the hardest times. Tim felt consumed by his suffering,
unable to rein in his tormented mind, and fueled by a still unknown
fusion of terror and loss. Although he sought therapy and could
occasionally rise above his pain, relief was brief and hard won. The
labyrinthine process of healing would take time. More than once, Tim
mentioned that if he had known how long it would take or how far he'd
have to go, he might not have been able to summon the strength.

Three more years passed, and Tim would periodically enter these
frightening abysses, absent of clear meaning and flooded with
grotesque images and raw emotion. During the more peaceful

periods in between, he worked in therapy to understand the legacy of his losses, as he continued to build a professional and social life. On any given day, Tim would appear bright and happy, articulate and pleasant to be with. Yet, a darker, more fearful side continued to lurk just below the surface. Tim rarely spoke about it. Except to his therapist, he was unable to communicate either the depth of his pain or his fear of "losing his mind."

> *I never talked to anyone outside my therapist about it in a way that felt meaningful. Clinical words don't convey what it's like from the inside, when you're going through it. "Terror" is a better word. I thought I was never going to survive this depression—that I was gonna be crazy, and that I was gonna be crazy, but aware! totally aware of it—for the rest of my life, forever confined to a hospital. I was assaulted by a hurricane of images which my mind could barely keep up with—faces, buildings, fires, explosions. I was so agitated I couldn't read or focus. I was severely insomniac. [It was] like living in a concentration camp.*

Tim struggled through crippling fear and confusion, and then, inexplicably, some small voice within would offer perspective, compassion, and even encouragement.

> *There'd be no relief for a long time, and then all of a sudden there would be silence—blessed silence. It was as if the silence were saying, "Listen, I know this is kinda strange, but you're gonna be okay." It wouldn't last long, but it gave me a little hope.*

Tim wrestled on. Agitated and exhausted, he was unable either to find peace or to silence the forces within him. For another six months, he fell prey to disorienting bouts of panic. Finally, the suffering built to a pitch that he could no longer contain.

I was falling into the depths of whatever it is—the stuff that Dante
writes about, the Inferno. I was smack-dab in the middle of it and
it felt like there was no "me" left. I had no protection. I was totally
aware of my terror, totally aware of the chaos and this insanity,
and it was too much for me. I couldn't imagine going on.

Traumatic loss exerts a gravitational pull back to its origin. It
demands attention. Through no weakness of character, or deficiency
in intelligence or humanity, Tim felt desperate. Despite his many
talents and his formidable resilience, he was badly weakened. Like a
ship that had sustained too many hits, Tim was slowly sinking.

———————

THE FAMILY SACRIFICE

I wanted her to see me and pay attention to me. She was really so
self-consumed and so gone on the drugs and stuff that she was just
never there. (Teresa)

Traumatic loss represents the most dramatic form of loss which
suicide attempters describe. The event, indelibly etched into the
body and mind, represents the moment when the world ceases to be
a nourishing place. Teresa's story parallels Tim's. Like Tim, she
survived the death of a parent. But long before that wound could
heal, she endured an entirely different class of losses—physical and
sexual abuse, and neglect.

Teresa ——————————————————————————

I used to have to pick my mother up out of bed and try to get her
going so she could go down and work at the restaurant we owned.
Sometimes I'd come home and there would be a note saying she
needed some time for herself. She'd be gone for weeks, to some
resort or some place to recover. So I'd skip school to take care of the

restaurant. I was twelve then. Sometimes she would just go into the
hospital for weeks and I'd come home from school and I couldn't
find her. I learned to go to the hospital and there'd she be.

In personality, Teresa is a study in contrast to Tim. Where he is
outgoing and ebullient, she is quiet and pensive. Tim is a physical
and emotional presence in a room; Teresa takes up little space, is
almost invisible, and speaks softly. A mother of two and a registered
nurse, she chooses her words carefully as she describes the manifold
dips and turns of her childhood and adolescence. She is cautious.
She wants to describe her experiences calmly and accurately. She
shies away from the dramatic.

My biological father died when I was three. He'd apparently been
drinking and hitchhiking, and was hit by a Greyhound bus. My
mother remarried, and a few years later my stepfather had some
sort of psychological breakdown and moved us from our extended
family in Prescott to Idaho, where he attempted to buy a guest lodge.
The deal fell through and we lived at a KOA campground for a year,
until we became the managers there. My stepfather drank a lot, and
began molesting me and beating my younger brothers.

When I finally told my mom what was going on, she divorced him.
Everyone blamed me for breaking up the family. My older brother
ran away. My younger brother got into drugs and was sent back to
our stepfather. My mom became addicted to Valium and tran-
quilizers. I felt responsible and guilty for everything.

Studies show that adolescents who are likely to attempt suicide
often live in families with the following characteristics: They are
chaotic, rigid and inflexible, and prone to conflict. Most often, the
needs and desires of the adolescent are viewed as unimportant and
ancillary. Their still delicate development is considered, if at all, only
after the needs of the remaining family members are taken care of.

At eleven, Teresa became the primary caretaker of the family. She dutifully managed the family restaurant, filling in for her mother, who was usually either drugged, or drunk, or simply missing. She would often work past midnight, preparing for the morning's customers, baking "ninety-nine loaves of bread and a hundred and six pies—I'll always remember the figure!" She'd get up early for school, and come back to wait tables in the afternoon and evening.

Teresa struggled to allay her feelings of guilt and responsibility. She believed it was her job to rescue her floundering family.

> *I was sent to a therapist because I was molested. I remember he asked me how I was dressed, and what I said, and didn't I want my stepfather to do that because I was jealous of my mother? I was stunned. I felt so insignificant. When my stepfather was molesting me and I was lying there, I just decided I wasn't gonna be there; I just went out of my mind and body, and I hated myself for that for years, because I thought I should've hit him, or screamed or something. I kept telling myself that I should have done something on my own to stop being molested, instead of telling. I should have stopped it somehow by myself. Somehow I thought this was my fault, and now he was telling me the same thing!*

The losses a child endures are rendered more ruinous when compounded with parental neglect, exploitation, and professional ignorance. In the absence of someone to provide understanding and comfort through difficult times, Teresa alone attempted to make some sense of what was happening to her. Yet she was still very much a child, and a child's world is bound by limited insight. So she crafted a set of explanations for her troubles in which she was the central protagonist and the one to blame.

> *It was my fault. I shouldn't have told my mother I was being molested. I'm responsible for the family falling apart. That's what I told myself.*

Therapists have discovered that children, in order to rescue some semblance of order from family chaos, decide they are at fault. If there are no adults willing to assume responsibility, children volunteer themselves. Others are more than willing to collude in the distortion. Our desire for a sense of order—for explanation—amidst patently irrational and cruel circumstances is so powerful that children, as well as adults, will create reasonable explanations for unreasonable events.

Unfortunately for Teresa, there were no adults present who could sense the burden she was placing on herself. Instead, she remembers having detailed conversations with her dead father. While walking to and from school, or while working in the family restaurant, she would talk with him to feel some semblance of parental connection. Thus, for Teresa, an intimate association developed between kinship and death.

> I used to fantasize constantly about him. We didn't have pictures of my dad around after my mother remarried. One day I stole this picture of him from my grandmother's house. Everybody was really angry and upset at me for that. I used to talk out loud when no one was around. I remember telling him, "I don't understand why you're not here." It was really painful. I also couldn't understand why he didn't come and save me when my stepfather was hurting me, and I thought that for sure I'd see my dad if I died.

Just as children create magical friends to confide in, Teresa imagined her dead father's ever-available ear. It provided comfort and at least a marginal experience of belonging to a family, especially because her day-to-day world was so bereft of compassionate human exchange. Teresa's relationship with the dead flourished to the degree that the relationships in her everyday life withered. But these fantasies provided only an illusory sense of connection, and the more she entertained the conversations with her father, the further they pulled her from the living.

At fourteen, her losses were sizable, her disappointment great, and she was quickly losing faith that this world held any promise at all. Slowly but progressively, Teresa withdrew from life by entertaining the possibility of her death. She had constructed and nourished a lethal equation: that in death there is solace and connection; in life, there is only despair.

> I knew he would be a much better person to be around—that he'd save me. Maybe if he thought I was gonna die, he'd come back. The day I attempted suicide, I remember sitting at the kitchen window, looking out and thinking, "If nothing else, maybe I'll finally find my dad."

As she grew into adolescence, Teresa's attempts to wrest some attention from her progressively addicted and self-absorbed mother failed, and she found herself more and more alone. She was a serious and unhappy young teenager, trained to be invisible but longing to be seen. Teresa was competent and responsible beyond her years, but inside, she desperately needed her mother's attention and love.

> I didn't know what was wrong when she first became addicted to Valium and tranquilizers. I spent several years taking care of her, and by the time I was fourteen, I had tried everything to get her back to a normal state. I tried acting out. I tried being really bad, or being really good, getting perfect grades or getting terrible grades, staying home, or drinking and going out with boys. I just went to all extremes. I didn't even want to do anything bad: the only times I did was when she was there and I wanted her to "see" me—really pay attention to me. My biggest ploy was to tell her I was pregnant, hoping it would stimulate some sort of reaction. Instead, she vacantly said, "That's okay, honey, we'll just deal with it."

Teresa had not always experienced such despair and hopelessness. In elementary school, intellectually astute and articulate, she would spend hours after school with the teaching nuns, discussing the war in Vietnam, creating projects for the needy in her small community, and engaging in lengthy conversations about world peace. In a predominantly white town, her best friend was a black girl, and she would steadfastly support and protect her from the often cruel remarks of other children. She vividly remembers the excitement she felt one day when her favorite teacher told her, "You are very special. You will do something great in life." These conversations quenched a thirst in her young soul, and formed the delicate foundation of her spiritual life.

> *Although I was very young, I had such purpose, and it was really direct: I was going to help people that were disadvantaged. There was no question in my mind. Then we moved, and everything changed. There was no direction and no purpose anymore. I remember the afternoon that I tried to kill myself, looking out the window thinking, "I'm not doing anything about anything I used to believe was important. Nothing is happening; and there's my mom, illustrating everything I think is wrong, and I've been participating in everything I think is wrong.*

Children who have been abused are particularly critical of themselves as they grow, and Teresa was no exception. And yet this passage reveals another important but hidden dimension of her loss. Throughout the history of humankind, those who have survived danger or hardship have almost without exception been able to draw strength from their spiritual faith. Whether prisoners of conscience, such as Mahatma Gandhi and Martin Luther King, or prisoners in concentration camps, people have survived through their prayers as well as their resolve. Victor Frankl, an eminent psychiatrist and author, was such a survivor. When held prisoner in Auschwitz during World War II, he was the object of negligence at best and unconscionable acts of cruelty at worst. A scientist himself, he began to study the differences between those who were able to

endure and those who succumbed. He discovered that many survivors were miraculously able to generate and nurture some sense of
everyday meaning and purpose, despite privation. They scribbled
poetry on scraps of paper; staged dramatic pieces within the inner
theaters of their minds; confided in their loved ones, both dead and
living; and planned to work for justice and healing after their
internment was over.

For Teresa, the second most significant loss was her loss of
purpose. She had been a passionately idealistic girl; altruism and
fairness formed the foundation of her young spiritual life. She
believed that people could be generous toward one another. Her
faith was strong, and despite family tragedies, such as the sudden
loss of her father, Teresa was still able to adapt and thrive. School,
the church, and relatives offset the confusion that swirled within her
nuclear family, by providing her a sense of belonging, and offering
her inspiration and an image of a meaningful future.

When the family moved, Teresa not only lost the safety net of her
community, but her still embryonic connection to deeply cherished
dreams and aspirations. She wanted to change the world, and as a
child's world begins with immediate family, the first world she
aspired to change was that of her family. This desire, nothing less
than a spiritual quest, kept her going.

But as Teresa's hope for her mother's attention waned, her spiritual vision succumbed to the futility of taking care of the family
business. She began to acknowledge the impossibility of rescuing
her family and, by association, the world at large, and a silent death
took root within her. Her faith collapsed, and she began to turn
seriously toward taking her life.

*I just accepted it finally, you know, instead of trying to change
the effect my stepfather had had on our family and to change
the feelings of guilt I had about it. I was fighting all the time to
change my mom and how she was responding to me, to get my*

brothers back, and to have somebody love me. I remember the only
thing I ever wanted was to be touched, and nobody would touch
me!

Progressively, Teresa grew more distant and unresponsive. She
passed her days in an altered state.

I was a zombie. I felt useless. I couldn't be part of anything. I felt
like I had a black rock in my chest. I became really hard. I couldn't
feel or be felt and I couldn't be touched, you know—nothing could
penetrate. Somewhere inside that rock was a soft spot, but I
couldn't get to it, and no one else could either. It felt that even-
tually that part was going to be dead.

As she felt more desperate for acknowledgment, Teresa's ability to
seek and recognize other sources of emotional nourishment grew
more limited. Her thinking became rigid and polarized—black and
white. She filtered the events in her world almost entirely through a
mind that was fixated upon her lack of belonging, and virtually
every exchange seemed to erode the already tenuous relationship
she felt with the world.

I developed this "good person/bad person" philosophy. People were
either good or bad. I was a "bad person," just because we were the
"bad family" in town. Or I was a "good person," but I still couldn't
be a part of other good people's lives. I remember this one dad who
sat me down and said, "We really think you're a nice girl and we
think you're very smart, and you're a good person, but we can't let
our daughter play with you anymore because your family is—
well, it's just not safe for our daughter." I remember thinking, "It
doesn't matter how good I am; I'm always going to be on the bad
person list and that's that."

Prolonged pain and suffering compromises our ability to think
creatively. They reduce our capacity for problem solving, for enjoy-

ing flexibility of mind, and for negotiating the complexities of intimate relationships. For a person contemplating suicide, a vicious cycle develops. Chronic pain narrows one's perceptions, and healthy options go unnoticed. The world seems circumscribed and toxic, and one begins to withdraw from it. In the absence of help, one's thinking eventually fixates almost entirely on the pain, and withdrawal intensifies. Caught in this deathly spiral, life begins to feel like a succession of insults, one after another, until a breaking point is reached.

> I remember having that feeling, sitting there at the table, thinking, "Now I know what's going on and now I see how my family really is, and if this is how it's going to be, I don't want to be a part of it." In the back of my mind, I was thinking, "Maybe if I kill myself, then it will have an effect on somebody—on anybody." I remember visualizing my stepfather [being] totally remorseful and making it up to my mom and repairing [things] with my brothers. I remember [imagining] one brother being sad [that he had] left. I imagined my mother just straightening up—just smacking into place like in the movies when someone gets slapped across the face and they come to.

These were the fantasies emanating from a spirit that had finally been broken. Despite a desperate desire to save her family and win attention and love, Teresa had to admit this was not going to come about.

ALIENATION

Two people who have sustained significant loss begin their decline toward suicide. Their losses are identifiable ones—the death of parents, sexual and physical abuse—but their afflictions are less concrete: emotional instability, episodes of mental illness, and the inability to communicate the depths of their suffering. Jason's story shares these critical experiences, and then adds another: a profound and chronic sense of alienation.

Alienation plays a double function in suicide. It is a palpable, debilitating experience of not belonging—to one's family, to one's local environment, or to one's culture. Belonging provides one with a context. It provides a feeling that life is meaningful, which in turn gives rise to a sense of one's purpose. These three elements—context, meaning, and purpose—have the power to sustain one's life despite its inevitable confusions. Together, they help people survive and discover meaning in life's adversities. Those who are isolated, however, cannot respond to conflict or disappointment with such flexibility, and do not see their alternatives. Without help, they become more likely to choose the path of their own demise.

Jason

> *James Dean was one of my biggest heroes*—Rebel Without a Cause, The Outsiders, *Indiana Jones, Fonzie. I grew up on Rambo films and* Playboy. *Tough guys were my idols. Smokin' cigarettes, stealing shit, comin' in the next morning all hung over. Living on the streets, sleeping in newspaper bins—these were my battle scars.* (Jason)

Jason is a ward of the state. An angular, handsome, seventeen-year-old—tall and lean, with jet-black hair, one side shaved, and with deep-set, dark eyes—he is an exceptionally intelligent and passionate young man. Only a teenager when I first interviewed him, Jason spoke colorfully, not only about himself but also about the isolation and sense of distrust that so many adolescents in American culture have felt. About to be released in his own recognizance, he is hoping to rejoin his friends near Los Alamos, New Mexico. Jason's father and mother have been forced to relinquish custody, as both have been deemed unfit to care for their son. Since he was twelve, he has often lived on the street. In one way or another, he has perched at the periphery, as an exiled member of his family and an unwanted member of mainstream culture. He is tightly bonded with friends of similar circumstances and, like them, is substantially alienated from everyday society. His is a chronicle of that perimeter life—its romantic and idealized highs, and its devastating and destructive lows.

> *In a way, you have to have suicidal tendencies to push yourself to the edge. You have to go out on the edge to really live and go after the dreams you really want. But you have to have balance. I was pushing the limits, you know. I didn't go to school, didn't have a job, didn't have a house, didn't have a bedtime—no rules. I just wandered around.*

Jason differs from the others interviewed for this book. He is still growing up. Many of those interviewed have had years to reflect on their experiences, but Jason's ideas about himself, his family, and his culture are still forming. His thoughts and feelings are continually updated as he searches for a sense of place. And yet part of the joy of interviewing teenagers is that one is exploring a "work in progress." There is a palpable sense that one's finger rests on the pulse of the future. When interviewing an eloquent and extroverted adolescent, one can feel the freshness of a mind not yet too socialized and of a heart that is in naked pain and yet still idealistic and hopeful. And while these teenagers may not be the final arbiters of reality, their voices represent the voices of the future and need to be heard. Beyond political forces which attempt to spin sanitized portrayals of life in America, when sitting with adolescents, you get the unedited versions.

> *I started realizing how much pain there is in the world, how much loneliness, and although I don't want to kill myself anymore, it still frustrates me how many kids feel like shit.*

We sit in a small meeting room provided by the residential care facility that has periodically been home to Jason for the past two years. As with most adolescents, he is a quixotic blend of child and emerging adult. You can feel the child in him, hoping to be acknowledged and nourished. He still looks to his parents for some sign of caring and concern, but is wrestling with their inability to provide it.

Jason speaks of the profound ethical and spiritual distance between his clan of struggling friends and the rest of American society, and he relates his perceptions with an arresting poignancy. Teenage suicide is once again beginning to rise; and I wanted to hear about it firsthand from a member of the generation precariously poised to inherit our legacy.

It pisses me off how many kids are molested each year. Most every one of my girlfriends has been raped or molested. We get the brunt of it. So many kids get fucked over it seems hopeless sometimes. Even now I still get hopeless and think, "Why go on?"

As I was listening to Jason, I remembered that only minutes before, as we were walking to the meeting room, a host of his friends, teenage boys and girls assembled nearby, were yelling encouragement to him: "Give 'em hell, Jason!" "You tell him what's really happenin'." "Don't you hold nothin' back, boy!" "Tell him the truth for us!" It was a show of tribal solidarity and support, but more deeply, it was a sobering reflection of the lack of opportunities our youth feel to be understood. These kids, white, black, Asian, Native American, and Latino, have been labeled "troubled." Some will need many more years of firm and consistent care before they are ready to embark on their own. And yet as the interview progressed, I wondered whether there wasn't at least some resemblance between Jason's experience and that of most adolescents in America.

I couldn't talk to my parents. They didn't listen, didn't want to, didn't understand; and I didn't know how to say it right. There was just no connection. They seemed to take my feelings as a phase or something, like it was no big deal. My father is still in denial. He says, "I'm here for you as soon as you get your act together." I don't even talk to him anymore, not even out of hatred. I understand where he's at—I'm the "troubled" one—and I'm not gonna subject myself to that anymore, so I just drop it.

Jason's family fell apart when he was four years old. His father moved out of state and rarely saw him again. His mother, herself a survivor of rape and incest as a child, began to recall more of her own traumatic childhood and became less and less functional over the next four years. She would alternately sleep in for days, and then leave town in a confused pursuit of her own healing. It took fourteen years for her to be diagnosed as suffering from manic-depressive illness.

There wasn't much food in the house, and Jason stole what he could to feed his younger brother and sister. By the age of ten, Jason was fitfully depressed.

I didn't know what the word meant— "depressed"—but I remember being angry a lot. I remember crying very easily, like even up to fifth and sixth grade. Now it's the opposite. It takes a lot to get me to cry. Sometimes I feel like crying, but the tears just don't come out anymore.

As he sprouted adolescent wings, Jason spent more time on the streets: skipping school; shoplifting food, cigarettes, or articles of clothing; and drinking. Soon he was experimenting with narcotics and hallucinogens. At twelve, he was arrested for possession and was sent to a group home. His mother refused to allow him to return to her house; and thereafter, for weeks at a time, he spent his days and nights on the street.

My mother's rejection really pissed me off. I was used to her
rejecting me in other ways, but this was pretty big. Later, when
I had actually graduated from the drug program—I did really
well—she still wouldn't let me come home. So after a while, I left
the state and went to live with my father. He's a social worker. We
had continual fights, and often they'd end with him beating me. I
spent all summer draining wine bottles, writing poetry, filling
reams of notebooks, and thinking that someday I might be famous.
I felt so much pain that year—constant headaches, constantly
depressed—I started thinking a lot about suicide. I started seeing
death as peacefulness. All I knew was I wanted to die.

Jason would never have been called an easy child or a docile and
cooperative adolescent. In quieter moments, he acknowledges that
he willfully stirred up some of the trouble that eventually backfired.
He became antagonistic in order to assert what he felt were his
minimal basic rights of self-determination: to express elemental
aspects of his personality, boldly and unfettered; to be seen with
understanding and encouraging eyes; and, when this didn't happen,
to protect the more wounded and vulnerable parts inside. His
defiance and iconoclasm bonded him to friends and offered some
possibility of survival in a world in which he felt an outsider. He
learned that no one would listen when he was quiet, so he grew more
vociferous: adopting a punk and New Wave appearance alarming to
most adults and speaking the truth as he saw it regardless of how raw
and irrespective of whether anyone wanted to hear. He acted provocatively when he was not heard and combatively when he most
wanted to be comforted.

I felt no one would listen to me—no one cared—so I just screamed
even louder—pushed it even further. Since I couldn't talk
to anybody, I had to take care of it all myself. No one was
there except for my friends, who were going through the same
trouble.

Jason survived by being clever, colorful, and resilient. He has endured familial rejection through his ability to find at least a small toehold in a makeshift clan with other adolescents. His appearance, his challenging manner, his ability to speak on behalf of many youths who feel dispossessed and misunderstood, have made him a kind of Pied Piper living at society's fringes. Friends trust him with the intimate details of their lives; and like many born leaders, he has the capacity to elevate their individual pain by giving it meaning in a larger context. Though in considerable turmoil himself, or perhaps because of it, he seemed able to galvanize the spirit of those around him.

> *So I created this group called the "Tribe of the Lonely Minds": people who have all these problems who can connect—this close-knit set of friends. We're like a group of people, naked, sitting around a fire holding hands—a communal circle of people, everyone understanding everyone's pain. We understand what's going on with each other. Maybe we say it, maybe we don't, but we all know what's going on. We'd talk for five or six hours. Through all this talking I started realizing how much pain there is in the world—how much loneliness.*

In June of his fifteenth year, Jason moved to New Mexico. Before that summer was over, he and his father would so antagonize each other that they regularly came to blows. Each was polarized and inflexible, and they flew out of control. In an altercation one smoldering afternoon, Jason hurled obscenities at his father, and the house seemed to explode.

> *He began beating me, and I yelled, "Fuck You!" He grabbed me by the neck and slammed me into the counter in the corner of the kitchen. He wailed into my stomach. I had fist marks all over and lacerations on my chest. I picked up a butcher knife and tried to stab him, but he smashed my hand into the drawer. I felt crazed*

*and began to run barefoot through the desert to a friend's house
two miles away, picking up tons of thorns in my feet.*

Jason and his father had reached a dangerous impasse. Neither
had the vision or skill to become reconciled. Jason fell prey to both
his father's rigidity and the inflexibility of adolescence, and he
became locked in a titanic struggle. He was unable to express the
difficult combination of rage and need that he felt, and his father
was unable to reach beyond the conflict to address the pain and
disappointment each of them carried. It was even more perilous for
Jason. Having been exiled from his mother's home, he found in his
father's company his only remaining family connection. However
minimal the affection between them, however tempestuous their
relationship, their small home provided a modicum of belonging
for a child who already lived on the periphery. This house in the
high desert formed a buffer for Jason between having a home and
itineracy; between belonging somewhere and alienation. As much
as Jason romanticized "life at the edge," like most teenagers, he
wanted to belong, to be a part of a loving family, to be someone's
son. But from that episode, it became clear to Jason that this would
not come to pass. At an age when even a less troubled life can be
confusing, Jason felt defeated and without resources.

As Jason related the intimate details of his family life, I noticed
that I was listening from two perspectives. As a family therapist, I
understood that this disorganized and shattered family had projected its collective pain onto Jason, identifying him as the "problem," the "bad one," the "patient." As torturous as this was for Jason,
it provided him with at least some identity as a family member, and
he played the part more than adequately.

The "identified patient" becomes a lightning rod for family anger
and pain. A family in chaos is battered by an extremely complex
network of forces, both interpersonal and intrapsychic. Often a
family will assign blame to one particular member, if for no other
reason than to remain afloat in the turbulent waters. It seems to

simplify the problem. Unfortunately, it can also lead to simplistic and often painful "solutions."

The "identified patient" is also elected, albeit covertly, to broadcast the family's pain. Through self-destructive behaviors—starting fights, setting fires, stealing, drug use, and promiscuity, among others—he or she acts outrageously enough to be noticed by members of the community. In fortunate instances, clergy or mental health workers become involved early on. Quite often, however, the family's pain is first deposited at the door of the local police precinct or hospital. Jason was both a lightning rod and a flag-waver. His banner broadcast that the family had spun out of control. Beneath this lay another perspective—one beyond blame, beyond finding fault with anyone in particular. In Jason's battered family, it was clear to me that everyone had succumbed to tremendous unresolved torment. Just as Jason was an adolescent alienated from family and from mainstream culture, his family was also isolated, living on the edge of collapse, unable to secure the help needed to survive intact.

I asked Jason, "If there was a neon sign painted on you at that time, what would it say?"

> *Pain. Just pain. To you, to me, to everyone. I looked like I was saying "Fuck you" to everyone, but if you looked at my eyes, you'd see this hurt, lost, sad person. I was like an animal in pain, scared and terrified.*

I imagined that each member of Jason's family might say the same.

————

Jason provides a vivid portrait of an adolescent's experience of alienation. However, this chronic sense of feeling disaffected—out of synch with one's culture—is experienced not only by the young. Suicide rates for middle-aged men and for the elderly remain the highest for any age-related subgroups. Although members of other groups attempt suicide more frequently, none of them so consistently complete the act and die.

Vic

Vic is nearly thirty years older than Jason. Mostly he spends his time alone, as he has done throughout his life. Born with a severe deformity to his right arm, he has struggled through medical complications and innumerable hospitalizations since birth, having numerous surgeries before the age of ten. Although as a child Vic was most often cheerful and strong of will despite his difficulties, he necessarily found himself spending much time alone. He avoided his young schoolmates, who would often be coarse in their remarks; and he would rest in bed, waiting for another operation or recuperating from one. Early in life, he pulled away from the world. He learned to entertain himself and take care of himself. He wanted to relieve the burden he felt he placed on his family. In a slow, southern cadence, Vic recalled how it felt:

> It was bad. It really brought me down. I remember I used to go to school so happy and ready to go and then come home with my chin hittin' the earth. You know, kids can be so cruel when they don't understand something. My parents were goin' through a lot with my medical problems and I didn't want to burden them. They thought I was very happy, everything was peachy. They didn't realize what was going on.

Vic has lived his life outside the mainstream. Quiet and unobtrusive, he more than ably survived, but mostly by himself. He developed two strategies to deal with his difficulties: he distanced himself from others and he remained mute about his pain. No one, including Vic, would realize that in the soil of these early strategies the seeds of alienation were being planted. With the passing years, when Vic felt pressured, lonely, or depressed, he would withdraw further from those he knew, attempting to solve his problems himself and remaining reticent about them.

I decided to depend on myself, I'd put the whole thing, whatever I was feelin', on myself. I was not like everyone else. I was different. I blamed it all on myself, and I expected me to take care of it all.

Vic left South Carolina, where he was raised, and moved to Jacksonville. He knew no one there. It took him almost two years to find work, and as work had often been his only vehicle for inter-personal contact, he grew exceedingly lonely. Weekends were the worst, and he'd try to fill the void with puzzles, solitaire, and novels. For a year and a half, he and a lover lived together. During that time, his silence was temporarily broken and he gratefully let companion-ship into his life. When he and his lover separated, however, the loneliness fell around him again, familiar and complete.

It was always hard for me to make friends, except at work. After she left, it seemed I spent all my time alone. Weekends, nights. In a way, it was nothing different. That's how it had been all my life.

Vic communicated more sparingly, telling neither his family nor anyone else of his creeping depression and collapsing self-esteem. Through the help of a local psychologist, Vic was placed on anti-depressants, and he made weekly visits for individual and group therapy. He found this to be helpful, although the group seemed to unnerve him when people raised their voices and became angry. Eventually, even therapy felt dangerous. His therapist asked him to face his backlog of accumulated suffering in an effort to move through it, and Vic found himself beginning to drown in a sea of unprocessed and long-held grief. There were evenings when he would repeatedly bang his head against the wall, attempting to exchange the emotional torment for a more tangible and familiar physical pain. When his head began to hurt, he would at least forget about his emotional turmoil for a while.

One evening, on his walk to the group, Vic discovered he was entertaining two different trains of thought. He was worried that he might have to let go of his only supports—individual therapy and the group—because his insurance was about to expire. Although his therapist was already offering him one free appointment a week, he expected this couldn't last. He also found himself musing, ". . . how nice it would be to have all this misery behind me—not have to worry about it anymore."

> I put on a good show that night. Everyone was jokin' and laughin' and having a good time. My therapist asked me a number of times if I was okay, and I just said, "Yeah, I'm okay"—not letting on, not talking about anything. As I walked home, I wasn't even thinking that that would be the night.

Two

The Descent

The tales of Tim and Teresa, Jason and Vic, have begun our exploration of suicide. They have given us intimate access to the experiences
that upset the critical balance between hope and hopelessness. Some
of these accounts are dramatic while others are more subtle, but they
all share elements fundamental to the experience of the descent into
suicide—that psycho-spiritual period during which the very fabric
of one's world seems to stretch, tear, and then break apart.

As these stories unfold, we can identify critical components of the
decline toward suicide. The stages of the descent are these: Pain and
suffering remain unaddressed by compassionate others. The person
then withdraws behind a façade designed to protect himself or
herself from further hurt and to cloak the suffering underneath.
However, the façade only intensifies the slide toward a suicidal
trance. Ultimately the trance narrows the person's perspective until
the only inner voices that can be heard are those that enjoin him or
her to die.

We will hear from Tim and the others again, but they have already
illustrated two of the most crucial questions we must ask about the

accelerating slide of the descent: If suffering visits all human beings during their lives—if no one is exempt—then why do loss and pain propel some people to attempt suicide, but not others? What ingredients must be present to override our self-preservative conditioning and incline us toward suicide?

Researchers already know many of the factors that commonly appear in suicidal episodes. Proximity to an effective means of killing oneself, depression and hopelessness, a well-defined plan, a history of suicide in one's family—all are important variables to consider. Yet, the direction a life takes is influenced by an enormous range of forces. Researchers in the physical sciences investigate the biological and chemical antecedents of depression and suicide, while social scientists study factors associated with psychological makeup, family history, age, gender, class and ethnicity. All these are pieces of an intricate puzzle, but none of them explains why a particular person attempts suicide. What can we conclude?

First, there is no single cause of suicide. Because one's motivation stems from a complex web of pressures and drives, the human condition cannot be so neatly explained. Second, regardless of which factors figure most prominently in an individual suicide attempt, most attempts share two characteristics. The first is an early pain that has gone unresolved and is compounded by current adversity. (To one who contemplates suicide, it feels as though salt is constantly being rubbed in an ancient but open wound.) The second characteristic involves what I call the unacknowledged pain: the absence of psychological and emotional support during or after a trauma.

UNACKNOWLEDGED PAIN:
THE INABILITY TO MOURN

I call my childhood "Happy Days: The Documentary." My father died when I was five. He was a drunk, a gambler, and a womanizer, and was deeply hated by my mother. His casino

burned down, and he was killed. She remarried and we were never
to speak about him again. No talking. No grieving. Nothing. All
the pictures were destroyed. From then on, regardless of how we
felt, we were to exercise extraordinary self-control. The truth was,
he was the grand passion of her life, and the only way to manage
his loss was to pretend he never existed. (Virginia)

Whether our suffering is great or small, when the difficulty is met with compassion and understanding at least some of the hurt is soothed, and the agony can begin to give way to a feeling that our burden is shared. Internal resources are taxed less strenuously and the difficulty can be integrated into a broader, more complex understanding of the world.

But when the suffering is caused by "significant others," or is not acknowledged by the people nearest to us, it can overwhelm our capacity to endure. Then the extreme states of body and mind begin to emerge that are characteristic of the descent toward suicide. People who have attempted suicide almost universally report that regardless of the type of trauma they had suffered, there seemed to be no one available to offer the critical insight and compassion so necessary afterward—and no one who could see beneath the adaptive coping and attend to the person who was suffering so. More alarming, when sources of comfort might have been available, the person in pain did not recognize them.

Perhaps the most deleterious consequence here involves one's ability to grieve. In the absence of emotional support, mourning is prevented. Mourning is an individual's and a family's most basic and necessary response to loss. Mourning allows a family to pause from its routines, reflect on its loss, and express whatever its members are feeling. When mourning is allowed to continue to its natural completion, people are able to reenter their lives, often with a renewed sense of engagement and a deeper, more profound appreciation for family and community, and for life itself.

When a family or community is unable to honestly acknowledge the trauma, mourning remains incomplete, for days, or months, or sometimes for years. Families will create predictable patterns of relating that prevent mourning of their losses, often through denial, or by blaming or alienating the most vocal or most bereaved member.

In the histories of those who have attempted suicide, an overwhelming proportion of people relate experiences of loss and trauma which they were not able to openly mourn. Ruth's story dramatically portrays the progression through the stages of the descent, in the absence of attention, care, and the permission to grieve.

Ruth

"I'll be the heavyset one waiting for you in the hall," she said over the phone. Ruth doesn't mince words. She speaks the truth as she sees it, and looks slightly askance at me, as if she doesn't expect to be understood. She practices medicine in Boston. A highly skilled physician and now a psychiatric resident, she is dressed informally today, wearing a kufi—an African skull cap—and jeans. We talk in the steeply raked lecture room at the university and sit alone amidst 500 empty seats, our voices echoing softly in the amphitheater. She is a curious combination of guarded and forthright, somber and yet ready to laugh and enjoy my company for a moment or two.

Ruth was raised in Harlem by a stern and sometimes abusive grandmother. Her mother was a prostitute and drug addict who lived nearby. Her father, also an addict, had long since left the family. She grew up smart and streetwise, and she survived by hiding significant aspects of her life from others. Against her grandmother's wishes, she discovered who her mother was (she had originally been told she was a distant aunt), and would sneak off for forbidden visits after school.

My mother was in the drug world, so I would see her at times when she was bloodied and beaten up by her pimp. I'd see her for a while

after school. She'd fawn all over me—tell me I was her princess. It
was the only time in my life I felt special. I didn't realize until
much later how irresponsible that was. I just thought my grand-
mother was keeping me away from her.

She also hid the fact that she was being molested. From the age of
six to thirteen, she surrendered to sexual contact with her mother's
boyfriend's son, a teenager who had also been taken in by the
grandmother. Her grandmother was unpredictable in her affection,
alternately angry and nurturing, and this left Ruth feeling that,
aside from stolen moments with her mother, the only person who
really loved and cared for her was her "stepbrother."

He would take me out to play and stuff like that, so when it came
around to him wanting sex, I felt, "Sure, whatever you want to
do." It reached a point where it took on this kind of quality where I
would go and bother him and I think what I wanted was just to
hang out; but my punishment for bothering him was for us to have
sex, and then after that we could play.

Lonely and confused, Ruth became a tough and intimidating
teenager. She was exceptionally bright, and with little effort she
maintained good grades; yet her school years were often spent in
detention after having fought with classmates. She could identify no
one who could understand her pain, and she decided that there was
not likely to be anyone in the future who could, either. Instead, she
defended the tender and vulnerable places within her with a sharp
tongue and quick fists.

I had a big mouth. I didn't take anything from anybody. If they
yelled at me, I would punch them in the eye! They used to call me
"Blackie," you know, 'cause that was the early sixties and being
black wasn't cool. I ended up feeling I didn't want to be black
either, so I would start a fight when someone called me that.

Her mother died when Ruth was thirteen, and the next year her stepbrother, whom she still loved despite the abuse, was killed in Vietnam. By the time she was fourteen, she was smoking marijuana in an attempt to mute the unhappiness she felt.

My mother overdosed on heroin. I came home from school that Monday morning and everybody was crying. My aunt told me, "Your mother died last night," and I remember vividly this knot in my throat. She told me it was probably better off since she was suffering. I didn't understand that. I was thinking, "Maybe for her, but it's not better off for me." After that, it was like, "Nobody can do anything to me that's worse than that."

Ruth had made a decision. Even family members demonstrated time and again their inability to understand the depths and complexity of her feelings. Often they meant well, but instead of asking her how she felt, and what she needed, they consistently told her what to feel and what was best. By the time she had survived two deaths, she had already begun to withdraw, convinced that life was a battle that she would best wage alone.

I copped this attitude: "You can't mess with me." I started running the streets. I was mourning my mom, and then when my step-brother died, it deepened. I had fantasies about marrying him, living with him, since we weren't blood relatives, and when he got killed, it was the beginning of, "What am I living for?"

Ruth's life proceeded in stark contrasts. She was gifted academically, and she almost always excelled in the activities she attempted. In high school, she played interscholastic basketball and was the captain of both the volleyball and track teams. Upon graduating, she was acknowledged and given awards for her achievements. But during the same period, she would succumb to crippling depressions. They continued throughout college and medical school, and were so debilitating that she sometimes had to leave for a semester or two. At times her hopelessness was so great that she would find herself lying in bed, crying for her mother. Ruth felt isolated in a world filled with people; the aloneness she had felt since childhood only intensified.

> *The big suicide episodes were all in medical school and early residency, because I really had no preparation for this. I mean, medical school is just a totally new world for anybody, but at least some of the people seemed to be able to connect to each other. They seemed to come from similar backgrounds and have similar interests and experiences. I mean, the first time I ever heard about the stock market was in my histology class, when students were reading* The Wall Street Journal!

The physiology of the human heart is identical whether one is African-American or Korean, Hispanic, Caucasian, or Native American. Its needs remain consistent whether it beats in a woman or a man, a boy or a girl. The care that Ruth needed was not to be forthcoming. Her family had been ripped apart by drugs, violence, and considerable societal pressures. Slowed at times, but undeterred, she would continue to pursue her dreams. Ruth refused defeat in her quest to become a physician, but she would face formidable difficulties along the way.

Ruth's story highlights central components in the descent toward suicide. Loss, often sudden and impossible to prepare for, can be powerful enough to destroy the fabric of one's life, either temporarily or permanently. Traumatic events can overwhelm an already fragile family system, and in response to the trauma, family members grasp for protection in whatever ways seem most likely to dull the pain: drugs or alcohol, adopting new and rigid belief systems, geographical flight, becoming reclusive, and even abandoning the role of parent. Like soldiers strewn on a battlefield, the trauma leaves the family deeply wounded, with communication disrupted and its members alone and divided. When devastating events occur, the most powerful resource for healing—the family itself—is powerless to address its own hurt.

In the absence of compassion and care, the original trauma leaves an individual highly sensitized to further hurt and disappointment. To protect themselves, people construct a series of postures toward the world. In fact, however, these postures leave one progessively more insecure and unstable. Each posture becomes more rigid as it proceeds unchecked, and each is self-reinforcing. The first of these is the withdrawal.

THE WITHDRAWAL

I felt like I couldn't penetrate anybody or make them feel, or know how I felt. I was on the outside of everything and I just couldn't get in. I've called it my "black cylinder." I couldn't see out and I couldn't get out. I could hear everybody on the outside but they couldn't hear me. It was a zombie place where I just couldn't be a part of anything and I couldn't notice the things happening around me. I was just all alone. (Teresa)

For those who have experienced it, the withdrawal is a tangible, emotional, spiritual, and even physical pulling away from contact and connection. Sometimes misperceived as a casual decision to remain aloof, the withdrawal is nothing like nonchalance or apathy. Instead, it is an active response to intense, unabated suffering.

Withdrawal contains two components that further isolate a person and compound the pain. First, people report either the flooding or the numbing of emotion and physical sensation. Tim, for example, experienced both of these at various times during his descent. The feelings arising from the sudden deaths of his parents were overwhelming for a young adolescent. Quickly and quite automatically, he became numb. A second component of withdrawal (and this hastens the descent) involves a separation from the environment in which the painful events have been occurring. Teresa grew distant, living in a world of fantasy and lost in the pain of her mother's neglect. With each day, she retreated further, decreasing the possibility of more nourishing experiences and reinforcing her view that the world held little promise.

Withdrawal can assume many forms. Some people may act in provocative ways, engaging in drug abuse, prostitution, or, among adolescents, "acting out"—being bad. Some people become less communicative. Withdrawal can also take softer, more subtle forms, such as Teresa's extra efforts to be "very good": These can be harder to discern and often more dangerous, for they don't call attention to themselves as dramatically. Regardless of the form of withdrawal, people become more removed, hiding their vulnerability and pain.

> *I had been feeling pretty miserable, but I didn't want to push myself on anyone, so I would kind of keep it light—not really go into it. I didn't want to burden all these people with what was going on with me. (Ian)*

It's as if they are moving farther and farther away. In fact, the withdrawal phase may be identified less by what is apparent than by what is missing.

Ed's story provides an arresting example of withdrawal. He actually hid from the world, while seemingly exemplifying some of the very ideals to which our society aspires. Ed literally became an all-American icon. No one could suspect, however, what lay underneath.

Ed

> *Most of the problems started when I was fourteen. My dad's business started going downhill. He had emphysema and he'd*

smoke all the time. I was preoccupied with him since early adoles-
cence, because I never knew how long he was gonna live. My
grandmother had Alzheimer's, though we didn't know what it was
back then, and my mother was going through menopause. Lots of
stress. Things started changing with my body. At that point, I was
a classic ectomorph, six-feet-four and 170 pounds. I started to get
all these sexual feelings. They were homosexual feelings.

Ed speaks graphically. Holding a listener in the powerful beam of
his attention, he says precisely what he feels to be true. He may
apologize for startling one's sensibilities, but he will not dilute or
sidestep the facts of his life. Ed is a large man, but one would be
mistaken to attribute the effect of his presence to size alone. Rather,
it reflects the breath of his spirit, which has woven together the
many disparate elements of his personality through a succession of
painful trials.

I thought, "What is this shit!" When I'd fantasize, the gay stuff
would come up. I'd like it and I'd be scared at the same time, and I'd
say to myself, or maybe to God, "Please don't let anybody find out."

Ed grew up in a small suburb just north of New York City, the
middle child and only son of a conservative working-class family.
The family's resources were limited, and yet through hard work they
managed well enough. Much time was devoted to earning sufficient
income to care for relatives, grandparents included, and to cover
their considerable medical expenses. Ed's was a loving family, if a bit
distant. Because of the local culture in which he lived, and largely
because of his father's open disdain of homosexuality, Ed kept his
secret well hidden.

I tried to live up to the beer commercials. I can remember my dad
and his friends saying—"faggot" this or "faggot" that. I started
getting very guarded. I didn't want to share any of my feelings or
fantasies with anyone.

Whatever the particular circumstances, people who attempt suicide decide at a crucial moment in their lives that the local world (and by association, the world at large) will either fail to understand their innermost feelings or judge them harshly. A young adolescent afraid of his sexuality; a grown woman who was once sexually abused or who who grieves for her failed marriage; a man diagnosed with a catastrophic illness; or someone who's dealing and abusing drugs are examples of such circumstances. Suicide attempters say they were certain that no one could possibly enter their worlds fairly, with compassion, and comprehend the depth of their suffering. In fact, most people I talked to have said that as they were beginning to withdraw, they were convinced that no one would even want to. Ed remembers this precisely.

I started having these conflicting feelings. I started being attracted to some of my friends. Some were girls, but some were boys. It was all normal, but I didn't know. I just thought even playing with my dick was weird and strange. I didn't tell anybody. That's when a lot of it started. I started getting introspective. I couldn't speak in front of the class without turning into a radish.

Withdrawal may begin in small increments, and from the outside it may not be easy to detect: little things left unsaid, eyes that don't look up to meet your gaze, a faraway expression. A loved one may seem preoccupied—it seems he is somewhere else—or for a moment he shows a flash of irritation or anger, sadness or frustration, and then it's gone, buried in silence. Speaking to him, you might get the sense that your words aren't heard—that they fall flat or seem not to impact—or his words seem slightly out of sync, absent of feeling, not about what's really going on. Alternatively, he may exert a little extra effort to make things appear okay: "I was just trying so hard to pass for normal."

Withdrawal is a complex process, with two complementary mechanisms. It offers protection, a cloak in which one may take refuge from the impact and reverberations of overwhelming stress. Clinicians who are specialists in the field of trauma understand this to be a natural response. In a sense, it is nature caring for itself. On the other hand, the withdrawal can become generalized—a habitual posture of retreat from the world, which insidiously becomes a life-style and then a trap. One begins by hiding particular aspects of his or her life, and this leads to additional deceptions. Over time, the person takes fewer risks and becomes that much more covert, eventually growing to doubt that a genuine encounter will ever be possible. The withdrawal phase represents the expression of that doubt.

Sharon is now an amiable and pleasant middle-aged woman. Referred to me by her therapist, who had treated her for depression over a number of years, she was intrigued with the opportunity to tell her story but also nervous about what would emerge. Sharon's mother had attempted suicide almost every two years while Sharon was young. She spent her childhood visiting her in the hospital, waiting for her to return, and then worrying about her while she was at home. The family was in constant crisis and could afford little focus on the children. Given the circumstances, play was considered a frivolity and an indulgence. Attention was given to the children to the degree they aided their mother, but was absent otherwise. Their father was kindly, but became overwhelmed dealing with such strong emotion and high drama. Increasingly, he called on Sharon for help, as she was the oldest sibling. A depressive pall began to hang over her as she learned to surrender her needs and feelings to the caretaking of her mother. Years later, she found it a formidable challenge to believe that someone would care about her.

I had gone to a counselor. One of the things he said to me—and this was very frightening to me—was that I had to learn to tell my own truth, no matter what the consequences. I felt an incredible amount of fear about saying or doing what I thought and felt and letting the chips fall where they may. It was terror. I was so afraid that if someone knew who I was I'd be left alone.

Sharon received direction from therapy, but the route would take her into pain that had accumulated for over four decades. She hovered at the trail's edge, unsure she could take the next step. At times, the tension of hiding caused even physical pain.

It was mostly in my stomach. Achy and tight. That's where the anxiety and dread of being myself lived. I would see the two people I had become: the person I showed in therapy, in tremendous pain, but honest about it; and the person I showed to the world— pleasant, attending to others. Hiding. Every day, I would feel the real chasm between the two. Coming out of hiding meant facing the pain throughout my life, and I just didn't want to go through it.

People who take significant risks can often call upon memories of other challenges, other chances taken, with positive results. Or there may be a family history of risk-taking—perhaps at least one family member who endeavored to push beyond the confines of convention. Sharon had neither. Imagining herself expressing the years of pain and disappointment (as well as her thoughts of suicide), she had only one set of images from which to draw. These images cemented her decision to hide.

It goes back to my mother—how she, also being suicidal, had dragged our whole family through her pain for years. I didn't want to do that to my husband or my daughter. I didn't want to drag somebody so close to me into it.

The withdrawal phase affects body, speech, and mind. People become less willing to listen or look for something positive. They are dubious of the value of sharing their pain, believing that it simply adds to the confusion. And through the progressive numbing of the body, they lose the ability to feel and to touch. The very capacity to register new information or engage in potentially liberating experiences diminishes, and so the bedrock beliefs which support the pain and withdrawal remain unchallenged, and are in fact reinforced.

By the time he began high school, Ed had been wrestling with these enormous feelings for three years. Quiet and gawky, he was a terrified adolescent, constantly censoring feelings and urges completely foreign to his family and to his small-town life. He was petrified of anything "leaking" into public awareness which might reveal him.

I felt that everything was conditional. If they ever started seeing under my fantasies—oh shit, man, no way! I told myself, "You cannot open up! You cannot open up!" If you ever look beneath me, you're gonna destroy me, so even if you suspect I'm gay, please don't let me know.

Adolescence is a time when it is common for one's self-esteem to be shaky, but Ed's problems were compounded. Searching for confirmation of his normalcy amid considerable internal doubts, Ed took the advice of friends and teachers and tried out for football. By his senior year, Ed had grown physically, and by lifting weights he had added to his dimensions. A six-feet-five, 233-pound eighteen-year-old, he was relieved to be winning the approval of family and friends and happy that he could excel at the most popular sport in town. His popularity soared, and for a while the adulation provided the opportunity for him to hide—in plain sight.

I made all-county and then all-state. I had a pretty good year, but it also put a lot of pressure on me. "Why doesn't he have girlfriends?" I'd imagine people wondering. I put all my energy into sports. Not

wanting to face my inner feelings, pretending I was too busy to do
other things with friends. I actually took a girl to the prom. I knew
she liked me, and I did have attractions to certain women, but
toward the end of that year, the guilt of it all started really hanging
on me. "Oh shit, man, how is this ever gonna work out?"

Ed was offered numerous football scholarships and chose the
University of Pittsburgh, one of the best teams in the country.
Almost, but never quite, outrunning his fears and anxieties, he
entered into a near-Faustian bargain with the world:

I can play football. I can do that. And I can pretend, but please
don't let them see underneath. Looming over me was the big
question: "Are they gonna know I'm gay?"

Ed entered the ultramasculine world of collegiate football, with
its rabid fans, its overly intrusive alumni, and its single-minded
obsession with victory. He was a young Adonis—strong, carefree,
sexually attractive. He represented heroic America, and he did his
best to throw himself into the role.

I played the game. I got tanked up and fooled around with some of
the co-eds, and I enjoyed it, and I'd say to myself, "This was okay. I
must not be gay. I'm not a fag!" I really hated those words and
I really hated feeling this. Underneath, I was just very lonely. I
wasn't preoccupied with it all the time, but a lot, because it clashed
with what I thought I should be. I wanted to be so much like
others. I started communicating less and less. I thought it was like
dominoes: if I ever communicated even some of my intimate
feelings, it would unravel and people would hate me.

The pattern had been established. Ed projected only the thoughts
and actions that supported his idea of what he wanted other people
to see. Everything else was censored.

I hated myself in many ways because I didn't like this—this double
life I was trying to lead. I liked to write poetry. I liked to write
things like that and be sensitive, and whenever a damn teardrop
hit me, I'd say, "You fucking chump! What are you feeling that
way for?"

THE FAÇADE

As the withdrawal phase progresses, people become increasingly
trapped within a closed system. They prevent others from seeing
their anguish and they miss the opportunity to experience responses that are understanding and compassionate. Their inner
turmoil, and in large measure their humanity, remains concealed.
The belief that no one could possibly comprehend is then
compounded.

In the roughest times, Mattie could always call on her wit, her joie
de vivre, and her considerable intelligence. People naturally gravi-
tated to her, as she was attractive, genuinely caring, and unpreten-
tious. Her most frequent complaint was that she didn't have enough
time for all her friends. No one knew the self-loathing she carried, or
that she was bulimic and often contemplated suicide.

There was something inside me that was just horrible or bad or
needy or painful, and it didn't match the outside, because I'd
always been so extroverted and everybody thought I was happy
and normal and well-adjusted and I got straight A's. I was a good
person, you know? I was just trying to pass for normal.

People in the throes of the withdrawal spiral become their own
judges and juries, deciding ahead of time that their concerns are
either pathological, impossible to grasp, or not worthy of another's
attention. The turmoil intensifies and remains unaddressed, and the
chasm widens between one's silent suffering and the image of

oneself that one projects. As time passes, that image becomes a façade: a mask designed to hide the pain.

Deborah is a medical secretary who lives in Colorado Springs. She spent the day of her suicide attempt calmly and unobtrusively sitting at her desk in the office, writing suicide notes. The mask she wore was virtually impenetrable.

> *Nobody could tell that anything was going on. The notes gave me something to focus on so that I could do my job without thinking about it and be really occupied with it. I was able to do it by rote, going through my role but not being there consciously. Nobody seemed to notice, except one. When I came back from lunch, one woman asked me if I'd been crying. I went to the bathroom and washed my face and I did not talk to anyone again the rest of the day. No one bothered me!*

Cynthia lived her life separated from intimates, friends, and even acquaintances. She was angry and she was alone. At the age of seven, she was molested in New York City. She told her mother, who— overwhelmed and fearing for her child—sent Cynthia away to live with a foster family. Upon returning to the city as a young adult, Cynthia grew isolated and sullen, and constructed a formidable barrier to intimacy.

> *I was hostile. I "acted out" for years—didn't communicate with my parents, hung around the university bars uptown, and sex- ually acted out a lot too. I was pretty promiscuous and I drank a lot. I didn't talk to anyone. No one. I got into the blues and listened to Billie Holiday records.*

These stories illustrate the many forms the façade takes. Mattie was the happy extrovert, Deborah grew more robotic, and Cynthia became silent and hostile. As time passes, the spiral grows tighter. The pain continues unabated and the perceived need for the façade increases. One pulls further away from genuine interpersonal exchange and, over time, loses a sense of who or what could be helpful. It is as if a person has become lost in the forest and finds a cave in which to sleep for the night. The territory is foreign and the sounds alien. Every rustle of leaves or crack of a twig is interpreted as a sign that something alive and dangerous is drawing nearer, and one pulls back into the cave, withdrawing deeper and deeper. The further the person retreats from the cave's mouth, the less the possibility of his or her distinguishing fact from fear, help from danger.

> *Never in my life had I known such uncontrolled fear. Did I tip anyone off as to how I was feeling? No, of course not! At six-feet-six and 240 pounds, could Big Ed admit to anyone, even himself, that he was going under? I mean, totally losing it, and only partially being aware of the fact?*

By the end of college, Ed weighed almost fifty pounds more than when he enrolled. Most of it was muscle. He invested enormous amounts of time and energy in becoming imposing and formidable:

> *. . . using my physical armor as a way to prevent others from getting inside. "Oh, he's too big, let's not piss him off."*

He was celebrated on campus as one of the better football players, and when Pitt won the national championship, he was invited by the New York Jets to their tryout camp. His prospects soared and friends and family were pulling for the Ed they thought they knew. The adulation and his inner torment built to a near-equal pitch.

Each day there was a battle to resist his urge to relieve the tension and tell someone. He would not permit himself to divulge his secret to friends, but he felt he was about to explode. Agitated and confused, Ed made an anonymous phone call late one night to the university crisis center.

I remember going to a phone booth, looking up the counseling center number, and talking a little bit, saying, "Hey, I don't want you to know who I am, but there's a little problem. I think I'm a little bit queer or something." We talked just a few minutes—I don't even remember what was said—and then I hung up. I remember it felt so good just to say it. And that she didn't know who I was and didn't care that I was well known or not. It felt so good knowing that somebody somewhere knows a little bit about me, even if they don't know my name. It felt like it popped this internal balloon, relieved the pressure just to talk about it. I felt pleasure for months after that, but I didn't realize and look closely that this was the way to go—talking about it. I didn't capitalize on it and use it as a learning experience. I went back to football— back to the same stuff, the same old thing.

Ed spent a few weeks living out the dream of a lifetime for any college football player. He practiced with some of the best athletes in the country, but although he played well, he was clearly not one of the best prospects. After three weeks he was cut from the team. Ed was relieved. Although worried about his future, he saw the end of training camp as possibly the end of the pressure on him to be someone else. Ed fantasized about living a freer life-style, "letting loose" and exploring his gay side, discovering the supressed dimensions of his personality.

But the reality proved different. The double life he had cultivated so meticulously for over a decade would not easily give way. To his horror, his façade seemed to have its own life, and grew stronger. He became a bouncer at a local club, and moved furniture to supplement his income. In his private world, Ed wrote down his innermost thoughts and dreamed he'd someday be famous. Free of football and the moment-by-moment pressure to support his image, he began to write poetry in earnest. Writing poetry then gave way to composing songs and learning the rudiments of music, but this too he kept secret. "They're gonna laugh at me and think I'm sissy-ish, so let me keep it to myself and do the jock stuff on the outside."

Alone in his room, Ed would compose verses designed to reflect his truer self—songs about interpersonal tenderness, the meaning of life, and with greater frequency, songs about death.

> It was when John Lennon was murdered in 1980 that—it sounds strange, but that inspired me to look into myself and start realizing that maybe I have a talent here. I was amazed how one man could influence the world with such words. To my thinking then, it seemed all the great ones—Lennon, Martin Luther King, Kennedy—they die and they go out with a boom. Elvis, Buddy Holly, Ritchie Valens—the message to me was "Do your thing and do it quick and powerfully before you go out with a bang." Something about that turned me on. Something about how they went out and how they were loved afterwards. I thought, "If I can do one one-thousandth of what Lennon did, maybe I can accomplish something in this world. Maybe one day I'll spring a hit on everyone and they'll look back and realize that Gallagher just didn't play football and physical things—that he had some kind of brain.

Secretly, Ed began to romance death. Each day, he would read the obituaries, studying who died and why and fantasizing the effect of these deaths on others. Living at home again, Ed was witnessing the slow and agonizing demise of his father from emphysema. His father was a stubborn man, too weak to work but unwilling to stop smoking.

The disparity between his "inner" and more public selves felt glaring to Ed, and his actions grew more impulsive and more clandestine. Early one morning, about three A.M., he stole into New York City to hire a prostitute. He was afraid of what he felt inside. He desperately wanted to affirm to himself that he wasn't gay.

It was the same old shit—feeling so split—but I was glad after-
ward. I was thinking, "Wow, I can really do this. Maybe I'm not
gay. Maybe my friends won't suspect I am." I was still playing the
jockish part of my nature in public. I said to myself, "Let me write
these songs secretly."

But Ed's forays into the city to study songwriting bore unexpected
side effects. He began to receive support for his writing from one
of his teachers, and he began to venture a bit further from the
protection of his persona. Combining visits to music classes with
explorations in Manhattan, Ed ventured into Greenwich Village,
specifically the West Village, where the gay community lived in high
concentration. It was there he had his first encounter with the life
he'd so surreptitiously fantasized about for over a decade.

I started seeing all aspects of life. I was curious, but I acted
disinterested. Wearing the mask, but underneath being very inter-
ested. Very guarded, very intrigued. I'd start to hang out more
frequently, still not even entering one of the gay bars—just walking
past it, looking in but acting nonchalant. I did that many times—
eat by myself, walk past a bar, going to Washington Square.
Finally one evening, I said, "Fuck, man, I'm twenty-seven years
old! I can do what I want!," and after having a bite to eat, and
getting a little bit tanked—not too much, but I feel good—I go into
this bar—I won't tell you the name of it—and I feel different. I can
talk with guys and feel good about it. I can be myself! I was gonna
leave, but this guy asked me to his place. I'm thinking, "He's really
good-looking, and I say to him, "I never really did this stuff
before." He said, "It's okay, I'll help you—I'll show you." He was
coming on to me, I know, but he was also nice, not pushy. I'd never
even kissed a guy, let alone done anything else. I felt so comfortable
to be myself. I had a real nice time. It also helped I was a little
tanked!

That night, Ed embraced his longing for a man, and for a few precious moments he felt whole. Yet at some deeper level, the binary construction of his psyche, the sharp division of self that he'd been living with for so many years, began to reassert itself. Driving home the next day, Ed became consumed with fear.

I started thinking, "Now what? You can't go back to your old life-style! How can I look my friends in the eye, my friends who think I'm straight as an arrow. You never told anyone and then just because you walk down Greenwich Village, you get involved with someone!"

The intensity of his self-flagellation increased, and Ed, alone more than ever, grew frightened and became savage with himself.

Then I started thinking of AIDS, of which I knew next to nothing. "Was I careful? Was I not? What did you do, you son of a bitch! You stepped into this new world and then you get AIDS! You're gonna kill anybody you come near." I remember going to work and not wanting to breathe near anyone. I would wake up in the middle of the night and look in the mirror and my eyes would just start getting real wild. I'd scream at myself, "You're a disgrace to your family!" I'd continually be thinking, "How am I gonna rebound from this?" Three, four, six, eight days and it got worse and worse. "I never had an experience opening up to anyone and I couldn't do it now," I thought. I did try to call the guy in New York on the phone to ask him how you deal with this, how do you keep going, but he never answered my calls, no matter how many times I called him. It made me feel worse, like I was suckered. It exacerbated all the loneliness I felt.

Ed was locked in dread. Having remained isolated and in conflict for so many years, he knew no way to reach out for help. His thinking became more rigid; he saw no solutions. One night, amidst a flurry of self-recrimination and fear, he found an image of peace and order: his suicide.

THE TRANCE

Early in the withdrawal phase, people still make some effort to stay in touch with the world and hope for at least some promise of better things. But when hope finally dies, people no longer see or hear anything outside their own minds—the tight spiral of thought that tells them to die. While this shift may occur just moments before a suicide attempt, it can be months or years in the making. A colleague of mine from Louisiana, an experienced therapist for many years, contemplated suicide for over a decade. She describes this mental state as "an almost totally separate reality, in which your world may not look or feel so limited and painful to anyone else, but it does to you. You enter into a very powerful trance."

During the latter stages of the descent, people lose faith that their predicament will ever change. Their strength is depleted, and they are deeply stressed. Some people are never able to leave their chronically destructive surroundings. In other cases, there is just no one able or willing to push past their façades. In yet other instances, people are no longer able to recognize support when it is in fact available.

A successor to the withdrawal phase, the suicidal trance carries with it its own set of chronically held beliefs and expectations, inflexible and life-denying. The trance is a state of mind and body that receives only the kind of input that reinforces the pain and corroborates the person's conviction that the only way out is through death. The trance marks the moment at which the world becomes devoid of all possibilities except one: suicide.

Mark is a curator and a professor of art history at a small college in northern Connecticut. Using the idioms of a painter, he wrote of this moment in his journal:

His was a landscape painting. Two triangular wheat-yellow fields,
one on each half of the picture plane. Two central bands of green
tire tracks incised into a mauve-red road. A blue sky. Little did he
suspect that after placing everything into its proper perspective, he
would disappear beyond the vanishing point. In his mind's eye the
yellow and the green, the red and the blue, all turned black. The
black on the canvas darkened the entire studio until all he could
see was black. One way only to escape the blackness in front of his
eyes and the blankness in the back of them.

Most of us have grown up with preconceived ideas of what a
trance is: a voodoo-induced somnambulance, or the behavior of
a person under hypnosis, who does things he or she might
not do when fully conscious. Trance, however, is rather common
in everyday life. It is simply a state of mind (and body) in which
the focus of attention is reduced to a few inner realities and is
increasingly fixated on a narrowed range of perceptions. We may be
preoccupied about a problem in a personal relationship, for example, or worried about the outcome of a meeting to be held next
week. Trance can be the rapturous state of falling in love, or parents'
sleep-deprived delirium in the first weeks after the birth of
their child. Or the determined mind-set of a student confronting
her final exams, or a steadfast resolve to finish the yard work before
lunch.

The suicidal trance, however, is severe and deadly. The person's
attention becomes constricted, his emotional range is compressed,
and his awareness focuses more and more on his pain and isolation.
It is similar to withdrawal, but immensely stronger. As in a fortress
under siege, the gates are locked, the bridges have been raised,
reserves are dwindling, and hope has all but evaporated.

During this stage of the descent, Mark found himself overwhelmed by the intensity of the suicidal trance. His thoughts
relentlessly turned toward his death, and colored everything he
perceived.

At that time, I lived in a poorer neighborhood in the city. Directly across from me was this old couple—retired, obviously—and they always sat by their window. They were the last thing I looked at before I went to sleep, this old man and woman. Each night I'd think, "They're gonna live beyond me."

That was between July 7 and July 20—these two weeks. I had no idea that there was a state of mind like this. Everything turned black. There was such a depression hanging over me, I started thinking, "I have to get out of this. I have to kill myself." This is the only way I could think of getting out, you know? I had suicide on my mind the whole time. There was no question what my intentions were. I thought about suicide day in and day out.

Despite differences in detail, everyone who attempts suicide enters the suicidal trance. Tim checked himself into a hospital, unable to subdue an unrelenting series of suicidal images. Teresa became single-mindedly focused on the pain of her mother's rejection. It was as if no experiences existed in the world except that. Both Vic and Ruth had become so isolated that they felt no one would care if they died.

Suicidal trances can be identified by certain common characteristics.

- They may appear extremely logical, with a premise and a rational series of arguments that encourage suicide as a reasonable response to pain. These arguments are powerful, especially when created by someone who has become emotionally deadened—whose reservoirs of faith, trust, and hope have run dry.
- Suicidal trances are self-reinforcing. They become stronger with each additional setback, and become more insistent as the descent continues.
- Suicidal trances appear as resignation, in which a person stops caring at all about the state of his or her life. They are frustrating and frightening to family and friends: it seems as if there is no

force strong enough to persuade the person to act on his or her own behalf.

- Suicidal trances "beckon." As the trance intensifies, it becomes more insistent that the person finally complete the act. These urgings most often take the form of voices entreating him or her to take the final step, or of images presenting a picture of the final act.
- Finally, this type of trance includes a particular vision of the future: an illusion of eternity in which the future is projected as an endless repetition of the present pain and disappointment, never-ending and hopeless.

Trance as Logical

> The chief mourner does not always attend the funeral.
>
> EMERSON, *JOURNALS*, 1832

I started to list the people who wouldn't mind if I wasn't around. I clearly wasn't a good wife for my ex-husband. He wouldn't miss me. And I never felt that comfortable in my role as a mom—didn't feel like I was a good mom, necessarily. He'll remarry and she'll be a better mom for the kids. The kids will be sad, but they'll get over it. I was never looked highly upon by my original family members. I've sort of been a fuck-up there. It's like I'll be a burden off their backs. Clearly their lives will be enhanced because I'm not around. At that point, I honestly felt I was doing them a favor. (Deborah)

Deborah stared at her desk in a trance. From the outside, it looked as if she was doing paperwork, but inside, she was organizing the rationale for her suicide; ordering her reasons carefully and thoughtfully, and even projecting herself into the possible reactions of those to whom she was related. In fact, she accounted for everyone in this equation but herself.

The suicidal trance creates a logic for death, and an alarming change in one's sense of self occurs. The focus of attention narrows almost exclusively to the torment one feels. Scarcely a minute passes without an assessment of the pain's severity and a determination that it will never end. Concentration lapses and the capacity for enjoyment ceases. One *becomes* a "person in terrible, immutable pain." And yet people who enter into this particular trance, and the distorted logic it carries, begin to think of themselves less as human beings and more as objects or obstacles in the lives of others. They are no longer part of the equation: they are forgotten players in their own demise. When the trance takes this form, all that remains is the dispassionate execution of a plan. People deep in the suicidal trance have abandoned hope of reclaiming their own lives and apply their creativity to their own removal.

> *I started watching TV. Just sat there till about eleven*
> *o'clock and then I said, out loud, "It's a nice night." (Vic)*

Vic withdrew from the therapy group as fast as he could without arousing suspicion. Although his therapist was concerned, Vic deflected all inquiries. He was no longer looking for help. Walking home as if he were taking a stroll, he anticipated the end of his struggle. He had entered the suicidal trance.

> *I was in a happy state of mind, kind of cheerful. I knew there*
> *wouldn't be too many people comin' around for the next few days,*
> *so I filled two new litter boxes for the cat, and put lots of food down*
> *for her. It looked like she thought I'd gone nuts!*

Within the strictures of the trance, Vic felt relief. Even before he consciously realized it, he became someone with a plan.

> *It seemed like when I started doin' it, everything had been planned*
> *before. I was just followin' the plan. I went and got my best suit*
> *and hung it up on the door. That was for my funeral. I got some*

change of underwear, stuck it in the pocket so people would see it,
to make it easier for other people. I sat down and wrote letters to
my parents, to my boss, to the group, and to my therapist. I wanted
them to know it's not their fault; it's just something I have to do. I
told them how much I cared for them, how much I loved them. I
was trying to take care of everybody else, like always. If I had just
taken a few minutes to take care of myself, you know, I probably
could have kept a lot of people from going through a bad time.

The suicidal trance resembles an altered state. One may feel
completely different—calm, even merry—although one's predicament remains essentially unchanged. An observer might notice a
brightening of mood and might even feel relief that his friend's or
lover's suffering has abated. Alternatively, the trance may seem
impenetrable, as though no consolation, no change of perspective,
will be received. A decision has been made against which all alternatives pale. One has become fused to suicide as the only solution.

Trance as Self-reinforcing

Once in the suicidal trance, a person changes how he or she
perceives the events of the world. The trance filters stimuli from the
outside and interprets them in highly limited ways. The only information permitted entry is that which corroborates the suicidal logic
and reinforces the trance. Little can get in, and very little emerges.
Each moment of pain further insults an already beleaguered psyche,
and the ability to seek help has by this time become seriously
compromised.

During the withdrawal phase, Karen grew so distracted and
confused that even simple tasks felt impossible. A graduate student
in mathematics, she continually had to choose less challenging
employment just to get by. Each setback served to reinforce her
inclination to die.

I remember sitting at this adding machine in this insurance office.
These ladies were bossing me around and I'm adding numbers,
and even that was hard for me. I couldn't even do it as well as
them! I decided right then: I already felt dead. Everything I did, I
felt more dead. Nothing felt alive and nothing would help. I just
felt it would be more congruent to be dead. Just not to have this
body to keep being in.

Karen, like others, lost faith that any input could be healing. At
the same time, she lost any ability to communicate the depths of her
suffering. Dialogue dissolved into monologue, and it was heard
only within her own mind.

Tim graphically describes the self-reinforcing quality of the
trance:

You're committed to the act of dying. You're consumed by the
impulse to die and you don't hear and don't want to hear anything
other than that. The only things that get through are the ones
which support suicide.

When one is in the trance, signals from the outside world are
heard only in relation to the original trauma. Even if the times and
places have changed, a person in the the trance sees the present only
in terms of the painful past. Every new event seems like a repetition
by rote of earlier hurtful events. And because the past is so alive in
one's present, one's sense of self remains dated, as well, as if he is the
very same person he once was. As the trance deepens, the person
comes to expect every bump in the road to produce the same inner
havoc and to leave him or her as bereft as before, if not more so.
The trance is then reinforced, and the person is left more vulnerable to the next repetition of pain. This was Deborah's state as she
composed her suicide notes, each one strengthening her resolve
to die.

I just started writing. I realized I was justifying my nonexistence. It
was straight from the past! I'm the fuck-up in my family. I'm the
only one in the family that's ever been divorced, much less twice. I
realized that I've never been looked highly upon by my family
members, and this just confirmed it. I started thinking, well, they
won't have to worry about where Deborah is going to fuck up next.

Umberto

American culture was still new and strange to Umberto. His mother
had moved the entire family from Guatemala to the United States.
She wanted better schooling for her ten children, and hoped that
they would fare more comfortably in California. His father, in his
late seventies and twenty-five years older than his wife, was more set
in his ways and resisted leaving Central America. Eventually he
acquiesced, but no one could foresee the pressures that would
silently build within this gentle, aged man.

My father killed my mother and then killed himself. He was old
and wanted to go back to Guatemala. They were a loving couple.
They never fought—maybe when I was a kid, but not for a long
time. He left a note saying he couldn't live here and he couldn't live
without her. I was thirty years old then. I loved them a lot.

Umberto is one of only three people included in this book who
did not actually attempt suicide. His story is instructive, however,
because it vividly describes the self-reinforcing nature of the suicidal
trance, and because he came so close to killing himself. Umberto
visited my office in his workman's overalls—cleaned, but with faint
stains of automotive grease. A descendant of the indigenous peoples
of Guatemala, he had a mountain of black hair and on his rather
large frame, he wore a shy and boyish expression. He spoke hesi-

tantly, still mastering the new language and describing very painful circumstances.

> *When I first found out my father killed my mother, I wanted to kill myself out of anger. I couldn't really understand why this had happened, and I felt like I wanted to join them. But when I saw my brothers and sisters and they were crying, I knew I couldn't leave them. It was now my job to give them a better life.*

Umberto, much older than his siblings, assumed the parental role in his traumatized family. He bought an automotive repair shop—a second business—in an effort to boost his income and provide a stable home. His new wife pitched in as well, ushering the kids to school, cooking meals, and attempting to reestablish some normalcy in the home. Umberto's role afforded the family some peace, but at a cost. He began to share less of himself.

> *I never told them how bad I felt. My brothers and sisters and I talked about our parents, but we never told each other that many of us were thinking of killing ourselves. I never told them.*

Umberto tried to bury his feelings. Some days were better than others: on the good days, he wouldn't think about his parents or feel oppressed by the enormous responsibility he had inherited. But the tragedy left him preoccupied and vulnerable. Two years later, he was notified by the Internal Revenue Service that he was violating the law by claiming his brothers and sisters as dependents. Upon checking, he discovered that in fact this wasn't illegal, but the IRS remained adamant. Unable to communicate adequately in a foreign language and unable to find help, Umberto felt trapped. Once again, he began to think of suicide.

> *That was the real reason I came so close to killing myself. They wanted me to pay back, not just for one year, but all the years.*

They wanted $20,000, and I didn't have the money to pay. I tried looking for legal help, but I couldn't afford it. I couldn't find anybody in the city. It was then I started thinking about it.

Umberto was torn between the role his culture demanded of the oldest male in his family—to be stoic and responsible—and the volatile feelings he hid within. In response, he withdrew into his pain and left a mask in its place.

I was always thinking about my problems. My wife knew a little, but I didn't tell her how much it was on my mind. I'd go out at two or three in the morning, pretending to go to work. The family was sleeping. I say good-bye like I will never come back. I kiss each one. I felt so bad. I was crying, crying.

Weeks passed, and Umberto was unable to sleep at all. Each letter from the government, each rejection from yet another lawyer, reinforced his resolve to die. Eventually he gave up looking for help. He entered the suicidal trance. He began spiraling further from connection with his family and from any measure of clarity.

I couldn't sleep. Just thinking, thinking about the problem— nighttime, daytime, all the time. If you cannot sleep—you have to live it to know how it feels in your body. I felt crazy. I remember a few times I drove through stop signs and red lights and didn't know till after.

I was also trying to understand why my father killed my mother. I just couldn't understand and it bothered me. Then, the more problems I had with the IRS, I started thinking, "Maybe he was wise to do it. Maybe it was okay, his way," and I thought I understood why he did that. Every day, there was a little more power in me to do it, and it kept building as things got worse.

Umberto's was a mind deeply wounded by his parents' deaths. In the trance, each new setback reinforced a final prescription. As his withdrawal continued, the only thoughts he registered were the ones rehearsing his own suicide.

A train would go by my home every morning about five o'clock. I say to myself, "I'm gonna do it. I'm gonna jump from the small bridge to the rails." I would walk to the bridge and time the train. I would sit there with my feet hanging over the side, thinking about killing myself and thinking about my father.

Loss of Will

> *Now I have lost myself, I am sick of baggage.*
>
> SYLVIA PLATH, "TULIPS"

The chronic and pervasive erosion of one's will is perhaps the most common characteristic of those who seriously contemplate suicide. Consistently, people describe this aspect of the trance with the words, "It was just too much work to go on." At this juncture, the inner resources that have permitted survival despite considerable pain are finally exhausted. Nothing helps—not intelligence or a sense of humor, not patience or perspective. Mental, emotional, and physical systems have shut down, and only a shell of the once whole person remains.

One summer afternoon, Teresa was baby-sitting next door to her home, spending time with her neighbor's newborn and earning some extra money. She looked away from the baby for an instant, and he fell from a low counter to the floor and stopped breathing. She quickly administered cardiopulmonary resuscitation and the baby revived, startled but unhurt. Teresa, however, was deeply shaken. As she sat at the kitchen table, a profound and cumulative despair began to pour through her. In her mind, she perused every aspect of her life: her brothers who had left her; her boyfriend, with whom she kept company only to irritate her mother; her feelings of not belonging at school; her exhaustion; and most importantly, her deeply disappointing relationship with her mother. From Teresa's perspective, it simply wasn't worth being alive anymore.

I was sitting at the table. I was pretty upset, thinking that I wanted my mom to pay attention and if I didn't get it, it didn't matter if I was alive anyway. While I was thinking this, I looked out of the window, and there was my mom, in a car, having sex with the delivery man out in our driveway!

The surreality of having a private view of her mother's sexual activities served to shatter all remaining hope. Immediately thereafter, Teresa gathered the materials for her suicide.

It is difficult and perhaps irrelevant to attempt to determine which components of the suicidal trance are the most debilitating and most dangerous. Any one of them—the sterile logic, the relentless reinforcement of a poisoned world view—strangles the spirit and provides a convincing rationale for an early exit. The loss of will, however, and its near-total dissipation of effort, is a more final state in which people feel themselves without reserves and absent of alternatives. It feels as though one has fallen into a bottomless hole, without a safety net or rope, and without a clue of how to reverse the fall.

Rennie's life provides a striking portrait of this fall.

Rennie _____

I had a lot of friends who were prostitutes. I tried it, but it wasn't my scene. Everything else was lucrative enough. There were rivalries going on in the red light district, weird and violent stuff; it was pretty dark. It's actually quite silly that I tried to kill myself, because I could easily have gotten somebody else to kill me just by going to the proper places. Things got pretty bad, and I started to "funnel."

The course of Rennie's life was tortured and circuitous. She grew up in a small village in Germany and always felt herself to be an outsider—in town, in school, and most painfully, in her own family. She felt suffocated by traditional customs and conventions, and had long abandoned hope that she would find interest in an ordinary life. "If you could be a certain way, and that was pretty narrow, you were accepted. I couldn't do that, so I always felt like a stranger." As a young adult, she moved into a seedy flat in the back end of Mannheim, and learned to support herself hustling pool, playing cards, and selling drugs. Living at the edge, she relied on her temerity and stamina to survive. But these qualities were finally worn thin by the constant challenge of street life, and Rennie found it difficult to envision a future. Her story exemplifies the loss of will which leads to the attempt.

> I'd burned out a lot of my other friends so I was really alone. I had just come back from Morocco, the most beautiful place I'd ever been. I wanted to go back. I had this vision of myself there—you know, the simple life, away from the drugs and the violence. The first thing that happened was that the man I lived with totally destroyed my apartment—smashed everything, left it in ruins. So I was just sitting there in this smashed-up apartment. I could barely handle being there. I thought that maybe if I could make a lot of money it would make up for being alone, but it seemed like there just wasn't enough money to be made to make up for that. I was living with somebody who was beating me up. It was horrible, but you know, I didn't even care.

Wherever she looked, she saw people who had made the same decisions as hers, only they were older and had been around longer. Their lives seemed to foreshadow her own future, and Rennie lost the will to continue.

> It didn't look like it was ever going to be different—like being in this deep hole and all the people I knew were in it too. They were

*out to make money and cheat each other to do it. I mean, everyone
that I knew was in a place that was as bleak as mine.*

*And then, there was another reality—people who had more
money, but they weren't any better off emotionally—so I didn't
know anybody that was happy. I hated Doris Day movies! I really
hadn't ever seen anybody that happy in real life. I was scared a lot,
really scared. I felt that it wasn't going to make any difference to
anybody whether I was there or not.*

The Beckoning

At this point in the trance, the inner pull toward suicide dramatically intensifies. Often it comes in the form of a voice. In fact,
mention of a voice is so common that I've learned to inquire directly
about this during interviews. This voice grows in volume with
the stress of the suicidal ordeal. It demands increasingly to be
heard above everything else, and it begins to occupy a greater part
of the person's psyche until it smothers more reasonable voices
altogether. Often people experience this voice as relentlessly
driving them toward self-destruction. Tim heard the words actually
leaving his lips, "Die now!" in a demonic exhortation to take his
own life.

Sometimes, however, the voice is less audible. Instead, the beck-
oning is experienced as an unceasing, almost magnetic, pull toward
suicide. Teresa continually felt the siren's call to rejoin her father and
escape her pain. She would imagine scenes in which, after her death,
the family would finally come back together, and all of them would
appreciate the suffering she had endured. Sometimes she herself was
included in these scenes, and sometimes she was a distant witness.
Either way, she was free of heartache and was finally being
acknowledged.

Images of the method of suicide, of one's participation in the act,
or even of the peace on the "other side" beckon the person to

suicide. These images contain tremendous power. In the trance, only they, to the exclusion of anything else, offer relief, and the promise of release.

Robert

> I remember having this rope, and I made a noose and I hung it up in the garage. It was there for about a week. Nobody seemed to notice it. I kept saying to myself, "Should I or shouldn't I?" (Robert)

Robert, a shy young man, has just turned eighteen. We meet on a break from his classes at junior college. Reticent at first, he answers my questions in terse phrases and sentences. He avoids eye contact, wrestling with how honest and graphic to be. Robert seems afraid of the power of his story and what feelings it may arouse. As the interview continues, however, he grows more comfortable with me, and relieved, I think, to be be describing his experience in the past tense.

Robert was a teenager when he attempted suicide, although he feels the seeds of his suffering were sown long before. And although he is happy these days, the safe bet a few years ago would have been against his very survival.

> I'd say it was a process of a long time. When I was nine or ten, my dad—he was an alcohol distribution manager—would come home every night and have a few scotch on the rocks. I remember one time I dressed up all in black. I'd been watching a lot of Bruce Lee movies, and I was gonna be a "Ninja." I was hiding under cars, running through the neighborhood, just being a kid, basically. Some cops had been patrolling, 'cause somebody had been stealing hubcaps in the neighborhood, and they decided it was me. They came to the house and said to my parents, "We followed your son here," and they implied that I was the one. My dad took me to the

back room and held me down and basically beat the hell out of me
because he thought I was stealing hubcaps for drugs. I didn't even
know what drugs were at that age.

Robert began to feel a stranger in his own home. His father grew
more unpredictably violent, and his mother passive, as Robert
entered adolescence. He continually felt undeservedly blamed, and,
more debilitating, he felt his father was almost exhorting him to
bring out the worst in himself.

When I entered high school, I was really having a hard time. I had a
lot of anxiety. My clique of friends were not very popular, and we
were kind of outsiders: leather jackets, white tee shirts. We were
"metal heads"— "stoners"—whatever you'd like to call us. My dad
would yell at me, really degrading things like, "You're a loser!" or
"You'll never become anything. You're gonna be a doper the rest of
your life!"—that kind of thing. It really hurt. I know I was kinda
hyper, and maybe I was a problem child, but I was never taken to a
counselor and nobody knew what was really going on. Nobody knew
until after the suicide attempts that I had learning disabilities.

Robert reacted to the pressure by dabbling in the punk scene. It
was fun for a while—going to concerts, dressing in black, and
wearing his hair in a Mohawk. He also began to drink and to
experiment with drugs. "It was pretty much a rebellious scene to get
back at my father for the way I'd been treated. It was a way of hurting
him."

During his sixteenth summer, Robert's maternal grandmother
died. His father lost his job and began drinking to excess. It seemed
that he and Robert could never find enough distance between them.
There was an ever-present feeling of impending confrontation, and
Robert was becoming fitful with anxiety and rage. Robert also fell
in love for the first time, and increasingly, he sought refuge from the
family's distress in that young and delicate relationship.

She was the first girl that I fell in love with, you know? Teenager love. And she had to move with her family to Washington. I was holding on to her for security, like when a child has a security blanket. When she left that summer, it was like "God, I have nothing."

The back of the family garage was poorly lit, and Robert's rope continued to hang there unnoticed. It hung silently, quietly waiting for Robert's decision. He would visit it a number of times during the week of his girlfriend's departure, staring and imagining what suicide would be like. Then he'd leave, not ready to go through with it. By the end of that week, however, the family tension had escalated precipitously and Robert reached a breaking point.

I remember this day, as my dad was yelling at me, thinking, "Yeah, if I killed myself, I'd show them, I'd show them," and then I started thinking, "It's not really for them; I'll show me!" I was just too stressed. So one day, I walked into the garage. It seemed pretty morbid, like it was a dungeon—scary and really dark—and then I noticed I was pretty tranquil. I was thinking, "Hey, I'm not going to be pushed around or hit anymore. I'm gonna be with the family that loves me—my grandma, my aunts."

Illusions of Eternity

The suicidal trance is a severe alteration of consciousness. Ubiquitous and convincing, it is extremely difficult to disengage from. To one who feels suicidal, it seems no more possible to change one's perspective than to suddenly part the air and step into a different dimension. The pressures are further compounded, however, as the suicidal trance begins to mutate one's vision of the future.

I thought about the future except there wasn't anything. There was a wall in front of me. It was black.

*I couldn't see into the future. I just couldn't be calm enough to sort
through things and think, "Okay, we'll just keep going and see how
things turn out." I was up against the brick wall again.*

These two statements describe the same state of mind, for the
same person, but are separated by more than twenty years. Catherine's first suicide attempt came just after her father died and as she
was entering her twenties. In the second, she was a working mother
of two children, on her second marriage, and desperately fighting to
wrest her husband from the debilitating clutches of cocaine.

For almost everyone I interviewed, the suicidal trance dramatically changed his or her image of the future. Regardless of gender,
race, ethnicity, and age, visions of the future were strikingly similar
for all those I talked to: Never-ending pain, equal to the present pain
or greater, and continuing forever, without respite. These visions
bespeak a terrible hopelessness.

Chris, now a psychotherapist, expressed this as a response to a
simple question: "When you were in the midst of feeling suicidal,
what couldn't you hope for?" She replied without hesitation, attempting to describe the feelings which, like a black hole, swallowed
all sense of possibility.

*To ever feel better. I was saying to myself, "I'll never feel better
than this. Even if I'd feel a little bit better, this feeling will always be
there ready to attack me—this feeling that it's never gonna change,
that I'm always going to feel powerless and rotten.*

Tim's response was virtually identical, but focused on the pain
which seemed so enduring.

*Forever. Eternity. That meant I'd never be able to be in a relationship with another human being: I'd be alone, isolated, in pain and
in solitary confinement within myself, with the clock ticking for*

sixty seconds on the minute, sixty minutes on the hour, tick, tick, tick, for the rest of my life.

Visions of the future are necessarily reflections of our past and present. In better moments, we can imagine ourselves in an environment that inspires us to develop our deepest talents and achieve our aspirations. We can picture ourselves in a community of people who understand our idiosyncrasies and accept our foibles; who can encourage the best from within and who can support us when we're tired. A healthy and happy present provides the inspiration for envisioning a healthy and happy future.

In these stories, however, we see the opposite. When the present is one of unabated suffering, and when that pain cannot be dealt with, one's likely response is withdrawal. As injury is followed by further injury, people become less and less able to perceive their environment accurately—less capable of seeing beyond the trance that surrounds them. They lose their balance, bewildered in the present and unable to comprehend the future. It is at this juncture, for almost everyone interviewed, that the stage is set for the final act.

Three

The Attempt

*My decision to die was really sort of a boring one—
wasn't really dramatic or anything. I was trying to drive
in L.A. traffic and I couldn't focus or concentrate like one
needs to. I used to be able to do this and lots of other
things; it used to be easy. I hit somebody ahead of me; a
little tap. It startled me. I got out of my car and just sat
down on the freeway. There's all these millions of cars
lined up in traffic around me and I began thinking,
"What am I doing on this planet? If this is what existence
is gonna be, I don't want it." (Karen)*

In this chapter we will examine a realm of experience that is
ruinous, where ceaseless pain suffocates the spirit and consumes the
will to live. These are the moments of the suicide attempt: the
"whole catastrophe," as Zorba declares. Here are all the feelings,
thoughts, and actions at the threshold of suicide—the extreme limit
of one's ability and willingness to endure the pain and still remain
alive. Suicide cannot be understood by isolating any one moment in

the process. In order to explore the mystery of suicide, we must listen to all its voices: both its naked, unremitting pain and its cool and methodical planning. Important questions emerge: What frightful clash of internal and external forces would point one toward self-annihilation? What abandonment of hope could so challenge our basic innate instincts toward self-preservation?

As we listen to those who have decided to end their lives, we find some answers to these questions. Each story is different, and yet they all have significant commonalities. The story of suicide begins with loss or trauma, an unbridgeable sense of alienation, and a deep need to hide one's pain. Withdrawal begins and then deepens—gradually, almost imperceptibly. Eventually, the person who was once here is no longer present. She may still live in our home and eat at our table, but she only goes through the motions of living. Hiding behind a façade, the person is isolated, and vulnerable to the urgings of the suicidal trance. Unchecked, the trance draws him or her to one fatal choice.

THE TUNNEL

And then I went to bed and thought that would be it. I remember lying there. The window looked out over the river and it was a beautiful scene. The moon was full and I was feeling this real peacefulness. I said to myself, "It's a beautiful night to die." I got into this whole other state, of knowing I was gonna die and accepting it and really wanting it. It's like when you go to weddings, you take pictures to remember everything that happened. Well, I was taking mental pictures to remember this. (Chris)

At the brink of the attempt, the suicidal trance intensifies to a frightening pitch. People feel extended beyond their capacity for survival. Some describe a deafening cacophony of voices, while others relate an otherworldly stillness and certitude. The suicidal act itself may be fraught with emotions of anger or grief, or it may be purposeful, even peaceful, and virtually without feeling. The ability to consider options has been so truncated that the person sees his future as though through a narrow tunnel, at the end of which is only one possible outcome. Time exists only as the succession of moments between the present and this one final act.

Chris's experience of this tunnel was so intense that everything she thought and felt seemed to further confirm her desire to end her life. She was not to be thwarted, either by a change of heart or by outside intervention.

Chris _____

When I got married, I had this whole picture: the good wife and mother, the good daughter, the whole American pie-in-the-sky picture. I just worked so hard at it: to read all the child-care manuals, to be the perfect supermom, to make sure the house was spotless, to do everything for my husband. And then the whole picture died. I did all the stuff other military wives did, but I was blamed when he wasn't promoted. I just wasn't a good navy officer's wife.

Chris met me in her office. It was summer in Santa Rosa, dry and hot, and the indoors provided some relief from the sun. As we sat down, registering our initial impressions, I was immediately intrigued with her. Chris is a large woman, big-boned and a little heavy. Her arms were muscular, her hands veined and rough-hewn. This is a woman who has lived in the country, worked the land, canned her own food in the summer, found a way to make things work in difficult times. She is not afraid to be physical. She isn't averse to hard work. She has a ready smile and a hearty laugh, and when she speaks about her life, she is straightforward and candid, eschewing both drama and false modesty. Chris's story vividly illustrates her paradoxical determination to wrest control of her life, by means of her death. It also reflects once again how traumatic loss, unacknowledged, may form the seeds of suicide.

As a young woman, Chris found herself foundering in a marriage that was painful and disempowering. She was targeted as the problem—the cause of all the family's misfortune—and after many years, she had come to believe it too.

He was an officer stationed in Oahu during the war. We got married, he went to boot camp, and he came out thinking, "What the hell am I doing married?"; but he didn't have the courage to just say, "We need to end this," and neither did I. So I hung out for the next eight years with him not wanting me and me trying really hard to be "good enough." I don't think he hated me; it was just all of a sudden he had this whole other life, the navy, thrown at him and he didn't know how to handle it. I became extremely sensitive to criticism—overly sensitive, you know. If anyone criticized me, I felt like I didn't deserve to live. He spent most of his time at the barracks, not coming home for long periods, so it was just me and our daughter, and he didn't care much about her because she was a girl. I got real depressed. It felt like this heavy weight descended on me. I felt lonely—scared—and was growing very tired.

Chris and her husband moved back to the mainland, bought an old farmhouse, and tried to make a new start, but nothing changed. He continued to distance himself and assign blame, and she grew morose and pained. The grief of his rejection was omnipresent and consuming. For months on end, they would barely speak, occasionally being sexual—for him a release, and for her a momentary respite from loneliness. Curiously, Chris seemed incapable of expressing anger, as though those feelings were being consistently short-circuited, undermined by sadness. She had no experience at being assertive. Demanding basic civility seemed inconceivable, and her self-confidence eroded.

I would get this sinking feeling, like the bottom would drop out of my heart, and these thoughts and feelings that "I don't deserve to

live," if I got angry at anybody. They could get angry at me, and I
didn't like it much, but I certainly couldn't reciprocate.

For almost all those I interviewed, there was a precipitating event
that occurred just before the suicide attempt. A cursory look would
lead one to believe that this particular event caused the act, but the
decision to end one's life rarely erupts so dramatically from one
source of stress. A precipitating event appears in almost every
recounting of an attempt, but shouldn't be regarded as the real basis
for it. Instead, the event serves to propel one further into the suicidal
trance—into the "tunnel." Ed's first homosexual encounter unleashed a torrent of self-hatred and fear. Teresa was horrified when
the baby fell, and she could no longer defend herself from the
futility and worthlessness she felt. Jason, unable to extricate himself
from the violence between him and his father, focused the rage on
himself. Some of these occurrences were clearly dramatic, while
others were mild, such as when Karen tapped the car in front of her
on the freeway or when Robert lost his girlfriend. In either case,
these incidents thrust people headlong into the tunnel. Rather than
awakening them from the suicidal trance, the precipitating events
cemented the conviction that there was no hope—no recourse.

Two events catapulted Chris into her attempt. The first involved
loss. She had been sick for three weeks—unusual for her, for she
rarely fell ill with colds or the flu. To her horror, Chris discovered
she was pregnant. She needed counsel, but talking about it with her
husband went predictably bad.

I had a lot of turmoil about being an okay mother—not being
abusive, 'cause that's how I grew up. I mean, I never abused our
daughter, but the temptation was always there. I was doing all
right with one child, but I knew inside that with another, I'd lose it.
And I knew I wasn't gonna get help from my husband.

So I said, "I really need to tell you that I just found out I'm
pregnant." At first he just yelled, "I'm not ever living with you

again!" When he stopped yelling at me, I told him I thought we should have an abortion and then he just casually said, "Oh well, that's probably a good idea. We couldn't afford a baby right now anyway." He didn't ask me how I was feeling at all! Some time went by and it suddenly occurred to him that he was fertile. He yelled, "Whoa! I got you pregnant!" and he became excited because he had always had a low sperm count and it bothered him a lot. So all of a sudden, he's on this ego trip, while my life is falling apart. I didn't even tell him what I was feeling. I just went ahead.

Chris numbed herself and had the abortion. She had calculated her options as best as she could. She felt that if they had the child, she might never pull free from her husband, and she realized that her situation would only worsen. She could not imagine bringing another child into her broken family, and she no longer believed that she could maintain the composure it would require. The weeks following were some of her most difficult. She wept unceasingly and her isolation felt insurmountable.

I couldn't stop crying. I couldn't regain the control I had, and after a while I couldn't even get a handle on what I was crying about. Every night, I sat on the couch crying. It felt like I even lost track of who was sad. It didn't make a difference anymore. It felt like all there was in the world was sadness. It permeated everything. I started feeling possessed by the house and possessed by the mood, so I would take walks in the woods and on the mountains with my daughter. She was three and a half. We'd spend the day in the fields, or by the river that ran through town, and I'd feel better. And then I'd come home and it would all descend on me again. I even made two trips to a town seventy miles away to see about moving, but all I could do was cry when I got there. I felt wrong for wanting to leave.

It was like a trap set on the floor of the forest, invisible and ready to ensnare the unsuspecting. Every effort Chris made toward self-preservation, deciding to assert herself and leave her suffocating predicament, would trigger waves of doubt and engulf her in self-recrimination.

> I'd ask, "What if it's just because I'm in a low mood?" Or I'd say to myself, "It's all my fault. I'm ruining my family's life. I'm breaking up my home. I'm just like my mother."

Chris could not envision a change. She could identify no one close enough, nothing powerful enough, to alter the downward course of her life. One night, after hurling invectives at one another, she and her husband began to hurl the furniture. A huge fight ensued. To Chris's astonishment, she heaved a Volkswagen clutch housing directly at her husband's head. He ducked just in time, and it crashed through the glass front door. They both stood frozen for a moment, shards of the pane diffracting the light from the porch, and then quietly, without another word, she turned and slowly mounted the stairs to the bedroom.

> The pain was up here in my heart, but in the pit of my stomach it felt like everything just dropped out of me, out the bottom. There was just horror. I had these two bottles of sleeping pills; the doctor kept prescribing them, and I kept on not taking them, just saving them. I knew that would be enough. As I was walking upstairs, I felt cold all through my body, but also determined. It felt like it was the only reasonable thing to do.

This was the second trigger. Chris had finally become angry, but she felt her rage to be poisonous. The fight and her interpretation of it only pushed her further into the tunnel and hurtled her toward her attempt. As she walked upstairs, she thought how much better it would be for her child with her mother dead. She would be relieving everyone of her toxic presence.

I was having thoughts like, "It will be better for my daughter. Her father can raise her. She needs not to be poisoned by me." I remembered that after my father died, his mother—my grandmother—came over in a rage one day and screamed at my mother that if it weren't for her and the kids, my father would be alive. Somehow, I was really bad for people.

A number of disparate feelings swirled within her at the same time. She felt a coldness within her. It penetrated her muscles and bones and she felt it in her heart, as if she were freezing. She also felt herself calmly determined. She wouldn't be deterred, and there was no need to be demonstrative. She would simply take the sleeping pills she had saved, fall asleep and not wake up.

When someone is deep in the tunnel, all events are seen through one exclusive filter. It is too late for subtle cues or inferences to change one's mind. Peripheral vision is impeded, alternatives are not considered. There is only one path, only one "finish line." Chris methodically swallowed two bottles of sleeping pills and went to bed. She lay there looking out the window, with a feeling of acceptance.

It was like the Last Supper. I was lying in bed, thinking, "These are my last memories." I was savoring them. I wasn't feeling scared. I just felt peaceful and cold.

It was not clear how much time passed, but suddenly Chris noticed a presence in the room. Her daughter was standing by the bed. She had awakened and come upstairs—something which had never happened before—and she was looking at the bottles. She seemed to understand, and became frightened. In an instant, she grabbed the bottles and ran downstairs to her father. A dramatic chase ensued—a desperate series of events in which Chris fought to die.

I was thinking, "Oh, shit! This is not what I planned. I overheard my husband calling an ambulance. The nearest hospital was

*twenty-five miles away, with winding roads, so I got up and
dressed as quickly as I could. I was getting pretty drowsy, but I ran
downstairs to go out the door. He grabbed me there, but I got loose
from him. I was thinking, "You're not gonna stop me!", and I
started running down the street. It's about one A.M. in this little
town of sixty people and my daughter came out screaming at me,
"Mommy, don't go! Mommy, don't leave me!" It just tore up my
heart, but I couldn't change my mind at that point. I was just
unable to be rational anymore, and I still thought it was the best
thing to do for her.*

Each obstacle reinforced Chris's determination. She knew the
small town well, and ran to a spot hidden beneath a bridge down by
the river. It had been her secret hiding place, where she knew she
would not be found. She lay down, and discovered herself beginning
to calm once again. Her legs felt rubbery and a drowsiness began
descending upon her.

*I was losing muscular control and it was getting harder to move, so
I just lay there, and I realized I'm back in this beautiful scenery—
the river, the full moon. I wasn't going to let go of that. I absolutely
had to have that as I drifted away.*

Once again, though, her fragile tranquility was shattered. In the
distance, she heard a noise. It seemed out of place so late at night, in
such a sleepy little town. She barely noticed it at first, but it grew in
pitch and volume. She sensed it had to do with her.

*I heard bloodhounds! My husband ran to a neighbor with a piece
of my clothing, and suddenly I'm being chased by these stupid
dogs. When they were about half a block from me, I pulled myself
up and headed for the center of the bridge. I remember thinking,*

"Well they're not gonna let me do it my own way, so I'll just jump."
I was really determined. I didn't doubt it. I just didn't want to live
anymore.

Chris felt a mix of panic and anger. She was alarmed that her husband would thwart her plans, and angry that her autonomy was being compromised. For Chris was not simply fighting to die. In the tunnel, in this highly exaggerated state, her wish to kill herself represented a number of conflicting desires, all highly compressed and highly charged. First, suicide served as an exit from the pain with which she had labored so long. Second, as if she were executing a death sentence from somewhere or someone else, her wish to die reflected a deep self-loathing. She actually believed that everyone would be better off after she died. Finally, and perhaps most paradoxically, she was also struggling to assert her right of self-determination. The wish to kill herself represented a desire to manage her life as she chose, as she wished, in whatever form, even death. Self-determination was a critical experience that had eluded her all her life, and she wished for it now.

Inside I was screaming, "Why can't I just do what I want to do for
once in my life!" I felt, you know, all of these years that he didn't
give a shit what was happening to me and now that I've decided
this, why the hell does he care! When I really needed him, he
wasn't there, and now that I don't, there he is with a half a dozen
men and these dogs! Why is he doing this to me?

Even as her body was beginning to falter, her mind methodically clicked through contingency plans for her suicide. Feeling the press of the chase, she ran to the center of the bridge and climbed onto the railing.

I felt this incredible determination, you know, like, "No one can stop
me." It was a tremendous sense of power. I jumped from the railing,

but as I was in the air, they grabbed me by the ankles. I was hanging upside down, swinging my arms and trying to get free. I was furious! Then they pulled me back onto the bridge. I've never felt so enraged in my life. I was fighting them and then I was biting them. They all had their hands on me and were holding me down and I was kicking and screaming. I really hated them at that point. There was no way I wanted to go with them. Somebody took his jacket off, and wrapped me up in it and they just held me down till the ambulance came.

Even in the ambulance, Chris had thoughts of bolting when no one was looking. In this state, she would try whatever it would take to complete the attempt. But she was strapped in, and shortly thereafter the sleeping pills took hold.

Everything just went kind of fuzzy and blank. I got really dizzy and tired and then I kind of collapsed and fell asleep. I was going in and out when I felt them begin to slap me. God, it was a miserable ride. It seemed unreal, feeling so angry and sleepy and being hit repeatedly. At some point I remember beginning to feel horribly embarrassed, really ashamed of myself that people were seeing this.

For most, the first moments in the hospital are chilling. There is inevitably a frenzy of activity, focused on either resuscitating the body or sedating the mind. Doctors, nurses, crisis workers, and aides are often quickly on the scene, compounding the confusion as much as helping. Chris's experience was no different, and she would have to survive one hellish night and days of humiliation before beginning to take the steps necessary to extricate herself from her web of hopelessness.

THE ATTEMPT ITSELF

As people describe the details of their suicide attempts, we find that within the actual attempt to take one's life there exist smaller, highly powerful, and sometimes conflicting experiences. Just as a hurricane contains a number of discrete weather systems—the ever-intensifying winds portending the storm's approach, the full malevolent force of the tempest unleashed, and the eye at its center (often so tranquil that one forgets the storm will soon resume its deadly course), a suicide attempt is composed of many different mind states. Each of them contains its own set of thoughts and emotions, and at any given point great sadness can exist side-by-side with a feeling of determination, and volcanic rage along with calm acceptance. Experiences within the suicide attempt include:

- Fury and rage
- The methodical trance, and
- Intimations of death

The Fury

The central moments in some suicide attempts are silent and methodical, but others are filled with an almost unearthly rage and desperation. All of the frustration, disappointment, and despair converge during a few explosive moments in which one's energy becomes directed toward self-destruction.

As the summer drew to a close, Tim spent more time alone. Moments of rest and peace grew less frequent and were supplanted by long, withering bouts of confusion, fear, and depression. Tim drew upon every ounce of his composure and self-restraint, and yet they weren't enough. He was exhausted.

> I had done so much work on myself and I was still in pain. I figured I must be insane and I just couldn't live with suffering such insanity. Excruciating doesn't even describe it.

One autumn day Tim voluntarily checked himself into a local psychiatric hospital, but he didn't stay. Frightened and bewildered, he left only hours later and began hitchhiking to a town east of the hospital. Unexpectedly, he ran into a friend who, disturbed by Tim's state, took him home to his farm for quiet and rest. Sometime in early morning, having been asleep for only a few hours, Tim awoke, startled. A final dose of terror, rage, and pain roared through him. It shook the bedrock of his mind and destroyed whatever skeletal sense of order he had preserved. Unable to remain indoors, Tim bolted through the back door and into the orchard. It was pitch dark. The air was cold, leaves were blowing, and the wind was biting at his skin.

I heard screaming voices everywhere. I saw images of buildings burning, charring. Part of my psyche had been sheared off; the protective part was blown away. I felt hopeless beyond anything I'd ever felt, and I was enraged at my insanity. In those moments, I felt it would go on forever. The suicidal feelings I had on and off suddenly became a totally consuming roar in my mind, my body and my spirit. I had a kitchen knife in my hand, and I started slashing my arms and wrists. There was blood flying everywhere. I was screaming the whole time that I wanted to die and I'm yelling at myself, "Die now! Die now!" I felt that whatever I was carrying—this demonic, hellish consciousness—I needed to exorcise it, kill it. I needed to sacrifice myself and protect the world from me.

My friend must have heard me screaming, and by the time he charged into the backyard, I was a mess. He grabbed my arms, held them up in the air, and screamed, "What have you done! What have you done!" I went limp and just closed my eyes. I was exhausted. I was in shock. Just hanging there. I was also afraid: "Maybe I'm gonna live. What am I gonna do then?"

Tim's fury was directed at the demons raging within. When his friend grabbed him, however, the spell was broken. Tim had cut through muscle and tendon, and hours of delicate emergency surgery were required to repair the damage. He was in shock, profoundly fatigued and rarely communicative for weeks thereafter. His hands and arms were heavily bandaged, and they had to be kept immobile. They were useless to him. He would try not to think about what had happened, but two apparently conflicting thoughts would periodically surface: Had he been more methodical, had his friend not come tearing out of the house, he might not have survived. Lying alone in his hospital bed, he felt lucky and "indescribably grateful." These were sentiments he had never remembered feeling. But Tim was also still frightened. There were moments of profound doubt, and sometimes he would even speak to the nurse about the possibility of euthanasia. Something, however, became painfully clear to Tim. He wasn't afraid to die. Tim was afraid of living. Living seemed unfathomable. He simply could not yet imagine what alien blend of patience, courage, and effort would be required to rebuild his life.

How can we understand the rage that surfaces during a suicide attempt? First we can see that it represents the explosion of a psychological-emotional charge that has been building over time, like a volcanic eruption that finally reaches the surface of the earth, unleashing tremendous destructive power. Second, we can ask, "Toward whom or what is the fury really directed?" In Tim's case, there were two answers. He wanted to destroy his insanity—the death-seeking forces in his mind, which he experienced as both demonic and overwhelming. And at a deeper level, he was angry at his deceased parents. Tim harbored dark and unspeakable rage at them for the vacuum and the broken family they had left behind when they died.

I was furious at them for deserting us—for abandoning me—and when they were alive, for making me have to take care of them— my mother especially. I couldn't talk about it with anyone, so I would get into the car and drive and scream. The depression was so

*consuming sometimes that all I could do was yell for a while to
release it. I was just trying to cope.*

These were difficult emotions to admit and express. His parents
were unable to hear his complaint, and he felt his friends and
remaining family would not understand. Instead, the pressure increased until it exploded in a self-annihilating rage.

Most suicide attempts enacted in such rage exhibit this duality,
even when the "significant others" are still alive. The fury is targeted
both at the unbearable pain and at those who are seen as unreceptive
to the person's torment. This second target reflects a virtual collapse
of communication, sometimes between spouses and sometimes
between children and parents. To the person attempting suicide,
suicide seems the only way left to be heard—the only way to express
how much these relationships have degenerated—and to admonish
those who seemingly don't care. This anger is a volatile mixture of
unrequited need, deep pain, and rage; and in a suicide attempt, it is
turned inward on oneself.

Gary was only eighteen when he attempted. Born into an upper-
middle-class family in a fashionable part of Princeton, he had
sampled most of the recreational drugs available and was a consistent drinker by the time he was in his teens. He was chronically
bored and unchallenged with suburban life, and as time passed, he
and his family grew alienated. They were unable to find common
ground and inclined to blame each other for the discord in the
family. The more unaccepted Gary felt, the wilder his behavior
became—both artistic (for which he had a flair) and destructive
(which more than once had introduced him to the local police). He
wasn't fully willing to leave his home yet, but he refused to observe
its rules and restrictions.

Gary's father had over the years displayed a tendency toward
physical and verbal abuse. Father and son frequently argued and
occasionally came to blows. One night they both lost control. No

other family members seemed able to intervene. Gary was beaten severely and then tied to a chair.

> *He began to shave my hair off, pulling it, tugging it. There was blood from my scalp running down my face and he was yelling, "This is how you're gonna look if you live under this roof, and you're gonna behave just like any other boy!"*

> *It was finally too much. I was light-headed from sobbing so hard and I was feeling so crazed and angry. I was shuddering and my muscles felt like they were moving me, rocking me back and forth. I didn't want to die, but I needed the pain to stop, and I wanted them to experience my pain.*

Gary had entered the tunnel. His self-control, already compromised by drugs and alcohol, simply wasn't strong enough to contain such charged emotions. With all means of protest rendered futile and with no possibility of overpowering his father, he felt only one avenue available to him. Gary's attempt reflected a dual desire: to squelch his pain and to broadcast how violent his family had become. Having no power to communicate this while alive, he chose to do so by attempting to die.

> *I went down to the workshop in the basement. I just poured the biggest shot of alcohol and just sucked it down so I couldn't feel a thing. Then I strung these thick stereo wires over the pipes. It was pretty high—the ceilings were high—and I just kicked the chair away.*

He was told afterward that their dog, old and placid, had come downstairs and begun to bark wildly. It was a family joke that the dog never made noise, even when strangers entered the house. His mother came down to investigate. Gary had lost consciousness and was found within minutes of losing his life.

Catherine's story was similar, although she was middle-aged at the time of the attempt. Furious at her husband's chronic unwillingness to heed her warnings about their crumbling family, she despaired of ever getting through to him. After a particularly vicious exchange, and when everyone had left the house, she ran into the garage. Although it was years later when we spoke, she wept as she told me of her attempt.

> I wrote a suicide note saying that I wanted my sister to take my two girls; and I proceeded into the garage. In a rage, I pulled everything out of the garage, put the car in there, shut the door, and turned the car on. I was so angry—I had so much adrenaline pumping through my body—that I wasn't thinking clearly. It was just anger piled on anger piled on anger. I was in there thinking, "Just breathe in the fumes."

Neither Gary nor Catherine could find an outlet for their rage. Their angry protestations leading up to the suicide attempt seemed to fall on unreceptive ears, and so each had decided, categorically and finally, that there was no one who could help or cared to. Their attempts reflected the sum of all their frustration and fury, turned, in one dramatic act, against themselves.

The Methodical Trance

Suicide attempts expressing strong emotion are dramatic and highly disturbing. For Tim in the orchard, Gary in the basement, and Catherine in the garage, there seemed to be no outlet, no target toward which to direct their emotion other than themselves. Suicide was the only channel they could find for their overwhelming rage. Hearing their stories leaves us uneasy—perhaps even frightened—to realize that internal and external pressures can escalate so precipitously.

It is surprising, however, that most people who attempt suicide experience relatively little emotion during the event. In fact, only a handful of those interviewed in this research said that there was a wild emotional tone to their suicide attempts. Instead, most spoke of a more methodical and purposeful demeanor, muted in emotion.

After his therapy group that night, Vic calmly wrote notes to everyone, set out a new suit and fresh underwear, and even apportioned a few days' food and litter for his cats. Similarly, Deborah, the medical secretary who wrote suicide notes at work, experienced an eerie flatness in her mood during the attempt:

> I was just matter-of-fact about the whole thing. "Okay, now I'm going to do this"—switching off anything else that might possibly enter. It was as if I was following a recipe. I mean, if you're baking a cake, you don't have a lot of emotion wrapped up in, "Oh boy! We have two cups of flour, isn't that wonderful!" You just get the flour out, measure it, and pour it. So I began to drink heavily 'cause I figured it wouldn't hurt so much. I finished a bottle of José Cuervo tequila and I started taking aspirin, because I heard it thins the blood. I ran the bath with warm water and was planning to open my wrists and then let the blood flow into the tub. In the meantime, I continued writing notes, writing to the most important people first just in case my timing was off.

What allows one to become so nonchalant? Psychologists refer to this as process as dissociation, in which people separate or distance themselves from painful or frightening emotions and memories, sometimes splitting them out of awareness altogether. This unconscious mechanism is quite effective as a temporary way of dealing with overwhelming stress or trauma. Over time, however, it leaves one's emotional life truncated and shallow. The suicidal trance is an extreme example of this. It is as if there are two people present: one is in unbearable torment and the other is calculating the best way to eliminate the former and thus eliminate the agony. At worst, as with Karen, one may feel already dead, simply waiting for a final release.

I wasn't crying all the time. I wasn't upset. I just felt dead. I didn't feel connected to anyone or anything, even my body. My body felt more like a vehicle. The aliveness was severed. It just felt weird being on the planet—just this side of dead, like suspended animation, waiting.

———

It was a delicate situation for Ruth. Understanding that she needed help, she sought psychological care away from the medical school. She was afraid that if her emotional condition were discovered she would be found unfit for psychiatric training. Ruth had already made a number of suicidal gestures in her life. As an adolescent, she intentionally walked in front of a truck barreling down the street. Once, in medical school, she opened the window of her fourteenth-floor dorm room and sat on the ledge, debating whether to jump. Another time, she tried to hang herself. After taking an anatomy and physiology class, she cut through the arteries and veins in her arm. The worse she felt, the more clinically methodological and more technically sophisticated her attempts became.

It was weird, because I was thinking to myself, "If you cut through here, and then there—" I'd give myself lidocaine so I wouldn't feel pain. This was the beginning of this very detached way I'd attempt. I'd be thinking, "Just do this, then this, and you'll just bleed out and then it will be over." I remember there just wasn't very much emotion.

Compounding her isolation, Ruth was also embarrassed about needing hospital care. In more critical moments, she felt ashamed for not completing her suicide attempts—for "fucking up dying." She was hospitalized eight times in total, and for the most part found that these events helped her to find equilibrium and to let go, for a time, of the desire to kill herself. Each time after Ruth was hospitalized, she bounced back. With a replenished psyche and new sense of direction, she completed courses left unfinished and passed those she had failed.

Almost a decade passed, and Ruth assiduously worked to relieve the anger she carried inside and to heal the crushing sense of loss that lay beneath that. She sought psychotherapy, and entered one of the most rigorous in-patient programs available. It was hard work, but beneficial for Ruth because it provided a protected environment, gave her a sense of belonging, and afforded her an opportunity to express the layers of rage she felt without hurting herself.

I fought them every step of the way. They'd say, "Ruth, this is yellow," and I'd say, "No." They'd say, "It's green," and I'd say, "No." My psychiatrist really understood what the problems were and helped me concretize things. I would fight with him, but learned in the fighting that it wasn't him I was fighting. They made me take responsibility for my behavior, and made me see I was a "murderer." I was just murdering myself.

Ruth began to feel better, but the pressures of the medical world, the hardest part of which was the social isolation, affected her. In addition, an intern's hours were unconscionably long, and the responsibilities sometimes seemed daunting. Once again, her strength began to erode.

It seems like as I start each new sort of accomplishment, it's a time when I regress a little. It's still a mystery to me. The pressures of being an intern were much greater than I imagined, and coupled with how exhausted I was, I started thinking about killing myself again.

The suicide rate for physicians is approximately double that for the general population, and it is almost double again for psychiatrists. Most psychiatrists who kill themselves do so in the early years

of their profession, when they are still new to its considerable
pressures. Most are self-medicated and have been addicted to drugs
or alcohol for quite some time. Many have sustained either professional, personal, or financial losses. Perhaps, after aspiring for so
long and working so diligently to ascend to the top of their profession, as acknowledged experts in psychiatric illness and the care of
others, they are unable to see that they themselves are also people in
need. Psychiatrists often find it difficult to consult their peers for
help or to find someone with whom they can unburden their
psyches. Also, as medical doctors, they have easy access to the means
of killing themselves.

Some of these factors were already in place for Ruth before her
most serious attempt. It had been a particularly difficult year. Her
therapist was diagnosed as having breast cancer and was unavailable to her; her preceptor died; her aunt died; she was evicted from
her apartment; and she and her lover separated. Ruth felt defeated.
She seemed to have no feeling left. There was no room in her for the
grief of another loss.

> I was thinking, "Here we are, ten years later, and things still aren't
> right. There really isn't anything anybody else can do for me. I've
> had therapy. I've had treatment. My therapist cares for me and I
> care for her, but it's really not enough. I don't have my lover; I got
> thrown out of an apartment I didn't even like. I just can't take this
> anymore and this is how I'm gonna solve it." I said to myself, "This
> is a permanent solution." A kind of peacefulness and calm came
> over me, like "This is the right thing to do." It felt good.

During the next week, Ruth began to remove syringes, needles,
tubing, and heparin—an anticoagulant, which prevents the blood
from clotting—from the emergency room in which she worked.
Methodical and devoid of emotion, Ruth gathered the materials
necessary for her demise.

I was very matter-of-fact about it. I'd stopped doing drugs a while ago, but I had a beer, turned on the television, turned off the phone, and sat down to put all this stuff together. I unpacked the tubing, connected it, and set up a needle where the blood would flow into a big jug. It was very methodical. It was also very symbolic. My mother would put stuff into her with needles, and I was taking stuff out.

I laid back in my chair and watched it flow a little bit and then I watched some TV. It felt really good at first, still calm and peaceful. I started feeling light-headed, and then I got tachycardia—my heartbeat became irregular. I had lost quite a bit of blood. Then I noticed this debate inside me: "Ruth, you really don't want to do this. You really shouldn't. You can't do this to your therapist, to your niece and nephew." Then another part would say, "This will really work. Just let it flow and go to sleep and when you wake up it will be over."

Intimations of Death

> *I'd know everything. I'd be delivered from confusion and learn the meaning of my life, the reason for my being here. All the questions would finally be answered. (Ian)*

> *I'd finally be with my family—with the people who loved me. (Robert)*

Images powerfully organize our lives. We entertain images of our possible future, and memories of our past, and both influence our experience of the present. We envision spirituality in the form of gods, saints, and angels. If we're honest, most of us will admit that we have imagined the moments of our death.

As children, we wrestle with the incomprehensibility of death. "Will I still breathe?" "It must be cold under the ground." "Will Mommy and Daddy be there too?" "Do puppies also go to heaven?" As we age, we may ask different questions and our concepts of death may be more complex, but we still wonder what this enormous event will bring. Both the questions and the answers come to us in pictures.

People who experience being close to death call upon the visions they've accumulated during their lifetimes, for they offer guidance. These images may encourage certain choices and may discourage others, but they are always central players in the drama of our own mortality.

This is especially true in the midst of a suicide attempt. Each person interviewed had a characteristic vision of an existence after suicide and a particular understanding of how it would provide the perfect response to suffering. For people in suicidal pain, as for many others, images of death offer respite and future reward. In the suicidal trance, the images of death as release and as an entry into a better world are so powerful and convincing that they can determine whether someone will continue to endure the suffering or will attempt suicide. Robert saw his death as both liberation and deliverance: he would finally be free of those who didn't seem to love him and reunited with deceased members of his family who did. Mark, the painter and college professor, in his journal entry, envisioned death as the end of a life sentence of suffering.

> Thus the need to affix the proper period to a life sentence that had become run-on. Back to the bathroom, blade in hand, turning the shower on quite hot. He felt a pulse in his ears, cauterizing the flow of forevers.

Teresa's image of death was filled with levels of meaning. Her wish to die, born of tremendous frustration and yearning, was actually a desire to reconnect: with her mother, with whom life had felt so disappointing; with her father, toward whom she alternately directed her anger and her supplications; and with some spiritual force that would finally confirm what she had always hoped to hear that she was special, in some way, to someone.

> *I really wanted to kill myself but I didn't really want to die. I pictured myself being like one of those people in stories, who would die and then come back to life after they saw heaven or something. I thought that either I would die completely, so maybe I'd see that light people talk about, or it would change other people's lives and then somehow change mine. I remember sitting there after taking the pills, waiting, and thinking, "Maybe I'll see God and find out that I am special." Finding that out was important, because I felt there had to be something deeper than what was going on here.*

She needed to end her suffering and to secure that intimate bond, and she reasoned that killing herself offered the best chance to make it happen.

> *I wanted the experience of some deeper spiritual connection, to someone or something, because the [relationships] I had weren't satisfying at all. I was also taking my last real chance to be mad at my dad. I was tired of being alone. I wanted him here, with me. At the very least, I thought that I'll finally find my dad.*

Teresa projected a deeply personal vision onto the face of death. In her view, understanding would supplant ignorance and love would take the place of exploitation. Where there had been division, there would now be reconciliation. Even those who had died would somehow return, herself included. These images supported Teresa's attempt to die.

There were others interviewed, however, for whom intimations of death had the opposite effect: they halted the attempt right in the middle. Cynthia felt she learned the reality of death during her attempt, and it terrified her. In her acerbic style, she described an alarming confrontation.

This was no suicidal gesture. I wasn't messing around. I had no fear at the beginning. I had always envisioned endless sleep. This was the romantic ideal. I ended up vomiting, which wasn't very romantic, and then I got very high from the seventy-five Sominex I took. This wasn't the endless sleep I planned on.

Suddenly, I experienced nothingness—vast, black, and bleak, you know? It seemed like nothingness was ominous, all-pervasive, and all-encompassing. I thought, "This is not good!" Nothingness was not very appealing. Endless sleep was appealing. But nothingness? Anything was better than nothing! So I called up an old boyfriend, who came to my apartment and took me to the hospital. It was a struggle physically to get to the phone and speak. I had to crawl. I didn't remember going to the hospital. I was unconscious for three days or so.

Vic had merrily continued preparations for his suicide and was about through ingesting the antidepressants he'd saved.

I fixed a Coke and put it down on my end table, got all my pills, I guess sixty or eighty of them, and began taking one at a time. I must have taken forty or fifty; they said there weren't many left. All of a sudden it felt like a big truck came up and hit me. "What are you doing! This is wrong! You're going to go to Hell!" I guess it was my religious background, you know. Hell is where you go when you're punished. It's where you relive your sins and mistakes over and over without ever being able to leave, until time ends! I thought, "I can't do that." So I got into my car, probably the stupidest thing, and drove to the hospital. I was going only about twenty miles per hour, and I pulled over every time there was a car behind me. It was the longest ride I have ever taken.

Cynthia aborted her attempt after apprehending a kind of existential void—a nothingness extending formlessly and forever. Vic's images were classically Catholic, resurfacing from the years he had attended church as a child. Ruth's perceptions of death changed dramatically as she aged. The early versions supported her wish to die, while later ones, strongly influenced by her medical training, played a part in deterring her.

When I was younger, I thought that I would die and see everybody feeling sorry for me. But after four years of medical school and residency, I'd think, "Dead is dead: cold-slab-on-a-slate dead." What I imagine now is bodies in the morgue, or doing a "code" on somebody and they don't wake up. Not very attractive.

The Eye of the Hurricane

I felt a sense of satisfaction, of finishing the job. I wanted to make sure it really worked. Walking back to the bed I felt calm and peaceful. (Cassie)

It was a good day to die. (Rennie)

Suicide attempts promise a kind of certitude that those who suffer actually yearn for—offering to end a life sentence of unceasing pain and to eliminate the daunting complexity of human existence with a single act. Suicide attempts create a sense of freedom in those who long for escape. People commonly report that at the center of their suicide attempts there were sudden moments of stillness: feelings of acceptance, serenity, and peacefulness, and relief from pain. How can calm be found in such an improbable context?

In these moments, when, like Abraham and Isaac combined, one is poised at the altar as both executor and sacrifice, one experiences a heightened state of awareness. One's attention is powerfully directed away from the trance and the chronic fixation on pain and is focused instead on the moment-by-moment experience of the present.

At this point people report being able to disidentify from the world of suffering and enter a new world that is smaller, less complex, and manageable.

Suicide promises to eliminate the possibility of continued hurt. In a series of perhaps inalterable moments, a person can sever his or her relationship with the world, declare an end, and feel relief that the war is over. He or she suddenly senses the serenity of nature or experiences a clarity of perspective. One man I interviewed said, "Everything came together. I finally felt clear. I knew this [suicide] was the answer." On Robert's final walk to the hanging rope in the garage, although nervous, he felt filled with "tranquility and peace." Vic actually felt happy leaving his therapy group that night; and his ebullience carried him through most of the attempt. While Chris was being chased, she was twice able to experience the serenity of the full moon that would accompany her to her death. Throughout her attempt, she could feel the beauty of the night and the peacefulness of the moment.

> It was almost like a mystical experience, really. There was a very strange quality about it. I had made all these decisions to die, and it seemed there was this bigger energy around me, encasing me. It was a kind of peacefulness. I could feel the coldness as well, but it was like this serenity descended into my brain. It made me think that I was making the right decision, you know, because right inside attempting suicide, I am experiencing this kind of very beautiful state.

These experiences are powerful. Paradoxically, they can even offer moments of appreciation for the sacred and precious beauty of life, despite the fact that they are part of a suicide attempt. But they are ephemeral and short-lived. However potent, these experiences are still secondary to the intention to die, and they dissolve as the attempt continues.

AT THE HEART OF THE ATTEMPT

What drives someone, in these final moments, to carry out his or her plan rather than interrupt it? What is the nature of the momentum that continues one forward, often despite considerable obstacles? The answer to these questions lies in at least one of the following desires:

- To escape a dilemma that feels inescapable
- To gain control of uncontrollable confusion
- To send a message when all others means of communication have failed, and
- To kill the pain, even if it means killing oneself

Escaping the Inescapable

> *I felt a relief. It was the only time I felt a little bit good during those twelve days. I really decided that that was it—the only way I was going to relieve what I was going through. (Ed)*

Human beings want to avoid pain. It is a natural and normal thing to do. We may decide to leave a job or to sever a relationship when it is chronically unsatisfying, or when it leaves us continually upset or feeling disconnected with ourselves. In some ways, the attempt to calm such turbulent waters is the same during a suicide. When the intensity is too great to bear and one sees no indication that change is possible, suicide seems like a reasonable attempt to escape what seems inescapable. Many who tell their stories describe a state of mind and body filled with turmoil and chaos. Roiling waves of anger, fear, and self-hatred batter the mind until virtually nothing else can be sensed. The chaos that assaulted Tim from within and the abject hopelessness that Chris felt are good examples.

Mattie's attempt was the product of years of self-loathing, born from early child abuse, and reaching unbearable proportions at the end of a relationship. Now a mother and a psychotherapist and living in Seattle, she attempts to describe inescapable suffering:

> *I just couldn't live with these feelings. They were out of my control, and I couldn't stand it. I felt so dirty and bad and horrible. I wanted it to go away. I wanted my lover to make it go away. The utter shame—that was the most difficult. I felt so bad and dirty inside, and so chronically unloved and uncared for at the same time. I've never been very good at describing the shame stuff—it just feels like you need to disappear. If there was a hole in the ground, I'd gladly step into it and be swallowed up by the earth.*

People in difficult circumstances will often try to escape those circumstances by any route available. The amalgam of pain combined with the other elements of the descent brings them to a crossroads. One road represents the continuation of chronic suffering and the other represents liberation. However, their perception of available options is so narrowed at this point that their only means of escaping the pain or quieting the chaos seems to be suicide.

Hours after the fight, Jason's father finally found him across the arroyo at a friend's house. Distressed, he pleaded with his son to come home. He withdrew his threat to call the police and promised not to hit him again. The fight had left them both frightened and shaken. However ill-equipped they were to deal with each other, both knew that this had gone too far. Jason's father wanted a reconciliation, but didn't know how to bridge the enormous chasm between them. And despite the beating, Jason, a young teen, still hoped for his dad's love and protection.

> *Before I went inside to talk with him, I was sitting outside, smoking a cigarette. I was thinking about my father and I remembered a song from this rock group. The song's called "Had a Dad,"*

and it's about this guy whose father beats the brothers and then leaves, and then the brothers are fighting and the family's falling apart, you know? So I'm thinking, "I have a dad! He's right here!" and I felt like I totally came to terms with him and forgave him. Then I walked in and he was real mad. He yelled, "Don't you ever take that tone of voice with me again, and don't you ever say I was wrong because if you do, I'm gonna beat the shit out of you. You haven't seen nothing."

Jason, no stranger to emotional pain even at a young age, simply couldn't contain his sense of futility.

I felt so stupid for letting myself believe it was gonna be all right. I went into my room and said to myself, "I quit," and I began to cut my wrists. I just gave up.

Ed could not conceive of living life as a gay man, nor could he endure one more day of the vicious and corrosive self-hatred which was consuming him. Having decided to kill himself, he only needed to choose a method. One winter's night, Ed left the house with codeine Tylenols and some sixteen-ounce beers. He would walk into the woods, remove his clothing, and freeze to death, quietly, and with luck, painlessly. He tried, but couldn't do it. It was taking too long and he returned home with his secret. He stayed away from work that week, not wanting people to guess his state of mind, sense his crushing loneliness, and interfere with his plans. All he could think of was the pain he felt, and the inescapable impasse he felt himself in. If death would rid him of these feelings, he preferred to be dead.

What I really wanted was a part of me to die. Life didn't stink, but that situation did, and it was a huge bruise that I had to heal and couldn't. I did not want to throw away the whole thing, but I did not know how to heal the bruise at the time. The only way I knew was to throw away the whole apple.

The next day he went down to the basement and hit himself as hard as he could with a baseball bat. He'd remembered newspaper clippings of people hit on the head at baseball games, leaving the stadium apparently unharmed, only to die the next day of internal hemorrhaging. There was pounding in his chest, his eyes fluttered, and he could taste blood in his mouth. It was done. Upstairs, he lay on the bed and watched TV, relieved that it would only be a matter of hours.

> *I laid there. I wanted to lie awake and feel what death would be like. I was really scared but also relieved that maybe it was gonna be over. I started writing some notes, to my friend Rex, Jack, some girls, some family, just saying, "Please forgive me, but I can't handle what I'm going through." I drifted to sleep, and had some dreams—angelic females telling me it would be all right—and I thought to myself, "I must be already dead."*

Hours later, the phone rang, waking Ed, who reflexively answered it before realizing that his plan had failed.

> *What the fuck! I'm alive! I look outside and there's my '77 Thunderbird, I'm still in my clothes, its March 1, 1985, and I'm still here!" I said to myself, "Let's start the month out right and get out of here." I also knew that my sister, brother-in-law, and other family members were driving down to see the family, and if I did it now, they could console each other. I knew there was no way out. I even grabbed the phone book and looked up suicide centers, but then threw it down thinking, "That bullshit ain't gonna help me now."*

There's a dam in upstate New York outside of the small town of Armonk. It lay in the shadow of where Ed had been a high school all-star. He drove close to the top knowing that in its seventy-year history, none of the forty people who jumped from it had survived. This would be final. It was a sunny day, warm for early March, and

Ed paused for a half-hour or so, looking, thinking, feeling frightened and relieved. He noticed a voice inside, and it began competing for his attention, getting louder with each moment.

> *Do it. Do it! You're gonna do it now. If you don't you're a real chicken bastard. I couldn't hear it, but I could feel it. I got on top and I said, "God forgive me," and I rolled off like being in bed. I hit once, twice, and then down another fifty feet or so. I don't remember much else. There was a medical student there that day; he was also real depressed, contemplating suicide. He heard a noise and he watched me fall. He raced to the bottom, shocked out of his mind. He said I was conscious and talking. He told me I asked, "Did I do it?" and he said, "Yes." I asked, "Am I gonna die?" and he goes, "I don't think so." I said, "Shit."*

Escaping the inescapable also reflects one's relationship with time. As we've heard, those who are suicidal conceive of their future as an immutable repetition of the present. Pain will compound pain throughout time, without respite. An entry in Mark's journal, written minutes after his attempt and penned partially in blood, shows the desperate drive to escape this oppressive future.

> *He walked into the bathroom to enter the mirror. Yet no matter how hard he pressed against it, eternity denied him entrance. Instead he opened the mirror, behind which he reached for a razor. For three minutes he sat still, right-handed razor poised over left wrist. Here he sat, a Cato without an army, a Chatterton without a poem, a Werther without a love, a Kirilov without logic, a Lucretia without a rape. The very absence of any logical, poetic, or passionate reason for dying reaffirmed the absence of any reason for living. Thus the reason to put an end to reason and its need.*

Power and Control

> *Up until that point, I just had this hopelessness, this powerlessness*
> *and the only power I had was knowing that I was going to take my*
> *own life. That was the only thing I could see and the only strength I*
> *had. (Ian)*

People who contemplate suicide believe that their lives will never change for the better. They reason that it is futile to initiate any activity designed to break through the crushing sense of defeat. They feel powerless. Backed against a wall or thwarted by an impenetrable shield surrounding them, they experience life spinning out of control, and their ability to stabilize it becomes progressively limited. It is paradoxical and tragic that, for many, the only act that can wrest a sense of power and control from such suffering is the attempt itself. The world must be simplified—reduced to one moment, one certain destiny. Anything more is too complex to contend with. In such a context, the phrase "taking one's life in one's hands" means exercising one's last right of self-determination: the right to kill oneself.

We can see this clearly in Chris's experience. The entire chase was a desperate and violent attempt on her part to decide her fate and control her destiny. Her rage upon being thwarted reflected the fury of having the direction and quality of her life continually impeded by others and feeling helpless in the face of constant adversity. She was angry at the colossal absurdity of attracting so much attention to her attempt to die, when her husband had been so uninvolved in her struggle to live.

Ian's attempt also expresses a desperate desire to regain a measure of self-determination and power. As a child, he had felt caught in the constant conflict between his paternal grandmother, a powerful influence within the family, and his father. The oldest child and the only boy in the family, he became a pawn in their battles. His grandmother wanted him to be worldly and cultured and would take him to piano lessons and museums, while his father, who considered this "unmanly," would forbid Ian her company. The marital tension between his mother and father augmented his confusion. Now a pharmacist, living in Olympia, Washington, he thoughtfully condensed his experience as a child into a few sentences:

Ian _____

> *I took it all internally. I figured there must be something wrong with me, because I couldn't please my grandmother and my father and I couldn't stop my parents from fighting. The whole family operated in denial, and somehow I ended up feeling responsible. I felt it was my job to make things better for everyone, but I couldn't change things, so I always felt like a failure.*

This formed the central confusion of Ian's life, and it surfaced in all his personal relationships. Underlying his excitement at falling in love and seeking an intimate commitment was the fear of his own inadequacy, and a feeling of certainty that he would at some point be judged as irreparably flawed. Inside, Ian felt alone.

> *It was a real complex mesh. I felt like I could never depend on anyone else to really care about me, but then I couldn't justify myself or give myself a sense of self-worth without being in a role where I was taking care of others. Being a caretaker—that's where I felt like I had an identity, where I was real.*

Ian and Kevin had been together for three years when they bought a house. It symbolized the lifelong commitment for which Ian had always yearned, as well as a deliverance from desperate feelings of unworthiness. The relationship had its problems, and Ian had heard rumors about Kevin's previous relationships and his propensity for having affairs, but Ian felt this relationship would be

different. He would care for Kevin as no one else had, and their
relationship would grow rich and strong.

The reality proved different, however, and very painful. Shortly
after the house was purchased, Ian discovered that his lover was
surreptitiously involved with someone else. Kevin also failed to tell
him that he had tested positive for the HIV virus, and over the
course of their relationship, had engaged in other sexual affairs.
There was a good chance that Kevin had exposed Ian to the HIV
virus.

Ian felt this to be an indictment of himself. Despite considerable
evidence to the contrary, he believed that it was *his* inadequacy
which lay at the heart of their trouble. Waves of insecurity and self-
doubt assaulted him, and he felt defeated, powerless, and alone.
Feelings from childhood—the panic at his family's falling apart and
the helplessness he felt despite his efforts to prevent it—began to
swirl inside him. They colored his perception of his current difficulties and left him feeling hopeless.

> *I turned myself inside out. I'd just spent three years of my life with*
> *this relationship being the focus of my life. All I could think about*
> *was me being alone, totally alone, and I was scared. I had always*
> *measured myself by what someone else did, and now I felt*
> *worthless.*

One afternoon, Ian and his lover had scheduled a talk. Ian bought
some yellow roses, Kevin's favorite, and put them in a vase on the
dining room table. He still hoped for reconciliation, despite the
betrayal and disappointment. He waited, but Kevin never showed.

Ian spent the next four hours agitated and frightened. A spark of
anger would emerge, only to be buried in self-recrimination. A
momentary sense of hope would arise, only to succumb to the fear
that he would never survive the crushing loneliness he felt. As his
aspirations for this relationship crumbled, Ian began to doubt
whether things would ever be different for him. His sorrow, hope-

lessness, fear, and self-doubt intensified, and he found himself in a pitched battle for self-control amidst what felt like untamable forces. He began to contemplate taking his life, and it was only then, as he perched at the edge of suicide, that he felt a measure of strength.

> *Suddenly, at that moment, I became focused. I hadn't felt that way for a long time and everything just came together. I felt like I had power: I was finally controlling my life. I felt calm and clear, and the pain went away. My whole body relaxed, and something inside me said, "This is it." It felt like an out for me. I won't be here to see what happens with my lover. I won't be here to take care of him or feel the pain anymore.*

> *I began to write notes and think about my family. I knew they didn't need another death, but I figured they'd get through it. I had a plan; I had the answer. I felt real clarity. I was living my life for the first time, as I was getting ready to end it.*

The Attempt to Communicate

After one has failed to communicate the depths of one's pain or the severity of one's fear and hopelessness, suicide attempts represent the delivery of a final message. We are familiar with the suicide note—a good-bye left on the scene to be found after the act is completed—but the attempt itself is also a message. Just as there are moments of fury within the attempt, and moments of desire to rescue a sense of power and control, there are also moments in which a person attempting suicide is consciously intending to send a message via the act.

Catherine's first attempt—the ingestion of antidepressants when she was twenty years old—left her in a coma for three days. It followed her father's death from advanced alcoholism. His death further estranged family members, and increased the bitterness between her and her mother. When Catherine talks about her

second attempt, two decades later, we can again hear the same anger
and frustration, this time centering on the conflict with her spouse
and her mother-in-law. Her husband, Peter, lied about his continued cocaine use, and his mother, to whom Catherine turned for
help, refused to talk to her son. Like the members of Catherine's
original family, her mother-in-law was lost in denial and confusion.
Catherine's two daughters were both younger than five, and she was
terrified that her family was falling apart.

> *I felt like I was up against a brick wall again! I was angry. I was*
> *furious at them for not taking this seriously and at myself for being*
> *a victim again. I was gonna show them. My husband took my*
> *daughters and said, "Come on, Mom's gonna off herself," and left.*
> *I was furious and totally hysterical and I couldn't deal with him*
> *ignoring me again. I couldn't see into the future or be calm enough*
> *to sort things out.*

Catherine's suicide attempt contained two levels of meaning. First,
she wanted her husband to stop his drug use and be a more responsive
husband and father. Second, her attempt reflected an enormous
accumulation of anger and hopelessness and a desperate desire for
change. Catherine was furious, and she was going to show them the
intensity of her pain and the consequences of their disinterest.

> *I was gonna show them how much I was hurting, and I was gonna*
> *make him sorry that he said that to my daughters. The statement*
> *in my attempt was that I wanted to live a good life with my*
> *children and I wanted my husband to listen to me. I was also*
> *saying to him, "Peter, you have a family here; family isn't with*
> *your mother or your father anymore. Your responsibility is here,*
> *and I can't do it all by myself."*

Teresa's attempt had a similar intent. Having failed to secure her
mother's attention for over five years, she looked to her own destruc-

tion as her only means of communication. As she sat at the kitchen table just before she saw her mother in the driveway, she was still thinking that somehow, magically, through her actions, her message would get through. As we've noted, the suicidal trance contains it own singular logic, which makes sense within the narrowed perspective of a mind in torment. Intent on killing herself, Teresa wanted to awaken her mother to her need. Although she would no longer be alive, she would be successful in delivering her message.

Ruth was lost in a world in which she felt invisible and her suffering seemed unrecognized. Years before her final attempt, she wanted her suicide to be public enough for someone, somehow, to receive her message.

> *I was in the bathroom of the medical school dormitory and I threw a rope over the shower pipe. But something was preventing me from doing it. I wanted to do it, but it wasn't visible enough. I'd be hanging in this bathroom all alone and nobody would see it, and I wanted people to see it. I wanted them to know how much I hurt. They were always talking about this intelligent, capable person, but they were not really seeing how much pain, how much suffering, I felt.*

Virginia, fifty-five years old, is now an organizational consultant in Denver. An adult woman drowning in a desperately unhappy marriage, she attempted to cope by utilizing the self-control she had learned when very young. On the outside, her family life appeared seamless, and even close friends knew little of her crushing disappointment and chronic hopelessness. Although she and her husband were a playful and engaging couple outwardly, they were rarely close and never intimate. She had married into a family not unlike her own, with their own set of stultifying rules and injunctions. In response to the lack of intimacy and to her unrequited desire to bear a child, Virginia exercised enormous self-restraint. She remained silent about her pain.

*I call my life, "Happy Days: The Documentary." My father died
when I was five. He was deeply hated by my mother, who was
tough, and my grandmother, who was even tougher! They would
call him a drunk, a gambler, a womanizer, et cetera, and it was
probably true. He was up late one night in his casino, counting
receipts, and he heard a noise. He opened the door. It was a
backdraft situation; he was consumed by flames. We thought it
was arson, but this was back in '46, and nothing was ever proven.*

*We were never to speak about him again. The idea was to simply
create a new life from that point on. No talking about him. No
grieving. All pictures were destroyed. The truth was that he was
the grand passion of [Mother's] life and she never got over him;
and the only way to manage was to put him in a closet and pretend
he never existed. Mother remarried a year later and then she
created "happy days": voices were never to be raised; there would
never be any fighting. No breathing allowed! Everyone was expected to do extraordinarily well. From then on, regardless of how
we felt, we were all to exercise extraordinary self-control.*

It wasn't until long after her attempt that Virginia realized how
faithfully her marriage replicated her original family life. In response to personal heartache, she learned to keep quiet, expect no
special attention, and maintain all outward appearances. She had
dutifully internalized the primary messages of her childhood:
"Don't speak about your pain! Don't let yourself be seen!" These
injunctions kept her restrained, hidden, and unhappy, and they
were now compounded and reinforced in her new family. Awkward
and inelegant, her suicide attempt signaled the end of her complicity
in this life-denying charade, an acknowledgment of her vulnerability, and finally, a public cry for help.

*Looking back on it, I think my suicide attempt was a public
admission that I could no longer do what I'd always done, and a
message that I didn't know any other way out.*

Killing the Vehicle

At the heart of suicide lies the intention to kill the pain, regardless of the consequences. Whether it is unrelenting physical discomfort, or whether people have exhausted their capacity to bear overwhelming mental and emotional pain, they endeavor to extinguish the agony, utilizing whatever means necessary.

The attempt to kill oneself requires a substep that almost all those interviewed describe. In order to initiate the act and execute the plan dispassionately, one must first separate from the parts of oneself that are suffering. Again, dissociation plays a role. Since the body and mind are the vehicle through which one experiences unbearable pain, the body and mind become the targets of self-destruction. It seems logical to eliminate the pain by eliminating the vehicle.

Karen said this during our interview:

> *I just wanted not to have this body. I didn't want to continue being in it. I wanted to get free of it. I wanted just to kill that thing and the reality it contained, and I didn't see any other way to do that other than to kill me.*

This form of dissociation is most often a gradual process. However sudden it seems, however surprised others find themselves in the face of a loved one's attempt, the seeds have been sown before. Teresa found herself trapped within her "black cylinder," increasingly unable to feel either herself or the world at large. As her medical studies progressed, Ruth saw her body mostly through its architecture. She would contemplate the physiological processes involved in suicide as if her body were part of a scientific experiment.

Tim's worst fear was not of dying, but of remaining "crazy" and being aware of it for the rest of his life. It was too much to imagine living with a constant barrage of self-destructive thoughts and images for decade upon decade; and although he didn't want to die, he needed to destroy the mind which had become so unsound.

Mattie's experience shows how killing the messenger requires dissociating to such a degree that one experiences oneself as something or someone else altogether. After the final fight with her lover, stunned by her self-loathing, she initiated her attempt. As she stared at herself in the bathroom mirror, Mattie felt disconnected. Standing with a huge bottle of aspirin in her hands, she was in fact startled to see a reflection there at all.

> *I was surprised to see myself, because I already felt like I was gone. I felt completely numb, and I looked at her and said, "Don't worry, you'll be out of your misery pretty soon." I just wanted to stop the feelings that I couldn't tolerate, and I couldn't stop them any other way.*

Generally, by the time one is ready to attempt suicide, the thought of it has been entertained and the scene rehearsed countless times in one's mind. And each time the scene is replayed, one dissociates just a little more, progressing through the withdrawal in its many forms and into one of the many varieties of suicidal trance.

Karl's unusual story portrays the progressive separation from unbearable pain and, ultimately, from his humanity. His life had become so alienated and corrupt that the only recourse imaginable to him was to end it and thereby end the suffering he was inflicting on himself and on others.

Karl

"You'll recognize me. I'll be the one in the airport who looks like Elvis." Our office was a 1984 Lincoln Continental, hurtling down the highway in central New Jersey just after rush hour. Karl seemed sandwiched between the seat and steering wheel, his huge frame filling one-half of the car as his thick hands gently guided the wheel.

Thirty-seven years old, he is a large man, six-feet-four and 240 pounds, but he still has more than a bit of boyishness in his face. A teacher of the Gospel, he organizes various inner city missions for the homeless and counsels those addicted to drugs and alcohol. He will be a witness for anyone who wishes to receive the teachings of Jesus, but he will wait to be asked. His life has taught him patience.

Karl is a minister of the nineties. Intelligent and folksy, he seems a cross between Billy Graham and Willie Nelson. He makes daily pilgrimages to the streets to buy meals for the hungry, but his ministry also includes singing rock-and-roll during his free time— an expression of his hard-won joy for life.

> *I grew up in a small mill town in Kansas. Mostly farming and steel, and when the steel died in the mid-seventies, the only thing that grew were the number of bars per capita. I was a teen then, and was always looking for the next bigger "rush." I played football and I wrestled, but after a while, that wasn't enough. I started drinking at sixteen, and pretty soon I was doing harder stuff—coke, crack— and freebasing.*

Life was arduous and boring for Karl on the family farm. Everyone worked late in the fields and there was little diversion except for TV and alcohol. He tried junior college after high school, but found it unrewarding. He discovered more excitement outside the law. To supply his growing drug habit, Karl became a dealer. He owned property in town in which he warehoused contraband cocaine, and he spent thousands of dollars on scales and other equipment for measuring and cutting it. As his business increased, so did his drug habit, and slowly, he grew colder and more fearsome. Inflated by his success, he increasingly felt omnipotent and indestructible. He was introduced to members of organized crime, and soon became an enforcer for the Mafia, occasionally inflicting physical harm. His behavior grew more heartless and he grew less and less human. No longer a boy, he was an explosive and intimidating mobster who carried handguns and knives wherever he went.

> *At one point, I owned three crack houses, and when I wasn't dealing on my job at the plant, I was dealing in the bars. I was drinking lots of shots of whiskey at a sitting, and was doing one or two grams of cocaine a day. I was making thousands of dollars a week, and smoking or shooting a lot of it.*

There wasn't much room to expand in this small town, and eventually, Karl became bored and sloppy. His relationship with the mob soured, and at the same time the FBI began to seize his property. As the net closed in from both sides, Karl took deeper refuge in his drugs.

> *I spent three days freebasing. Freebasing makes your mouth real dry, so I was also drinking a lot of [psychedelic] mushroom tea and whiskey. Things were bad, and I felt like I just wanted to end it, and go out with a bang. It was raining that night, and I drank twelve double shots of whiskey, did another three grams of cocaine, and started speeding down the highway. I was chasing this truck at about seventy and I was looking for a place to crash. I was thinking, "Now I can put an end to this poor pitiful life," and I slammed into a concrete divider.*

> *The car slid on the passenger side for hundreds of yards, sparks flyin'. There was a gorge on one side of the road and a wall on the other. I was so cranked that my hands stuck to the wheel and I was still sitting sideways in the seat. The metal was turning blue from the heat, and the only reason it didn't explode was because of the water on the road. I emerged with only a scratch on my face.*

Karl's survival was miraculous, but it failed to reverse his descent. He continued plying himself with alcohol and whatever drugs he could secure. Both the FBI and the Mafia were looking for him, and to elude their grasp, he slept in his truck, often suffering minor frostbite by morning.

Whatever glamour his life had held evaporated. Karl had exhausted his options. He had bartered whatever moral fiber he possessed long ago, and he was suspicious and afraid. The fall he'd taken was so precipitous and so sudden that it left him numb and immobile. He no longer felt human. He knew he'd try suicide again: it was only a matter of time. Karl's eyes watered as he told of the second attempt.

> I had bought some new shells and I loaded one gun in particular, a Ruger Blackhawk, my favorite. It was a .44, and it was so powerful that the recoil alone could dislocate someone's shoulder. It was gonna be another night in the truck, freezing, alone and scared, and I just felt like I couldn't do it any more. I was full of alcohol. It was late at night. I took the gun out, and looked at it for a while. Then I put it to my head, cocked the hammer, and pulled the trigger.

By most estimates, the chances are over 2,000 to 1 that a new cartridge will fail to fire in a working gun. It took Karl a few moments to realize he was alive, and then he fainted.

———

The Bubble Bursts

How are suicide attempts thwarted? What series of events intervenes unannounced to preserve one's life, and what happens then to one's suicidal trance? These questions take us into the critical moments of the suicide attempt and those that immediately follow it. There are people for whom the attempt fails and yet the trance and the desire to end their lives remain. Others experience the beginnings of a change, either during or just after the harrowing episode they orchestrated. Devotion to the suicidal quest wanes, but it leaves a vacuum. How that vacuum is filled strongly influences the trajectory of one's recovery.

Some suicides are interrupted by external intervention. The call that Deborah received as she was preparing for her attempt was unsolicited and unexpected.

> *The phone rang and I answered without thinking about it. I was drunk and disoriented. He asked, "Are you all right?" He's a real straight doctor, and he says, "My wife and I were about to go to a formal dance. I finished dressing, and I was waiting for her, doing a little sweeping in the garage. Suddenly, I saw your face, and there was black all around it and I got scared. So I called."*
>
> *I told him I was fine, but I'm sure he could hear something in my voice. He was over here in minutes, dressed in a tux! I didn't want to open the door, but it seemed like providence had stepped in. I thought, "Who am I to fuck with the universe?"*

There are people who, alarmed by unexpected physical distress—increased or irregular heart rates, uncontrollable muscle spasms, shortness of breath, extreme loginess—have abandoned the attempt and called for help. Others, like Cynthia and Vic, experienced disturbing metaphysical encounters—premonitions of death or afterlife, for example—and stopped. Some gave up when the method faltered, as for example, when their bodies rejected the pills they had taken.

Ruth exhausted her supply of anticoagulant and her blood flow diminished, although she had lost so much blood that she began to feel excruciating pain. In the depths of her suicide attempt, she found a small but critical reservoir of perspective. This helped her to change her focus away from killing herself, and to dealing with her isolation.

When I'm in pain, I laugh, and I started making jokes to myself about how this was gonna be a big deal if I didn't do it. I was saying, "'cause if you're not gonna do this, then you're gonna have to live!" Now that scared me! I pulled out the tubing, and then I cried and cried. If I was going to live, all I saw in front of me was more misery. When I'm doing well, I can check those thoughts, but sometimes, when the voices quiet down, then I just feel really alone. That's what I was crying about then—just how alone I was.

Sometimes the suicidal trance shatters during the attempt. The desire to die dissolves, at least temporarily, leaving the person shaken and unsure how to proceed. When the suicidal bubble bursts, people may feel overwhelmed with emotions they have long suppressed. The attempt seems to have organized all their thoughts and feelings into a vision of death and liberation, so that when the trance collapses, no psychological structure remains to handle the emotion.

Ian always chose to hide his concerns from friends and associates. Having refrained from telling others of his feelings during better times, he could not do so now. That afternoon, as he paced the house, waiting for his lover but knowing that he would never arrive, he chose a different alternative.

Being a pharmacist, I already figured it out. I knew that drugs wouldn't work quick enough and they'd be painful and messy. I couldn't see cutting myself, so I decided that carbon monoxide would be the way to do it, because I'd just go to sleep. I pulled the truck in the garage and plugged some of the air leaks. Then I turned on the radio and just sat there, thinking.

During the first thirty minutes, I was thinking, "This is really depressing, so if you want to be depressed, listen to country music." It's always about love and losing love, heartache and pain. I felt drowsy and I got a little scared, so I got out of the pickup, left it

running, and walked around the garage. I was pretty dizzy and I
could see the smoke in the air.

As Ian listened to the radio, he thought about questions he had
rarely considered: destiny and purpose, and what he still loved
about being alive—the summers in the northwest, for instance. He
fantasized death as a netherworld in which he'd somehow still be
present in the world, just not part of it.

I was thinking about God. "Is this a sin? Am I doing something
bad?" I come from a Mormon background, so all that started
coming in. I was raised to believe that we are here for a purpose
and when it's your time, you go. I was wondering, "Have I lived a
good life? Am I going to be punished for this?" I started wondering
about heaven and hell. "What am I going to experience? Which
one will I end up in?" When I got back in the truck, I was really
light-headed and woozy.

Ian began to anticipate the loss of his family—his father and
grandparents—through his suicide, but most of all he felt the loss of
his own childhood, in which his role was to take care of the other
family members and feel responsible for their happiness. Sadness
and loss tumbled through him until he felt he could think about it
no more.

So all this pain started coming back and I said to myself, "Let's just
get this over with," and I started pushing on the gas pedal, revving
the motor. It was at that point that the motor started dying. It was
having trouble idling and it was beginning to overheat. Then this
song came on the radio. It was the stupidest song I've ever heard in
my entire life! I think it was Roy Rogers, and he was singing
something like "Don't you give up, pardner. Things will get better.
The good ole days are just around the bend." Just this kind of
mindless "Da da da da," like a Disney version of country!

Ian's attempt began to fail, and the bubble of the trance burst. The pain that had been contained over the course of his life flooded through him. Slumped on the seat of his truck, Ian was overcome by near-volcanic outpourings of grief.

> I was stunned. The truck was dying. I'm feeling all this pain. It felt comic, like a sitcom or something—like some idiot who tries to commit suicide and everything goes wrong. All of a sudden, the conviction broke. I felt, "This is not what I'm supposed to be doing." I took it as a sign. Roy Rogers telling me, "Don't give up, hang on!" The car conked out after the song, and I just laid on the seat. All at once, there was this massive grief that just welled up out of me. All this agony, all this pain, came out, not only from now, but from my whole life. I started crying hysterically, really sobbing, and I couldn't control it.

As Ian lay on the seat, he felt that time slowed. He could feel every muscular contraction and every tear. It was a concentrated moment, compressed around deep, unacknowledged pain. This powerful grief, itself a kind of trance, seemed to neutralize the suicidal trance, and Ian abandoned the desire to kill himself. In its wake, he was able to feel, undiluted and for the first time, the suffering he had been holding at bay.

There are also some who complete the attempt, only to have it fail. It can leave them brutally injured, like Ed after his fall, or terribly shaken, like Karl. Rennie attempted suicide three times over the course of four years. The first two attempts occurred when she lived in Mannheim, and in quick succession.

> The first time, I was trying to slash my wrists. It was really difficult, because I hadn't previously realized that it was so hard to cut your own flesh. It's tough stuff and I ended up beating on my wrist with a knife for a long time to get it to go numb. It hurt so much to cut it, I thought, "Oh shit, this really hurts," and this other part of me

was saying, "You'll just have to ignore that; it will be over soon."
Finally, I got deep enough just as a friend who had keys to my
apartment came in and dragged me out.

Having been thwarted, she tried again the next morning. The
only thing that had changed was the method.

"I'd better do this one right," I told myself, and there was this
satisfaction in saying that. I was determined to get the job done. I
was still feeling pain, but there was light at the end of the tunnel. I
was telling myself, "You won't have to feel this way much longer."
There was a little bit of fear, but also a lot of relief. I didn't think
dying would hurt. It couldn't possibly hurt any worse than trying
to cut myself!

Rennie had called a dealer and secured a large stash of morphine.
She felt relieved that this would be much easier than the attempt
the night before. She was even happy in her walk to the pharm-
acy to pick up a syringe, to see the dealer, and then go home. She had
never injected herself with drugs and was sure this attempt would be
fatal.

When you inject yourself, the taste of the drug comes up between
your tongue and the back of your teeth. I remember everything
turning dark. I didn't feel the franticness that I felt when I was
cutting my wrist. It was more, "I just want to do it now." I was very
peaceful. . . . I was out for a couple of days. A friend told me he
came in, felt my pulse and listened for my breath, and split. The
first thing I remember, when I realized I was alive, was hearing
myself say, "Oh shit."

Days passed in a haze and Rennie felt rudderless. She became
reclusive, and only emerged when another dealer attempted to take
over her territory.

It was probably the best thing that happened to me 'cause my fighting spirit came out. I wanted to show them all I was tough.

It's strange. I was really down and out, but I would dress up when I'd go out so I'd look cool. I'd put on a really good show so nobody would think of taking over my territory. When somebody did try, it just didn't go over real well with me. I got really pissed off. I enjoyed the fight. And I really knew I was gonna win either way. I just knew I was gonna win, or he was gonna kill me, and that would be okay too.

Rennie prevailed in this showdown of fearlessness and bravado, and she actually enjoyed the opportunity to channel the rage and hopelessness trapped inside her. A few days later, glimpsing how truly hopeless her circumstances were, she capitalized on her new-found courage and decided to leave Germany. Within days she found herself in New York City.

Rennie was a keen observer of people. She had to be. It was just one of her many survival skills. She enrolled in a well-known drama school, but quickly learned that her proficiency in acting was not what was most sought.

At the student level, you literally had to fuck your teachers to get parts in school plays and I dropped out after half a year. I mean, I had never been into prostitution before and I wasn't about to start now. I was very clear what that was about.

Rennie transferred to Pratt Institute and studied her second loves, photography and illustration. She had an eye for people on the edges of life: the alienated aged and infirm on park benches; solitary figures at playgrounds in winter; wild, clandestine punk-rock scenes in anonymous buildings. She was inspired with her new sense of direction. Life seemed to hold some promise, after all. She had escaped Mannheim and was happily ensconced in the world's most exciting city.

Life was thrilling. Rennie truly felt that she had successfully left her dark life behind. But the tide turned rapidly. Almost a year after arriving in America, Rennie was felled by a severe sciatic condition which left her immobilized and in great pain. Her photography had introduced her once again to the drug world, and it was there she turned for relief and refuge. Professional opportunities seemed to evaporate and she began hustling, this time dealing in high-quality heroin.

> *I was dealing heroin out of my flat in the upper west side of Manhattan, making a lot of money at the time, probably about $2,000 a day. I was getting it imported from Thailand and it was pure. Of course, then I couldn't stop doing it. I was gone; there was nothing to fight anymore.*

> *It was spring, and again I wanted to die. I had gotten rid of a relationship, even though I didn't want to. I loved him, but he was seeing another woman and our fights were drawing complaints from the neighbors. I was dealing and didn't need the extra attention, so I forced him to leave. A friend of mine said, "You gotta get him out. You've already lost the relationship, and you're gonna lose your apartment. You know, it's harder to find an apartment than a relationship in New York City."*

Rennie felt bereft of spirit and hopeless. She called a suicide hot line, hoping for one last chance—for something she wasn't seeing—but hung up disgusted and angry.

> *It was an older lady on the phone and she said, "But honey, you have your whole life in front of you." I hung up and said to myself, "That's it!" I was thinking, "Hey, maybe for you it's nice to have your whole life in front of you. I don't know anything about your*

life, but my life is certainly nothing that anybody would want to have in front of them!" I wanted to give it one last chance and I knew she was trying to help, but that was the last thing I wanted to hear.

I wanted somebody to tell me something that would make life seem worth living. I mean, I had no indication that I was gonna have a future at all. Maybe if she said, "This is the worst time, I know. It won't always be this bad," or something like that. I don't know. I wasn't open to much.

The next day, Rennie attempted for the third time.

So I did about five times as much heroin as normal and I fell out for just one day—I mean, even less than the time before! It scared me. I hadn't realized what a humongous tolerance I had. When I put the needle in my arm, it was a sign of resignation. I had given up and it was a sure thing that I wasn't coming back.

Sometimes, the failure bursts the bubble of the suicidal trance. Most often, it delivers one into another state of confusion, a netherworld where people are neither strong or focused enough to make another attempt nor clear enough to envision the future. Sometimes just after an attempt, however, a glimmer of insight does emerge.

Rennie awoke stunned and disoriented. Lying motionless on her bed, she attempted to grasp what had happened. She felt perplexed and awed by whatever hidden force had interceded. "Some greater power must have prevented my death," she reasoned. "After all, I was *so* determined."

It was the first time I thought of God or faith or something like that. I was thinking, "I've tried three times—it must not be my time." I thought, "Maybe there's something else I'm supposed to do."

2

The Return

Sometimes you have to play a long time, to play like yourself.

MILES DAVIS

Four

Waking Up, Alive

Now you think I wanted nurses poking and prodding me, after I just tried to kill myself and failed? I felt like punching anybody I could, just laying there in the intensive care, miserable. I felt like screaming, "Fuck you, man! Fuck you, God! Fuck you, Devil! Fuck all of you!" That's an understatement. Please excuse all the expletives, but that's how I felt. All I wanted was to find another way to die. I wasn't out to make any friends."
(Ed)

After the attempt, one must face the reality of having made such a ghastly choice. The body suffers from degrees of trauma, and the spirit is left weak and fragile. One can barely conceive of a starting point more tenuous and devoid of promise.

What does it feel like to survive? How do people begin to wrestle with what has transpired, and then contemplate the enormity of what may lie ahead? We have come to the process of recovery. The struggles of those who attempt suicide are unique for each person, but all who survive their attempts and begin the journey back to life have experiences in common. While not every facet of recovery is evident in every story, these profiles, taken together, create a developmental portrait of the complex and often heroic passage from suicide to health. Success leaves clues, and in the following chapters we will learn how people reassemble their lives and how, from the brink of self-destruction, it *is* possible to begin again.

In this chapter, "Waking Up, Alive," and in chapter five, "The Road Back," we'll hear two stories at length—those of Ed and Chris. Their accounts portray clearly the process of rebuilding one's life after a suicide attempt.

THE PHYSICAL DAMAGE

Carbon monoxide. What it does is compete with oxygen for the binding site in your hemoglobin. I had attached about 30 percent of my hemoglobin. You don't need 100 percent to kill yourself, only about 60 or 70 percent. I was really sick. They had to put me on oxygen and force it into me to get the carbon monoxide out. I was there for hours—a long time. I had done a pretty good job. (Ian)

Finding oneself alive after a failed suicide attempt despite days, months, or perhaps years of fantasizing and planning is, for most people, a harsh reality. It is unexpected and unrehearsed. It is a consequence that one is simply not prepared for. For some, the suicidal trance is shattered. For others, the thoughts and feelings of the withdrawal and tunnel stages still linger, intimately familiar but strange in this post-attempt context.

Since the suicidal assault on the body can be ferocious, efforts to address the emotional pain often must wait while the physical damage is repaired. In a majority of suicide attempts, the injury, although quite serious, is temporary. Robert was rescued shortly after losing consciousness. The rope had strangled him and he narrowly averted having a collapsed trachea. He was left with lacerations and painful headaches.

Mark had swallowed 120 five-grain aspirin. Within the next two hours he became completely deaf and endured intractable pain.

So I'm walking along the railroad tracks and there's two kids coming my way, talking to each other, and I can only see their lips moving! Its kind of a rural area, north of Binghamton, New York. There wasn't anybody else around, and I just wasn't ready for the pain. It felt like my stomach was exploding. Not just burning— that doesn't describe it enough—but exploding like a fireball.

So I get to this gas station and ask to use the bathroom. It's really strange going up to the attendant and asking, and not hearing him. I thought going to the bathroom would help. Well, it didn't do anything, and there was a lot of blood that came out with the shit. I didn't know what to do. I walked away, sat down on the side of the road, and started trembling.

Chris swallowed close to fifty pills and needed emergency medical care.

They pumped my stomach. It was grueling; it was horrible. I remember feeling like a piece of meat—like they're wanting to keep this body alive—and I felt like I had already died. They forced coffee down me, and slapped me on the face. They were yelling; they were really angry. They'd scream, "God damn you, you're not gonna give up!"

Upon arriving at the hospital, Vic was in poor enough condition to require injections of emetics and slurries of activated charcoal. The results were ghastly and literally gut-wrenching.

*I just handed the bottle to the guy and he looked at it and said,
"Did you take all these?" I said, "Yeah, and more." He strapped me
on a gurney. I remember them placing a huge metal bowl in front
of me and then they shot something in my arm. The next thing I
knew was, "Whoa, here it comes!" Everything that came up was
black. It was sickening. I don't remember anything else until a day
and a half later.*

In other instances, the attempts have been too violent for the
body to bear, and physical recovery is rendered difficult or impossible. Tim slashed at his arms with such fury that he cut through
ligaments, tendons, and nerves. Delicate emergency surgery re-
attached the fibers of the hands and wrists, but could not replicate
nature. Months of physical therapy were necessary to regain even
the simplest of movements, and today there are still pockets of
feeling missing in his fingers.

Ed went by ambulance to Westchester Medical Center, where he
would remain for the next five months. He had broken his wrist,
one ankle, his neck, and the sixth and seventh cervical vertebrae. He
was paralyzed from his chest down and his hands were partially
affected. Ed would never walk again. The first days after emergency
surgery were uncertain. They had given him a tracheotomy and had
inserted two metal plates in his skull. The doctors were unsure he'd
survive. Although visitors said he was awake, the next date he
remembered was March 20, almost three weeks later.

LOSS OF PRIVACY

It's like a window in your heart; everybody sees you're blown apart.

PAUL SIMON

Ed could barely contain his frustration. Wounded and confused, he needed time to assimilate the gravity of his fate. He wasn't interested in rehabilitation. He wasn't even interested in talking.

I didn't want to hurt my family, but I wanted everybody to stay away from me. Seeing their faces, I felt tremendous horror and guilt at what I had done. I couldn't talk about it yet. They didn't know I did it to protect them. It was almost a noble thing, I told myself—any way I could justify it. Like if I'm alive, I'm gonna be a lot more trouble than dead. It was just horrible, horrible guilt, and I didn't want anyone to touch me. It stayed that way for a long time. I was so mad at the world. I didn't give a shit.

As is true for many in the post-attempt phase, Ed's world had changed beyond what was possible for him to comprehend. His body—his ally and nemesis, which earned him praise and glory, and which hid the more vulnerable parts inside—was broken. Yet as devastating as this was, something else had happened which was almost as distressing: his inner world, which for years had been so private, was now laid bare. Although it would be some time before Ed was willing to discuss the motivation for his suicide attempt, he could no longer conceal the fact of his pain. No amount of posturing could cloak his self-hatred, nor could he call on his machismo to deflect legitimate concern for him.

Perhaps this is the most difficult challenge immediately following the attempt. What was once deeply private has become public, known not only to family and friends but to scores of medical and mental health personnel. For a time, the rights to privacy and choice are surrendered. This is particularly agonizing for those whose attempts result in hospitalization, wherein the first hours and days prove almost intolerable.

Chris had to endure not only loss of privacy, but also reproach for what she had done. It didn't come from the hospital staff, but from the patients. It seemed as if there was a hierarchy of ill-nesses, an unspoken caste, with suicide at the bottom. Somehow her story quickly became public knowledge and she was exposed to derisive and malicious commentary. Hours after the attempt, Chris lay awake in her hospital bed, separated from her fellow patients by only a curtain. She was both hyped from the drugs and exhausted by her ordeal. She could see their silhouettes as they spoke.

> They put me in a room with two other women. I could overhear them: it wasn't hard; they were talking pretty loud. They were very angry that I was put in "their" room. They seemed to know why I was there, and thought I was horrible for wanting to kill myself. I remember them saying, "She should be ashamed of herself, when she has everything to live for," and "Why did the doctor put her in here?"

Cynthia had courted suicide for more than fifteen years: after she was molested on the streets of New York as a child; throughout the time she was sent her to live with foster parents; and during her al-coholic and reclusive college years. Hidden beneath her formidable intelligence and sardonic wit, suicide was her secret, held close and never revealed until she was admitted to the hospital. Within mo-ments of waking, it became apparent her plight had become very public.

I remember when I first woke up, and there were some guys in there actually nailing the window shut. They had sent me to the university hospital, where the head of the department, a German psychiatrist, decided I needed a father figure, and he started ordering me around. When I'd smoke, he would order me to put it out! And there were all these graduate students around my bed asking questions. My mother also showed up, which I really resented. She never showed up when things were going well—only on my deathbed.

THE HOSPITAL

A suicide attempt announces that one's life has spun out of control and that one is powerless to alter it. In the aftermath of an attempt, an almost unbearable vulnerability arises. People fall prey to the judgments, dictates, and even fears of staff, family, and fellow patients. Suicide attempts offer an invitation to comment that often neither clinicians nor onlookers can resist. Some hospital staff try to be kind, but are limited by inexperience and naiveté.

Toward the end of Mark's stay in intensive care, he found that five nurses and the resident physician had surrounded his bed.

The nurses would come in—they'd often send the prettiest one in—and say things like, "Gee, why would you want to do this thing, a young guy, a handsome fellow. You've got a good physique." One day when they were all around, the doctor, who'd said nothing to me the past three days says, "I hope you've learned something from this experience." So I just started espousing all my existentialist philosophy—all about the meaninglessness of life.

Many people feel overwhelmed by the frenzy of the emergency room procedure. They are slapped, walked, fed emetics, and forced to vomit. They are connected to monitors and IV drips, covered with bandages, or plied with sedatives. A medical choice is made in which the effort to save the body supersedes any attempt to heal the mind. The patient often feels like an onlooker witnessing a resuscitation. People who attempt suicide often continue to feel ignored and unimportant regardless of the endeavors to rescue them physically. At worst, the drama rises to a pitch that alarms even medical personnel, prompting them to react in clumsy and aggressive ways.

Teresa's experience was particularly difficult. Having survived, she then had to endure the onslaught of the physician on call that night. He was furious at her.

> *He was so angry he was stammering. "We oughta just keep you here! You know what we do to people like you? We tie them up when they act like this!" I felt so humiliated.*

Cassie is now an effervescent and very amiable woman in her late forties. A mother of two grown children, she is a highly skilled teacher of the developmentally disabled and is now back in school completing a doctorate in psychology. She attempted suicide as her marriage was dissolving in the wake of her husband's infidelity and during his endeavors to obtain full custody of their still-small children. Her experience in the hospital was milder than Teresa's, although the lack of attention and concern for her plight, on the part of both the nursing staff and the psychiatrist, left her bewildered.

> *I remember them waking me up in the emergency room. They were asking me my name and how old I was. There were lots of people standing around. Then I remember them asking the same thing again, minutes later, and having the thought, "I'm not any older than I was the last time you asked me!"*
>
> *The psychiatrist—ugh! He patted me on the head. All he told me was that he was putting more potassium in my body. There wasn't*

any conversation about why I did this or anything. I thought that a suicide attempt would come across as a cry for help.

Of all post-attempt experiences described, perhaps none are more devastating than when the anger is delivered by the family.

I was pretty young, that first attempt. I just magically wanted it never to have happened. About the third or fourth day I called my brother, who hadn't visited me yet. I tried to talk to him, but he was really angry. This was shortly after my father died of alcoholism, and my brother said, "You should have just died." My heart fell to my feet. I was completely drained—hurt. I thought, "Maybe he's right. Maybe I should've been dead." I felt like a terrible person. That was a hard one. It still hits the heart pretty hard. (Catherine)

Difficulties such as these were common in the stories told to me. And yet not all encounters were disturbing or assaultive. Many of those interviewed had positive experiences early in their hospital stays. These moments ranged from simple acts of kindness to unusual and sometimes enigmatic encounters.

After Sharon awoke from an overdose of sleeping pills, she had difficulty remembering what had transpired the night before. She knew she was in a hospital, however, and memories returned of hospital visits as a child, following her mother's frequent suicide attempts. This was the last place she would expect kindness. Sharon was disoriented and confused as the staff psychiatrist sat with her.

She just told me what had happened. And then she asked, "What was so terrible that you tried to kill yourself?" It seemed like she really wanted to know. She was really concerned, in a calm sort of way. And then all this stuff about my husband and my marriage just came out of me—all the pain.

In times of crisis, simple acts of caring are often pushed aside in favor of intricate technical interventions, both medical and psychological. For those who spoke about early moments in the hospital, however, acts of caring were the most treasured. Sometimes they proved powerful enough to ignite the first spark of life after years of courting death.

Chris's encounter with the attending physician was unexpected and startling. After enduring the comments of her roommates the previous night, she expected the worst.

> *I just felt really hopeless, like just not wanting to live. I had no idea what was happening to me. I was very angry. I was simmering underneath. The doctor came in. He was clearly very tired from being on all night.*

Chris had been braced for condescension and reproach, and stiffened when the attending physician walked in, but she was surprised.

> *He sat down and took my hand in his: he just picked up my hand and held it! He seemed very loving. Boy, I was dumbfounded! He held my hand and brushed the hair from my face and said, "I'm not even gonna ask you how you feel. I know you feel miserable. I don't even want you to tell me right now." I thought to myself, "This doctor is really cool!" Then he said, "And I'm gonna tell you a secret. You see, in this state, it's illegal to attempt suicide, and they send you to the state hospital for a month if you try, plus you have to pay a fine. You have to handle all the legal ramifications and it's real nasty. So I admitted you under a diagnosis of food poisoning, and you should know that my career's on the line and you are holding it in your hands"—and he squeezed my hand a bit. "I'm gonna have to trust you that you're gonna act differently than I expect you want to right now."*

In minutes, the years of isolation that surrounded Chris was gently pierced.

As he's talking, I realize that my actions are going to affect him. He says, "I don't expect you to want to live for a while. I know how you are feeling, but I also know your husband and your little girl. She's the most beautiful creature I've ever met." He lets that sink in a little, and then he says, "You know your husband. Do you really want him to raise her?" The question had never entered my mind! I knew this was the voice of reason.

For Ed, the process of emerging from hiding was more complex. Perhaps there were some caring and insightful staff in the hospital, but it would be a long time before he would let them in.

Ed spent five months in the hospital, recovering from the medical trauma and beginning rehabilitation. He had lost all memory of the first three weeks after the fall, and he awoke to discover that he was in traction. A tracheal tube had been implanted in his neck, and it would be three and a half months before he was able to speak. Regardless of how he was treated, he felt imprisoned and enraged. Where he was once a vigorous and self-reliant young man, he was now virtually helpless. Although some staff were attentive and even pleasant, Ed rejected their overtures. At times, he would even swing his fists at them. He could not afford to receive kindness. He needed to freeze time and obscure the reality of his new condition. If he didn't acknowledge people's help, then perhaps it had never happened. Perhaps he wasn't paralyzed, and he wouldn't need to attend to the terror which lay underneath.

Ed was transferred to a rehabilitation center near his home, whereupon it was discovered that he had developed an infection in his heels, osteomyelitis, and it caused a blackening of the bone. He would have to return to the hospital, and the initial prognosis was not an optimistic one.

*They're telling me—I got to go back to the hospital, and I was
saying, "Fuck you, man, I don't care!"—and I didn't. If anything,
it was a relief. I wouldn't have to go through this rehab stuff. I
didn't give a shit. One doctor told me that if they didn't take care of
this, I could die. My reply was, "Good. It's about fucking time!"*

What transpired next proved both startling and providential.
One of the doctors came to Ed's bedside and informed him of the
medical strategy they had planned. Ed imagined a course of antibi-
otics and physical therapy, but was horrified at what he heard.

*He says, "What we're talking about here is amputation, and we'll
need to amputate up to the knee." I couldn't believe what I heard. I
also couldn't believe this doctor. I mean, he's probably a decent
surgeon, but where did he learn his bedside manner? He was smug,
and real impersonal. Like he was reading the news. No intro, no
softening, just boom! "We're gonna amputate."*

The bubble burst. Ed was literally frightened out of the trance. He
could barely comprehend that his legs were paralyzed and he certainly wasn't able to contemplate losing one. Regardless of whether
he would ever walk again, he discovered at that moment something
he did care about. There had been enough damage. It was time to
stop. Losing his leg would be too much.

*I began to pray. I prayed to God, "Please, please, God. No more for
right now. I fucked up bad, all right, but please don't take my leg.
I'll try to do something with it. I must be here for some reason.
Please, let's do something about it."*

A turning point had been reached. Ed was still angry and remote,
but the fear of losing his leg stirred a desire to end this chain of
disasters. He sought second opinions and discovered to his great
relief that only a small portion of the heel bone needed to be

removed. The surgery was done without anesthesia, for there was no feeling in the leg, and he was soon released back to rehabilitation.

Remembering him as sullen and quick to explode, staff and patients gave him a wide berth. They couldn't tell that something had changed. With this last ordeal, however, a simple question had begun to supplant the self-hatred encamped in his core. It would alter his life forever.

Why did I survive? Why was I the only person in seventy years to live through that fall? I thought, maybe there's a reason. Maybe there's a reason to start pursuing life again. I think I developed a faith—not a rolling Bible faith or anything, but I really started thinking about things after the success of the surgery.

I started to wonder, "Maybe there are reasons why people live and die. Maybe you're supposed to do something with it." I had to desperately hold on to that in order to find some purpose for living. I started feeling almost special for surviving. I needed that to feel that I was here for a purpose. It was either that, or there was no point in pursuing rehab or anything else.

Ed began to bridge back to the living. He'd spend hours in his room writing poems, attempting to wrestle meaning from the past and purpose for the future. Sometimes he'd awaken in the middle of the night, stirred by a muse and needing to express the enormous range of thoughts and feelings that had once been locked inside. Writing became a release, and the creativity that he once hid so completely became his lifeline. Late at night, confined to a wheelchair, he was able to travel farther than ever before—beyond his persona as a tough football player, beyond the approval he had alternately aspired to and felt oppressed by, and into the world of image and emotion, rhyme and meter. He felt inspired. There *was* somebody inside, and connecting with his seemingly limitless fount of creativity confirmed it.

I just started trying to be more Ed Gallagher, a person not connected to football or a suicide attempt. John Lennon's song, "Starting Over," which he wrote right before he died, was a big thing for me. I was starting over. I started writing all types of things—poems, prose, aphorisms. I just let myself cut loose.

Ed was opening. His writing offered a way to connect with himself, and slowly, cautiously at first, it served as a bridge to others. When no one was looking, or at night when no one was in the rehab lounge, he'd tack a note or a poem on the wall. Someone would respond to his work, describing how it spoke to his or her experience, and they'd find time to talk. He had always kept a distance from fellow patients, but now he sought their company. His desire for connection grew, and he found people with whom he could genuinely and authentically relate. As he did so, he discovered his capacity to enjoy others. He felt drawn to them and felt them being drawn to him.

And, I started talking. I wasn't ready to talk about the trigger incident—that would take a while—but I started talking about everyone else: feelings, my life as a football player, suicide, what happened when I kept myself locked up. Pretty soon, I discovered I was seeing the beauty in others. I remember thinking as I was talking to this one friend, "You look pretty cool, so maybe I look good too!" It was funny, but it seemed like a big revelation!

After encircling himself in secrecy for years, Ed now wanted to be visible. It seemed to explode from him. A desire to communicate had taken hold and he wanted to talk about life's deeper challenges. He fervently sought opinions and commentary on his writing. He felt proud of his talent, and he wanted people to know.

I wanted people to know that I was more than a jock, or a bouncer, or a furniture mover. I wanted to advertise my talent instead of keep it under wraps. It got to be where I was both sharing my writing and myself at the same time. As I progressed into talking more and more, it felt very good.

Ed sent an autobiographical essay, "Ways to Ease the Pain," to a local radio station and was immediately invited for an interview. Accompanied by his high school coach and the minister at the rehab facility, he spoke about his former life and the one just beginning. He was nervous, and the words came haltingly at first, but then, as if he had always been behind a microphone, he discovered his voice—straightforward, sometimes graphic, funny and poignant. The time flew by; the interview seemed a great success; and Ed knew without hesitation what his next step would be.

I got home that night—it was real late by the time we got in—and I couldn't sleep. I was too excited. It was about four A.M. and I called this cable talk show, saying this is what happened to me, this is what I'm trying to do, I was just on the radio, et cetera. So they interviewed me on cable TV, and they said, "We like the way you came across. Would you be interested in hosting your own show?" That's how "Mr. Ed's Corral" started. Since then, I've done about 180 shows. It's a talk show, interview format, and we've talked about drugs, suicide, rape, gambling, incest, disability stuff, adolescence, animal awareness, acupuncture—even magic.

Ed was recovering from years of hiding, from years of self-hatred, and from the ordeal of the suicide and its aftermath. His new life was taking form, and he felt excited in ways he'd never before felt. Yet life still contained difficulty and heartache. His father had reconstructed Ed's bedroom and bath to accommodate the wheelchair, but when Ed moved back home, a great tension enveloped the house. His father was at a loss to understand the suicide attempt. He felt devastated by Ed's actions and became sullen and argumentative. Ed's suicide was a personal affront. He was angry, and Ed grew angry in return.

Arguments, loud voices. We went after each other a lot, and yet we loved each other. He was shattered and he couldn't understand, and I had this rage and survivor guilt. It was really hard, you see, 'cause I hadn't talked about the gay stuff, so of course it didn't make sense. He had these health problems: He was so close to death with emphysema and I couldn't tell him. I knew he'd never understand that part.

Ed felt trapped again. Still without a motorized wheelchair and unable to afford the hand controls he needed to drive a car, he stewed in the house between shows. The days began to assume the "double life" quality that had existed before his attempt, and everyone was edgy.

I used to think, "What can I do to get arrested, to get out of here? What can I break? What trouble can I cause?" My father wanted me to forget all this suicide stuff and get a "real" job, but it was like, "Hey, I can't go back to the shit I used to do." So, I'd just close the door and write poetry. That was my release, my escape valve.

As difficult as home life seemed, however, something had irrevocably changed within him. Ed no longer engaged in self-destructive outlets for his frustration. No stranger to discipline from his days as an athlete, he applied himself to his writing. Prose and verse were his confessors, and the refuge to which he turned when he felt alone and angry, impatient or hopeless.

It got to a point where I said to myself, "Enough. I'm not gonna live my life in a fucking depression anymore. I'm gonna try to make something happen." It's been really good. I've made a lot of good friends and contacts, and I found out that I can be me in many ways and be liked, and accepted and loved, and I can give something back—not just anything, but something that I really believe in.

Some time later, Ed's father died. After the funeral, Ed, his mother, and his sister, the only remaining members of the family, found themselves alone. Ed had been rehearsing this moment for a number of years, and finally he told the true reasons for his suicide attempt.

I eased into it by talking to some friends beforehand so I was a little more comfortable about talking. I said, "Maybe this is the best time to tell you what triggered everything." I told them, "I've struggled much of my life with gay thoughts and feelings," and they said, "Oh, we knew that!" I said, "Shit! Why didn't you tell me!" "Well, we decided that when it was time for you to say it, you would." My mother added that she didn't think my father would be able to handle it, so she never brought it up.

That blew my mind! I couldn't believe they had known the whole time. But, they were right in a way. Of course, I wished we could've talked about it, but I know I would have been very defensive. I was pretty elusive back then. I was wrong, you know. I built myself a prison of loneliness that I never had to.

There is no way to whitewash a suicide attempt. It is a real act, and it carries real consequences. Some of the consequences are terrible. It was only with a generous portion of newly learned compassion and courage that Ed could avoid being consumed by remorse.

When I got this motorized wheelchair, I started going to New York City again. I had to see, "Am I still good-looking? Am I okay in a wheelchair?" And to my surprise, I made some friends and had some nice contacts. I mean sex is completely different. I don't have a lot of feeling below my chest and it destroys me if I let it, you know? But I'm realizing that sex doesn't always come through your dick.

It was four years after the attempt. Ed had long ago moved into his own residence and spoken at two national conventions at Columbia University, and was invited to talks and presentations throughout the metropolitan area. He published his first book, *Will I Live Another Day Before I Die?*, and was asked to be an independent scholar for various psychiatric periodicals. The content of his speeches expanded from suicide prevention to creativity and its role in fulfilling one's potential, and he began to speak at schools of all levels. Ed has appeared in his own HBO special, played parts in daytime soap operas, and is the executive director of his own educational institute, Alive to Thrive.

> *Since the HBO thing, I've received so many calls and letters. I realize that whatever I was thinking or feeling back then that was so peculiar to Ed Gallagher is pretty common. I mean, the stories are unique, but the feelings are universal.*

Through enormous difficulty, he allowed life, which had once felt tortuous and cruel, to become a teacher. Life was now a challenge and an opportunity. Acceptance slowly replaced the self-abhorrence that almost destroyed him, and faith and confidence dissolved his hopelessness. In the crucible of his recovery, Ed forged his own brand of spirituality. He finally befriended life and God on his own terms. At the end of his book, Ed wrote a prayer:

> *Thank you, God, for the life you've given me and the life I want to live. Please keep me strong and healthy, and back me up with your power, strength, and trust. I'll pick up the rest.*

Five

The Road Back

FIRST STEPS

The doctor was right. I still felt I wanted to die. I knew I still wanted to die, but I was also angry. I realized there was no way in hell that I wanted my husband to raise my daughter. I didn't want her to feel as powerless and abandoned as I felt. It felt like he was giving me a task I could accomplish even though I felt so bad.(Chris)

Every journey begins with an intention and a first step. In ways varied and innumerable, a crack in the door appears and light penetrates where it may never have entered before. After the failed attempt, people cautiously entertain a change of perspective, an alternate reality which may have hovered close by but which remained hidden during the trance.

A voice of compassion had melted the armor that surrounded Chris. Patient and gentle, her admitting physician seemed to be the very archetype of the Good Doctor. Skillfully, undemonstratively, he empathized with her dilemma while challenging her to poke through her suffering and grasp a wider perspective.

> *I knew nothing about psychological innards at that point, but two things had happened all of a sudden that were new. First of all, he didn't put me down for wanting to leave my husband. Most everyone else seemed to think I was a bad person for wanting to leave him. And then, even though I still felt real dead inside, there was this other thing out here, separate from myself, that was a task worth trying to accomplish.*

This was the first step. First steps represent a subtle but critical shift in attitude. At this juncture, one can feel both the familiar desire to die and the first hints of wanting to live. In such moments, people simultaneously experience the pain of the past and a still embryonic sense of nourishment in the present. These are the moments when the suicidal trance gives way and one begins to entertain new possibilities. These are the first moments of recovery.

In one short stroke, Chris felt radically different. Someone had entered her world and acknowledged the legitimacy of her pain. She had also been compassionately challenged. The doctor related to her as an adult and as a capable person, despite the circumstances. This was precisely the kind of help she needed. It gave meaning to her present predicament and offered her a reason for living. Her daughter's welfare was critically important and she needed to devote herself to that end, but at the same time there was still much that Chris had to discover about herself. She had always been a set of contradictions: passionate yet timid, stubborn and strong-willed underneath and yet docile and conciliatory in personal relation-ships. The connection forged in a few minutes that morning awakened the desire within Chris to investigate the puzzle that was she, and for the first time in years she felt this might be a worthwhile project. Someone believed in her, and in an important and necessary step, she was willing, at least for a while, to suspend her doubt.

Encouraged by the doctor's generosity, Chris became willing to look within herself, to see and examine what was there rather than simply reacting. Lying in her hospital bed, Chris became aware of something about herself that would change her life. She chose her words carefully as she described this to me, wanting to be clear, not wanting to be misunderstood.

> *A part of me died that night. The part that always refused to stand up for myself died. Somehow, making the statement that I can kill myself if I want too, even though I wasn't supposed to—or allowed to. It sounds strange, I know, but somehow I was making a decision* for myself; *and it meant to me that I could stand up for myself. I know, now, it was a very serious way to prove that.*

Chris had spent her entire life anticipating the needs of others, and aspiring to an ideal of perfect womanhood and motherhood. In her original family and in her married life, this wasn't so much appreciated as simply expected; it was her duty and responsibility. Depleted and disempowered, her only avenue of self-assertion became self-destruction. Within the tunnel, the only way to declare her right to live was to die.

And yet Chris lived. The next morning, she realized that her desire to live also survived. Gingerly touching that part of her, she knew her world had changed.

> *I felt like a whole different person—like a different human being—afterwards. The whole image of being the all-American wife and mother—I just didn't care about it any more. I knew I was okay without that image and that I could go ahead and get the divorce. Somehow, I couldn't even remember who I had been before!*

There are times in our lives when we discover with certainty what is true; and although we can sometimes identify the exact moments of the discovery, it rarely happens all of a sudden. It often comes after much struggle and confusion. Chris was describing a pivotal shift in her very experience of being alive. She was finally able to glimpse a future other than her own demise, a future that contained hope. This glimpse was like a birth, but the labor had been long and difficult.

Later that morning, still weak from the night before, Chris gathered her things and made her way home. Her marriage was shattered and no effort was made to pretend otherwise. Her husband chose not to meet her at the hospital. He had thrown her clothes over the front yard and left. Walking through the house, she realized how much a stranger she felt there; and it was clear to her that she would move that day. Twelve hours before, she had raced from her family in suicidal fury, and now she was a single mother, beginning her life again.

Chris's feelings were both intense and conflicted. Slowly, gradually she allowed herself the feeling of freedom. It was only a day since her attempt and she still felt dubious about living. She was just beginning to sort through her inner life, and this would take some time and some help.

> I still felt like "I don't want to live," but at the same time, I thought, "Well, if I'm gonna raise my daughter, I'm gonna have to live. That means I'm gonna have to get through these feelings." It was so early, though, and I didn't trust my thoughts, and I didn't trust myself being alone. So I did the hardest thing of all.

In the profile of every recovery from attempted suicide, there is a moment on which one's entire fate balances. It is the first step, often hesitant and subtle, but a palpable beginning. First steps reflect a still nascent feeling that life may somehow unfold in a new and different way. Ed furtively pinned a few of his poems on the bulletin board in the hospital. This was his first move outward since his attempt. It was his way of asking, "Is anybody out there?" The response he received propelled him further.

Following the attempt to hang himself, and some weeks in the hospital, Robert returned to school. He had to return to school knowing that both classmates and teachers were confused, disturbed, and even fascinated by what he did.

> *How am I going to handle it? How am I going to handle the people, all the rumors, all my friends at school, and stuff like that? They didn't really talk to me about reentry when I was at the hospital. But I went back. I ended up getting a lot of phone calls from my friends, and a lot of cards. I still have a drawerful of cards.*

In such a small town as Chris's there was only one place where she felt she might get through the day. She was uncertain how she'd be received, but there was no alternative. Years later, she could still feel how fearful she had been.

> *There was this hardware store in the center of town where everybody came. It had a potbelly stove and tables, you know, and you could go in and have tea. That's where I'd hang out a lot of the time, and so did everybody else. Everyone would come in, have lunch together, and talk. I knew everybody in that town and I knew that everyone heard what I had done the night before. But in spite of that, I knew that I had to have people around me if I was gonna make it through that day, and so I took my daughter with me. God, I can feel the fear as I talk about it.*
>
> *I went into the store and I talked to the woman who owned it. I told her I needed to hang out all day. "Could I do that? Will that be okay?" She said, "Yes." And then she said, "And if anybody says anything, I'll kick them out!" She was really on my side and I needed that. A lot of people stared at me that day. They didn't say*

anything and I didn't know what they were thinking. I just forced
myself to stay there. It was really excruciating, I was so horribly
ashamed. But I needed to be around people if I was to survive,
whether they approved of me or not.

Chris did survive the day. At its end, she learned that an apartment was available just across from the hardware store. That night,
she and her daughter moved in.

I got the suitcases and our clothes and we left. We walked out the
door and I never went back in that house again. I was completely
focused on how to be there for my daughter, about how this was
gonna be. I was just amazed because she was happy as a lark. She
got her toothbrush in one hand and her little doll in the other, but
the toothbrush seemed to be more important. She staked out her
new room, and then marched to the bathroom. She placed her
toothbrush in the holder and said to me, "There, now I live here."

To support herself, Chris drew and painted portraits for locals
and for tourists passing through. Her art had never been encouraged and she was forbidden by her husband to earn money, so her
considerable talent had languished. For Chris, therefore, unpacking
her paint and brushes was a declaration of her independence. Each
morning, she would stand her easel on the broad porch of the
hardware store and paint. With each new color and each stroke of
the brush, she was creating a new world for herself, canvases replete
with depth and passion and filled with people who seemed to care.
Her delight was only matched by those who came to sit for their
portraits.

In the year following the attempt, Chris faced many challenges. She
had been discharged from the hospital with the agreement that she
receive psychotherapy, and this took some arranging.

I had to learn to hitchhike. There were no therapists in my town, so I had to leave my daughter with a baby-sitter and get a ride up the highway. I was petrified at first. I was scared to death standing out there. Everybody hitchhiked then, but it just wasn't me. But, you know, I always got the most incredible rides! Really fun and interesting people. People would pull over—sometimes I'd know them, sometimes I wouldn't.

Chris took her promise to engage in therapy seriously. She owed it to herself and she felt an obligation to the doctor who had treated her with such kindness and trust. She began sessions, both individual and group. Chris received the personal attention she needed in individual therapy, and in group work she experimented with creating relationships that were mutually respectful and empowering. It wasn't always easy, and over time, she found pockets of deeply hidden fear.

I was this dispassionate observer of the group, sitting up there commenting to myself on what everyone else was saying and doing. I was still very split, not really present, and I didn't think there was something wrong with that at the time.

I thought I was being pretty clever because nobody could hurt me. After months in the group, somebody said something nasty to me. I think she called me haughty, a know-it-all. She didn't like my "cool" attitude, because they are in there doing some heavy work, and I'm sitting there watching, thinking, "You guys are all crazy and I'm fine!" Well, she was right, and I got very upset. I started crying. It was the first time I was emotional enough for the therapist and group to work with me. I was always so cool and calm in the group. Suddenly, I'm screaming, "I just don't know who I am!"

For Chris, this was a watershed. She had locked so much pain inside her in the years before the attempt that she didn't know how to work with her feelings. Here in the group, she was being coaxed to the next level of her healing, and it was foreign and frightening. Since the suicide attempt, Chris had been protecting herself, keeping her life in order. She had fashioned a safe territory in which she could function and slowly acclimate to her new world. Now the group was asking her to go farther, and she hadn't a clue how.

The therapist asked me to play a game with him. He said, "I'll make a statement and then I want you to make a statement— whatever comes to mind." Then he said, "I love to go to the beach and just walk and feel my toes in the sand," and I said, "I love to go sit on the mountaintop and feel the wind blow through my hair." And he said, "And I love to just sit and watch and listen to my children laughing when they're playing," and that really hit me.

I hadn't thought about enjoying anything for a very, very long time, and these weren't things connected to how I'd be a good mother for my daughter. It was connected to me, and the things that give me pleasure. We went on and on and after ten or fifteen minutes, he said, "These things that you love give you a sense of who you are." It was like lightning struck. "Is that it? That's me! Well, those things are enough for the time being." It meant to me that the things that made me feel good are all I need to be, and that it was already there. At that point, I lost much of the heaviness of not wanting to live.

After a lifetime of struggle, Chris had finally given birth to the desire to live. Having discovered the rudiments of simple enjoyment, her focus moved to the more complex aspirations she had held before she married. She had always wanted to study art and psychology, and in a short time Chris and her daughter moved from the small town to be nearer to the state university.

Chris was learning to sense her own need, to take the action most likely to yield what she wanted, and to allow herself to feel satisfied and strengthened by her choices. What once seemed unthinkable and unattainable was becoming a daily reality. She discovered that the more she acted on her own behalf, the more sensitive she became to precisely what she needed and the more likely she was to obtain it. Her life was an experiment, and each day she looked forward to entering the laboratory.

I had many surprises and I had some great ideas. My daughter and I had virtually lived alone for three months after we moved—we didn't know anyone—and I realized, "I haven't been touched by an adult human being for at least six months!" So I went to my group and said, "I have this great exercise. I want to learn how to be hugged." The therapist seemed a bit dubious, but he went along with it and he separated the group into people who find it difficult to approach people and people who generally find it pretty easy. He had the shy ones, me included, hug someone first. That was pretty easy. I just chose someone I wanted and did it.

The next time, I had to wait and let someone choose me. As they were walking towards me, my legs started shaking. They turned to rubber and I fell to the ground. I just sat there and curled up. I started crying and I couldn't stop.

When someone wrestles with suicide over a long period, it becomes an intimate, a possessive lover, demanding one's sole attention and preventing more nourishing experiences from reaching one's mind and body. Imperceptibly but powerfully, people enshroud themselves in layers of protection and defense. Over time, avenues of contact and connection wither from disuse, and the most valuable products of human interaction—comfort, love, and feeling understood—become impossible for them.

When Chris rolled into a fetal ball that day in the group, it was as if her entire body expressed the pain of a lifetime of not being approached with love. The shape of her body in those moments reflected both the posture of an adult who was valiantly holding herself together, trying hard to act responsibly, and that of the child she had once been, needing simple human contact. Although Chris had recently become more assertive and felt it natural and easy to offer comfort to others, seeing someone approach her in kindness seemed to dissolve the years of protective isolation and reveal her yearning for caring. She was allowing herself to feel sorrow for what she had never experienced, as well as happiness at the abundance of the moment. A new certainty emerged. If such experiences were possible in *this* group, they might be possible in other parts of her universe as well.

"Isostasy" is a geological term referring to the force that lifts light objects when other forces cease to hold them down. It could also be used to describe what happened to Chris. Her passion began to surface; and from then on she pursued her renewal with a sense of adventure. Each breakthrough seemed to build on the one before it, and carry her on to new territory.

> *It was one awakening after another. I'd just feel a longing for something, and rather than sit around and get on my case and feel bad about it, I'd say, "I can do something. If you want a hug, get a hug! If you want something to be different, make it different." Then I'd realize, "Oh, my God, I had another experience there!" It was like growing a new way of recognizing stuff inside me that I don't think I'd ever had since I was a very little kid.*

Years later, Chris reached *the* turning point in her journey back to life. It came in the form of a memory, and it answered a fundamental question: Why couldn't she, except under extreme duress, stand up for herself and be assertive—even angry—when necessary?

> *I'd never remembered anything about my father before. One night, when my second husband and I and the kids were watching*

this stupid sitcom on TV, I had this flashback memory. Suddenly, the screen went black for me. I could sense everything going on behind it, but I began seeing something completely different. I saw myself as a little girl. Somehow I knew I was two-and-a-half years old. I was underneath the house playing in the dirt, wearing this little frilly dress. My father called to me. I could see his feet sticking out from below the siding, and then he yanked me out and began hitting me—spanking me really severely for wearing this dress in the dirt. He was holding me up and shaking me really hard and yelling at me. I was like a spectator up until this point, watching him, seeing him throw me around and then, suddenly, I was the little girl, looking at his face. I was hating him, wanting him to go away. I was thinking inside that I wanted him to die.

That was the night my father jumped off a bridge and committed suicide. I had a lot of flashbacks after that, many with lots more feeling, but now I know what I learned back then: that anytime I experience really angry feelings about anybody, when I get really furious, I immediately tell myself, "Your anger is terrible. You don't deserve to live." I turn the anger in on myself.

Chris realized what she decided as a child: "My anger can kill," and that she would sacrifice herself before experiencing such trauma again. This realization brought her tremendous relief and liberation, and propelled her toward her later stages of recovery. Her life would continue to be blessed with such insights, although it would also be visited by moments of heartache. Chris remarried, and for a time enjoyed a harmonious family life. Later, that marriage too would dissolve. She moved to a large metropolitan area to train as a psychotherapist, and then back to the country, where she felt at home. Her children have grown to be happy teenagers, and she is becoming increasingly respected in her specialty: providing intensive psychotherapy for families at risk.

3

The Anatomy
of Recovery

*I realized I don't have to kill myself. I can move. I can go
anywhere on this planet. The worst that's gonna happen
is that I'm gonna die, you know? And I already know
about dying! (Karen)*

There are many stories like those of Chris and Ed, and in each, recovery starts from the most improbable circumstances. The road back to life begins at death's door, after lengthy and unrelenting internal pressure toward self-destruction. And yet, as we can see from the above stories, healing is possible. People *do* recover from the attempt to kill themselves. More importantly, people recover from the ever-present *desire* to kill themselves.

This chapter describes the stages through which people progress in creating meaningful and satisfying lives for themselves, perhaps for the first time. As I've worked with people and listened to their stories, certain stages have emerged as the universal elements and the common threads woven through the process of each person's recovery.

- The first stage involves Dissolving the Suicidal Trance. It occurs as one discovers that it is the suicidal context, *not he or she*, that has to die. Suspending doubt, grieving, and learning to trust are the most important steps at this stage.

- The second stage of recovery, Rebuilding the Self, focuses on healing the past, taking responsibility for one's actions, and discovering new answers to the question "Who am I?"
- Thirdly, while building a new relationship with oneself, one must allow others in. This stage, Reaching Out, is the direct opposite of the isolation in the suicidal trance. It requires that one learn to ask for help, be willing to be seen, and invite the intimacy of others.
- The fourth stage, Allowing Others In, is enormously important. After reaching out, people must now allow themselves to accept what others offer and learn to let themselves be loved and be healed by healthy relationships.
- The final stage involves Giving Back. Having learned to receive from others in new and healthy ways, it is now time to offer what one has learned back to one's community. This stage serves to integrate and cement the gains made on the road back to life.

These stages contain watershed experiences that strengthen one's faith and help one to marshal the stamina to survive and progress through the inevitable periods of confusion and pain. Some of these experiences will be serendipitous and unexpected, while others will be consciously sought and hard-won. Nevertheless, they constitute major turning points in the process of rebirth. And while not everyone passes through the various stages in the same linear progression, people who recover do experience most of them at some point during the road back.

Six

Dissolving the Trance

Time stands still after an attempt. Ordinary concerns are eclipsed by the intensity of the event. For hours, days, sometimes even years, it seems as if the world remains suspended in crisis, waiting for the next step: the first inklings that perhaps there may be a better way than suicide.

The first stage of emerging from suicidal despair and hopelessness involves the dissolution of the suicidal trance. For many, as we have heard, the trance begins to break when one's inner world, once so secret, is exposed to intimates and to strangers. Perhaps the attempt is interrupted by the person himself or herself, or by a friend or family member, or perhaps the attempt fails and medical intervention is necessary. The intensity of the person's pain has been revealed, even if the details are not clear. It is as if the front of one's house has been torn away and the interior is visible for all to see. It is a time of great confusion, often of great humiliation and anger. Ed would barely let hospital staff come near him, let alone speak to him. Chris had to suffer the added indignation of judgments by other patients. Teresa found herself being accused of selfishness and insensitivity by the attending physician.

These are some of the humbling and virtually unavoidable beginnings on the road back to life. Despite the agony they cause, these moments play an important role in a person's recovery. When one has contemplated suicide for weeks or months or longer, it comes to represent relief and the release from all pain and suffering. It has become a goal and an obsession. It is after the attempt has proven unsuccessful, after that final option has been played to an unanticipated result, that one becomes willing to entertain other alternatives. In each of these stories, people report similar steps to dissolving the trance. They include:

- Suspending doubt
- Breaking the suicidal context
- Grieving
- Learning to trust, and
- Letting go of dying

SUSPENDING DOUBT

> *It seemed like some kind of spiritual experience. After I woke up, what I realized real strongly was that there was some sort of purpose to me being on this planet and that I'd better damn well find out what it was. (Rennie)*

The very failure of the attempt compels some people to consider the possibility that there were reasons—existential or spiritual—why the attempt failed. At this point, confused and dispirited, people tentatively consider the questions "Why didn't I die?" "Why am I still alive?" and ultimately "Is there any other way?" These first questions represent the suspension of the doubt that led them to suicide: doubt that life holds any promise whatsoever. They reflect the first internal shifts away from the desire to die, and represent the first life-promoting decisions. These decisions are often subtle, almost unnoticeable from the outside. Chris exercised a momentary willingness to look into her doctor's eyes and listen to his counsel. Sharon, startled by the attending psychiatrist's kindness, allowed herself to receive compassion and guidance. A modicum of trust grows where before there was only suspicion. These are first steps.

When Rennie awoke, she knew she had tried suicide for the last time. None of the attempts had worked, and she decided that three times was enough. A small spark of curiosity propelled her into the beginnings of recovery. It was vague and speculative, but it was enough to start her thinking. She wondered what kind of fate had intervened to halt her death. Her mind turned to ideas she hadn't previously considered: meaning, destiny, and the faint possibility that there was an unknown purpose to be discovered in her life. These were only whispers, but they hinted at freedom from her suffering. They intrigued her, and gave rise to her first concrete post-attempt decisions.

Rennie knew that nothing good would happen until she cleared the heroin from her body.

My whole life was just like from one shot to the next, and there wasn't that much space between them anymore. It got to the point where I had to shoot up every hour or so. It wasn't about getting high; it was about not getting sick. I wasn't gonna do the methadone program, because I had seen people on methadone and I was convinced it just substituted another drug. So I just decided, "I'm going to do it myself."

Rennie went "cold turkey." She called some friends, asked them to visit her for support, and began the arduous task of quitting heroin. They plied her with valerian tea and copious amounts of marijuana to survive the symptoms, but in the end, she had to endure a week of seizures, sweats, fevers, insomnia, and ever-present nausea.

The worst of it was after three days. I couldn't read anymore. Reading had distracted me from the pain, but on the third day, I went completely cross-eyed. I couldn't focus at all. I mean, if two people sat in front of me, it looked like they had switched places! I just lost total control of my body.

It seemed like a kind of purgatory—seven days somehow disconnected from real time. Despite the physical rigors of her withdrawal, or maybe because of them, Rennie felt herself in a spiritual journey, a dark night from which she prayed to emerge. In quieter moments, between bouts of muscle spasm and cramping, she would return to the memory of waking up after her last attempt and recapture the hope of a meaningful future. But there were many times in the agony of the withdrawal that she considered shooting heroin again and ending her misery. Each time, however, one thought would dissuade her.

I knew that if I didn't do it this time, then it was gonna be another time, and I'd have to go through the same thing again. I had already gone through this amount of pain and now it was behind me, but if I did the heroin now, I'd have to repeat the pain again and again.

When Rennie attributed meaning to her failed suicide attempts, she began to chart the path of her return to life. Her quest for a sense of purpose and the desire to discover her destiny gave her the strength she needed to withstand physical hardship and survive the inevitable periods of emotional confusion.

Abandoning doubt is a subtle and creative act, born from the rubble of the suicide attempt and from intimations of a better life. It leads to a new model of how one can live in the world; and although that model may take time to form fully, it offers a goal to which a person can aspire. Rennie now had something on which to focus—

something toward which to direct her attention aside from the drugs and her pain. It made the challenges ahead, if not always easy, at least bearable.

BREAKING THE SUICIDAL CONTEXT

It is necessary to separate oneself from the suicidal context in order to rebuild one's life. This separation may take a variety of forms, but essentially, one must radically alter one's relationship to the environment of suicidal despair in which the attempt occurred. In recovering, people learn to choose alternatives to old routines and the people associated with them—the quotidian reminders of despair and defeat. In the delicate stages of early recovery, people feel the stirrings of change within, but they also realize that the world at large may be less pliable. To change everything feels like an enormous task. Breaking the suicidal context reflects a desire to disconnect from the oppressiveness of the past and hope for a fresh beginning. It is a leap of faith motivated by the necessity for change. Although a person's plan may not be clear at the beginning, many describe having an inner certainty—a "knowing"—that they are on the right course. They often pare down their possessions, simplify their lives, and try to discover just what happened to them and why.

For Chris and Ed, it was isolation from which they needed to separate. It was essential to their recovery that they reach out to others and let others in. For Rennie, it was imperative to end the cycle of her addiction. Teresa was still a young teenager when she bought a one-way ticket to Prescott. She had to leave. Somewhere beneath the abuse and neglect, there was a kernel of recognition, even at her young age. Despite the sketchiness of her plan, she knew a change was necessary to her future.

It was a thirteen-hour bus ride. We had a layover from Idaho at Reno and I stayed in the station, waiting. I was still very calm and strong, and so far everything was okay. I had my money and my clothes—everything I needed. I was proud of myself. At some point, this big and sleazy guy came over. He was trying to get me to go somewhere with him. I didn't know what was going on then. I do now.

There was this elderly couple. The man must've been in his seventies. He and his wife just came over next to me. He pulled out a knife and began cleaning his nails with it, kinda nonchalantly, suggesting to this guy that he might want to leave! Then they took me to dinner. It was very comforting and nice. I felt even happy for a little bit there. We played cards and ate. I was happy 'cause they noticed me, and I wasn't being polite or "good." I started thinking, "Maybe I should go with them!" I think that was the first time since kindergarten that I felt that about someone.

Teresa created a new life. Just off the bus, she saw a help wanted sign in a restaurant window, applied, and was offered the job that afternoon. The next day, she enrolled in school. She made arrangements to live with some relatives—distant enough to allow her independence but understanding enough not to send her back to her mother. She wanted a new start. Within a week, she was back in school, had joined the track team, and was taking vocational courses at the local community college.

Vic also knew he had to leave. He was too isolated, and he knew that was dangerous. In his matter-of-fact way, he reasoned he had two choices.

Well, either you do it or you don't. You either make it or you stay back here. I got laid off—good ole budget cuts—so my brother, who lives out west, said, "Why don't you come out?" So I took a coin and flipped it, is basically what I did. It came up heads, and heads was for out west, so I came out.

As Mattie regained consciousness, the cold tile of the bathroom floor beneath her felt hard and unyielding. She hadn't yet remembered staring into the mirror a few hours before, being surprised to see her reflection, or swallowing a full bottle of aspirin. As she lay there, her hands could feel the smooth contours of the toilet bowl, and her mind could sense the crushing despair that was creeping back.

> It was despair that I couldn't even do this right, and that now that I'm still alive and I'm gonna have to go through this. It felt like my punishment, not to have died. I didn't know anybody in town, and I didn't want anyone to know about it, and Curt and I weren't speaking.

Although the breakup with her boyfriend had prompted Mattie's suicide attempt, she had no idea as yet that both her suffering and her fragile self-esteem had little to do with their incompatibility. She had no recollection of the incest with her grandfather, and she wouldn't remember it for almost twenty years. Sometimes she could sense the volatility buried deep within her, but it seemed alien and alarming. Mattie *was* certain, however—even hours after her attempt—that she needed to leave.

> I felt so dependent on him that the thought of me alone was like being in a vacuum—like I just didn't exist. I really needed somebody else around to say I was okay, but even just after the attempt I knew I had to get out of that relationship. I think that was probably the starting point in coming back to life.

Mattie began to separate from the suicidal context by letting go of a hurtful relationship and learning to assert and defend herself. Easily cowed and prone to feelings of great shame, Mattie would always devalue her importance in relationships. She didn't yet know that an experience was waiting that would change her life.

I got into therapy for the first time. You know, it wasn't a great therapist, and it wasn't the best experience, but it was the beginning, and I learned to get angry. I mean, I'd like to say that I had one of those wonderful experiences where I said, "Oh, I'm so glad to still be alive and on the planet, and I'm gonna change my life and get healthy." I think that's what started to happen, but I certainly wasn't conscious of it.

Therapy helped me to get really angry for the first time in my life. I got really angry, yelling, screaming, throwing things at Curt, and then I ended the relationship. It was almost an ecstatic experience! I was a little out of control, like I was over the edge, but I had been so controlled in my life. There was so much energy in my body. I felt very powerful. It was much healthier than feeling like I was a complete schmuck.

These first steps were thrilling. Never before had she stood her ground so ferociously. She had made a final statement to Curt, but perhaps more importantly, had spoken to herself. She would never again submit to a harmful relationship because she was afraid to be alone.

How does one know that such a decision will lead in a positive direction, toward life, and not just back into the suicidal trance? What guidelines are helpful to prevent a repetition of the painful past? What ensures that these new decisions will be growthful and life-enhancing and not repetitions of past confusion?

Decisions to distance oneself from the suicidal context are usually the antithesis of the suicidal trance in focus and intent. Where there was isolation, one now seeks the company of understanding people. Where there was certainty that life held little promise and meaning, the person now feels it has some potential. People who have lived (and almost died) in major metropolitan environments often choose to move to the country. Rennie needed to leave New York City and its drug world. Upon leaving the house she shared with her husband, Chris initiated a series of moves that would eventually find her on collectively shared land in the mountains. People make decisions of countless varieties, but all share similar desires: to lower their internal psychological stress and experience emotional stability and peace of mind; to leave relationships that are either overtly hurtful, prohibitive of their growth, or inattentive to their needs and aspirations, and discover healthy relationships; and to increase their sense of personal discovery and possibility.

Karen's story illustrates the endeavor to break the suicidal context.

Karen

It was a county hospital. They had a seven-day mandatory policy for people who attempted suicide. When I got out, the moment I got back to the house where I had attempted I just knew I had to get out of there. I walked into that level of reality, and I knew without a doubt that if I stayed there I would have to kill myself.

It was important to meet Karen on her own turf: twenty miles out of town on a single-lane macadam road running by a creek—pine, spruce, cedar, and the ever-present alder all crowding the road's edge as if pushing forward to catch a glimpse of the cars flying by. Karen is intimately connected with the land outside of Tillamook, Oregon, and to visit her there is to experience an essential element in her recovery: her life surrounded by nature. I pulled into a dirt drive, past a rusted iron gate, half-open. As I opened the door of the rental car, two huge, lazy collie-shepherds lifted their heads and then fell back asleep.

Karen is thin and wiry. As she turns off the lawn mower and comes my way in greeting, her face reflects many layers of experience. Despite the welcome, there is caution. Her eyes seem to search for a moment to assess the situation. There is a question in her gaze, and just behind that, as if she has found the answer, relief and a simple shyness.

Karen's story is unusual. After having returned from a six-month trip throughout Africa, she arrived back in America shaken and disoriented. She had never been exposed to other cultures, and although she was dazzled by their beauty, their devastating poverty horrified her. She had embarked on her journey as a young adult, a gifted math and dance major, a cheerleader from a prestigious university, and had returned unsure of herself, perplexed as to how to fit back into her former life.

On the advice of family and friends, she sought the help of a local psychiatrist. Tragically, the psychiatrist, along with an associate, began to overmedicate the new patient and sexually violate her. Memories of these events, once repressed, have only recently surfaced, through psychotherapy, and they include scenes of being restrained, molested, and tortured.

Karen's story strains our credulity, and yet it has been proven to be accurate. Presently, both psychiatrists have lost their licenses and have been required to pay damages. Karen's story is included in this book not because of the details of professional betrayal, however, but because her path to recovery, specifically her decision to leave the suicidal context, is instructive.

> I began to shrink and disappear. I didn't know what was happening to me. I was on heavy, heavy drugs. I couldn't think. I couldn't do math. I had gotten much heavier and I couldn't dance—I could hardly move. I became progressively dead inside—like suspended animation, just this side of death. I wasn't feeling connected to my body; my connection to aliveness just felt severed. All that gave me purpose and reason to be here was gone.

Karen didn't lose a parent to a premature death. She hadn't been molested by a relative or neighbor early in life. She was, however, subjected to violation and exploitation. The development of her sense of identity, so natural during early adulthood, was wrenched from its normal course and thrown into chaos. The chronic medicated stupor in which she was trapped began to erode her capacity to remember. Karen progressively lost all sense of who she was. The talents through which she had fashioned her identity became unavailable to her. The loss of her ability to dance and choreograph, and to perform complex mathematical tasks, was tantamount to an athlete's losing a limb, a painter losing his sight, or a musician suffering from incipient deafness.

One day, after suffering derisive comments from fellow workers because she seemed unable to accomplish the simplest of tasks, Karen left work early, only to be stuck in traffic on a Los Angeles freeway. It was there she realized that her life seemed meaningless and she felt chronically numb, and concluded that she'd be better off dead.

> *It wasn't like screaming or crying or anything. It almost felt like just going in and getting an apple. I just went in the bathroom and there were these bottles of pills—lots of them. I decided to take them all, just to be sure. I swallowed them all, and then went to lie down on the couch. Everything just felt very quiet. No chaos, like there had been—just very, very quiet.*

The act of attempting suicide had a paradoxical effect on Karen. As she lay on the couch, she noticed she was losing sensation and becoming foggy. But during those moments, as she began to feel the relief of dying, she discovered that she was also becoming excited. She could see the end of her suffering, and that meant freedom. At this point the bubble unexpectedly burst. Her excitement at her suicide suddenly changed into a desire to get out of her difficulty, alive.

> *I was lying there, and another part of me decided, "I don't want to die. I want to get the hell out of here!" Then I realized what a jam I*

was in. I thought I'd never be able to get out of this situation short
of dying. I never felt the choice to live until just then.

In those moments, Karen realized that it was the suffering that
she wanted to end, not her entire life. She called for help and was
taken to a county hospital for both treatment and the mandatory
one-week stay. That week was a difficult one. Although she had
deeply repressed the memory of her abuse, she still feared emergency medical and psychiatric intervention. She felt suspicious of
any attempts to help her, and dubious that the clinicians there were
even skilled enough. Karen became totally focused on surviving the
week and then leaving Los Angeles.

I had a sense of purpose. No one was ever going to catch me again;
nobody from the medical community, nobody with power over me,
would ever force me to do anything again. There was this feeling
that nobody was going to do this for me. You know, if I give it to
someone else, they're going to create chaos, devastation, and
trauma, and that wasn't nearly what I needed. If that meant I
would have to live away from society, then I would.

Karen left southern California and moved to the Oregon border.
For a time she lived at the edge of a small town and took classes at a
local college, but fairly soon she moved farther into the woods.
Coupled with the desire to be alone and to heal, there was an as yet
unnameable impulse inside her to flee. She would read an article in
the newspaper, or have a benign encounter with the college physician, and an overwhelming urge to move would come upon her. To
her friends, she appeared spontaneous and free, but like a fugitive,
she was driven to escape, without understanding why or from
whom.

Karen had flashbacks, but they were kinesthetic ones: they included no pictures. Her emotional reactions were subtle, like waking in the morning and feeling afraid to open her eyes, or not

wanting to wake at all. One day, her lover, the father of her newborn son, simply touched the front of her neck and she jumped across the room. She exclaimed, "God. You think I'd been raped or something!" She wouldn't know the truth about herself for seventeen more years.

A few months later, Karen left her lover and moved deep into the backwoods with her son. She only knew that she wanted to be alone, without phones, without electricity, without people. Occasionally she had a glimmer of insight, but it was fleeting. Psychotherapy wasn't an option. Although the memories of her abuse were still repressed, something inside cautioned her away from that kind of help. Instead she looked for a cabin as remote as she could find.

> I wanted to go way back there, for a long period of time, where I could just relax and feel safe, and I didn't really feel safe around humans. I mean, I had to [deal with them] sometimes, but it would engage the more streetwise part of me. I felt like I needed to take off all these shirts, these personalities, so that I could just find out what was really there aside from social expectations, fear, or pressure of any kind.

Karen could offer theories as to why it was critical for her to live in the woods, but they did not do justice to the power of the certainty she felt. She didn't know all the reasons for her choice, but she knew there was a place "out there" that was so far removed—so peaceful and undisturbed—that it would allow her to discover what being alive was supposed to feel like.

> I was very afraid at first. But it was breathtaking—the redwoods and the ferns, the meadow sloping from the back door. It was very quiet, and that's what I wanted. I wanted it so quiet that I could hear inside.
>
> It quieted my whole spirit down. My senses became so finely honed to where I could sense if there was a cheetah or mountain

*lion or a bear nearby. It was magnificent. I would think, "Oh, this
is what being on this planet is about."*

*I felt like I became an animal of the woods. Every now and then,
out of nowhere, I was leaping across the meadow. I would feel like
a gazelle and I'd wonder, "My God! Where'd that come from?"
There was a bounding spirit that I hadn't felt in so long, and it
would feel so wonderful. Every now and then it would peek
through, just enough to keep me going.*

Winters were damp and cold and without electricity; provisions
had to be stocked and firewood made ready; and extra work was
required because she was raising a young child. She applied her
creativity not only to constructing enormous wall hangings and
quilted sculptures, but to building a workspace for her son, as he
grew.

*There were stairs going up to it and he had his own small door and
a doorbell. We would work for hours, both of us, on artwork and
projects. We shared a lot of deeply creative, quiet time. He also felt
total courage on the land. He learned to sense what animals were
nearby, and would walk in the woods without being afraid, even at
night. The downside, like most only children, he could have used
more time with other kids. I felt guilty about that for a long time.
Sometimes, children would come over and Kevin would just throw
himself into the play.*

Karen had doubts, but this life-style offered the only medium
through which she could imagine becoming whole again. She
needed to recover life at its most elemental level, and go to its
deepest source. Time would have to be the judge of her success.

Many of the stories we've heard involve acts of dissolving the
suicidal trance that are powerfully dramatic. Other acts, however,

are more subtle. Some persons passed entire decades in the trance, besieged almost every waking minute, and even in sleep, by suicidal voices and images. When finally dissolving the trance, people feel a need to empty themselves of these toxins.

Some have entered monastic settings, protected from the world and isolated from social intercourse. Others simply get in their cars and drive. Perhaps they are searching for a new home, but hours tick away behind a wheel, or at a vista point on the highway, and they feel their past flowing out of them. This clearing-out process is not one of focusing one's mind purposefully, but letting it relax. Rather than analyzing one's thoughts and images, one seems just to notice them and let them go. It is a passive process—a time for rest.

When Rennie arrived in California, she found a morning job in a photo lab and a small studio apartment, empty and freshly painted. Her afternoons were unscheduled, and within a few days, she noticed that all she wanted to do was sit in her room and stare at the blank white walls. Something both subtle and powerful held her in that room, day after day.

> I didn't have any big plans. It wasn't a conscious decision. That's just all I could deal with. I had been overstimulated for so long. I lived pretty simply—I had only one friend whom I played backgammon with once in a while. It felt like my mind was stunned, in shock. So I would go into my room and look at the wall and my mind would empty.

In Japan, there exists a form of psychotherapy which utilizes complete relaxation and stillness as its primary form. In Morita therapy, the therapist might prescribe a week in bed, sheltered from outside stimulation, until the body and mind become quiet enough to resume daily activities. Rennie created her own Morita therapy. She hadn't studied meditation, and only months before had read her first book about addiction. Her recovery was still embryonic, and yet she was beginning to learn from experience. When something felt right or healthy, she'd try it again, and she would travel that road until it came to a dead end. The freshly painted room offered her quiet. It was the hue of emptiness and this was exactly what she needed.

> I didn't hang any paintings. It was just so comforting not to have any visual noise. Pretty soon, all the stuff of the past would come at me on the wall. There was this flurry of images and scenes of my past. It's a little hard to describe.
>
> It was a real cacophony sometimes, and I'd get pretty over-whelmed. But I'd just sit there. That's all I could do anyway. Pictures would come rushing onto the wall, and then they would fade to white. I had this sense, through it all, that I just needed to digest what had happened. I sat there every day for six months.

Karen also pursued the absence of stimulation. She moved further into the wilderness; and her longing for safety, anonymity, and rest competed with the fear of being so isolated. Nevertheless she stayed, and allowed the fear—just like everything else—to be a part of the landscape. As she wrote in her journal:

> And so life's journeys brought me here
>   surrounded by ferns and trees . . .
> The doubts, the questions, the horrors;
>   The nightmares and silent fears.

In the safety and solitude of the woods, Karen learned to observe her thoughts and feelings without acting upon them. She could now allow the feelings to emerge into consciousness and then clear. She learned patience and trust. Eventually she found that her fear was dissolving. Perhaps more importantly, it led not only to a deeper, quieter place inside, but to the first clues of the abuse she had suffered.

It took a while to run out all the tapes and the fears, but finally it happened. I felt totally safe there. And that's when the "trace" started to happen. I picked up that there was something else going on. Something pretty deep inside. One morning I woke up and my whole head and neck was swollen and my eyes were swollen. It took years after that to know what actually happened, but that was the beginning.

GRIEVING

It felt like I was grieving for everything at that point. I don't think I ever cried like that before, where I just cried and cried and cried. After a while I didn't even know why I was crying. (Ian)

To reorient oneself toward living takes longer for some than for others. Some people report powerful experiences early on the road back, while others describe a gradual healing. Many recoveries follow the progression of stages described here, but sometimes these experiences assume a different order. Whatever the individual differences, there is one stage of the healing process through which all must pass: grieving.

Although grieving occurs throughout the recovery process, it often first appears just after a suicide attempt. After his truck stalled, Ian lay on the seat, sadness pouring through him. A door that had been open for an entire lifetime had closed. He had tried suicide. He had used three-quarters of a tank of gas in the process, but events had conspired to prevent his dying. Now there was nowhere to go, and nothing to do but allow the torrent of grief to surface.

I didn't even try to control it. It seemed like sadness for a whole life of pain: Kevin being HIV positive . . . me not being positive . . . my grandmother . . . my father . . . my mother . . . my being gay.

Everything just welled up and came out. I lay there for about two hours. It was as if there was a part of me saying, "This is supposed to happen. Let it all out." I felt a kind of knowing about it, like, "Go ahead, you're supposed to let go of this."

The pain he felt that afternoon in the cabin of the truck had accompanied him for years: if it wasn't the melody, it was the backbeat. It dimmed his sense of possibilities and muted his happiness. And yet, consistently, he had refused to allow the pain into his awareness.

Grieving, however, demands just the opposite. Instead of turning away from the pain, one must face it. This is the acid test. For it is not the suicide attempt itself that galvanizes the spirit to return to life, but a willingness—perhaps for the first time—to allow the pain to surface without turning toward suicide, and to feel the grief, despite the fear of being overwhelmed by it.

Grieving allows long-held sorrow to emerge. The wound has already occurred, and that cannot be changed, but grieving provides an avenue for the original pain, as well as the pain of the physical, emotional, and interpersonal consequences of the suicide attempt, to surface and be healed.

Grieving is an integral and unavoidable component of recovery from any trauma. It is not an end in itself, nor is it a permanent state. The most common fear about the pain underneath is that it will never end and it will consume and overwhelm us. This was very much how Karen felt, in the years just after leaving the woods.

I had moved to Nebraska, where my partner was teaching at the university. I was starved for intellectual stimulation, so I joined a book group formed by university women. I remember we read Kinds of Love, *by May Sarton. I started to feel sad; then it quickly became this profound grief. Really deep. It was like staring into a pool and seeing another pool at the bottom; and then staring into that pool but* not *seeing the bottom. It was pretty scary.*

Everyone was crying, going around the room and talking about someone they loved who died. But I felt like I was grieving my own death! Like I was losing a child, except it was me inside. I didn't know how to make sense of it at the time. I felt it would be selfish to tell the group I was grieving for myself, so when it was my turn, I made believe that I was grieving about someone else. I even made up a name. But even though [the sadness] felt scary, I also felt drawn to it. After letting it out, I felt acceptance and relief. I also felt "innocent"—childlike again—afterwards.

The fear that we will succumb to the uncontrollable momentum of our sorrow—that the pain will unbalance our lives forever—is universal. The reality, however, is quite different. Grieving actually represents the successful beginning of resolving one's past. It reflects the choice not only to remain alive but also to dissolve the isolation arising from the pain. Grieving allowed Karen to recapture some of the innocence she had lost during her abuse. Even though the crucial memories would still be obscured for years to come, she was slowly able to reconnect with the younger Karen, the one who existed before the trauma.

True grieving occurs at the time when the trance breaks, either during or following the attempt. Grieving signals an initial, faint awareness that possibilities other than suicide exist. It may be frightening at first. Old pain rushes into the emptiness like water spilling over a dam.

For most, these first steps do not feel voluntary. The grief seems to emerge on its own. Allowing the pain to flow without resistance stands in contrast to the act of suicide, which is an attempt to stop this pain. The grieving does not mean that the person is becoming further enmired; it is, rather, an indication that progress is being made. Three subtle processes are occurring at the same time here. First, the pain emerges and is acknowledged—both the pain of original wounds and the pain of the suicidal trance. As powerful and deep-seated emotions surface, and one willingly embraces the grief and despair, self-confidence is strengthened. Second, grieving allows the development of compassion for oneself. In place of cruel self-judgments, grieving enables one to develop tenderness and forgiveness. Slowly, in the quiet of surrendering, people begin to catch the first glimpses of who they are beneath the pain. As one woman said: "It came after fully experiencing the grief, the despair, and the rage, and feeling what seemed like the very first moments of peace."

Finally, grieving represents the "revaluing" of oneself. When people allow their pain to surface, they make a statement that they are important and worthy of attention.

Ian's sadness erupted moments after his attempt, and by allowing it to continue, he created a bona fide turning point in his life. Karen's grief emerged roughly five years after the abuse. The timing is different for each person. Sometimes weeks, months, or even years elapse before people allow themselves such an experience, and yet regardless of *when* the grief emerges, the healing effect is undeniable.

Madeline

While driving, Madeline would still have fantasies of veering off the road or into an abutment. "For a long time after the attempt—for years—I deeply regretted not killing myself." A mother of four grown children, Madeline is an intelligent and devoted political organizer. She won national recognition for her life's work in the fields of community economics and nonviolent action, and yet, deep inside, she still wanted to die. Madeline is now in her mid-seventies. Thirteen years ago, her husband left, never to return. No matter how hard she worked, no matter how many causes she applied herself to, the shock of her sudden divorce lingered and the pain felt undiminished.

For three years after the attempt, she continued to feel actively suicidal. She dutifully made the rounds of therapists in her area, and was given numerous antidepressants, but nothing took away her deep sense of loss. At one point, Madeline even requested electroshock, believing it would erase her short-term memory enough for her to forget her suffering. She tried traditional psychiatric approaches as well as those more avant garde, sampling everything from psychoanalysis, with which she felt frustrated, to past-life therapy, which surprisingly spoke to her experience of the pain.

Everything helped a little, and eventually she ceased constantly rehearsing her suicide in daydreams and fantasies; but she still held herself back from close relationships and there were times when she still thought of suicide. Mired in the pain of losing her forty-year marriage, she felt unable to let the relationship die. Madeline found herself fervently holding on to the past and stalled in the present. She was painfully stuck. Nothing replaced suicide as her back-door option until a crucial therapy session in which she decided to let the marriage die, instead of herself.

I was asking my therapist, "When is this going to be over, because I'm still in terrible pain about it." It was my familiar complaint. He studied me, and then said, "I want to try something with you. I'd like you to lie down and close your eyes, and I want you to tell me the story of when your husband left, as completely as you can remember—every detail, every word, every minute." So I did that, and as I did, I began sobbing. Then I began sobbing at absolutely every step along the way. Every detail, I'd cry harder and deeper than I thought I could. It felt like my tears were everywhere.

The grief went on for a long time. Finally I sat up and he handed me a box of Kleenex and said, "Now let's talk about this." I was drained, and he had my complete attention. He said, "That was like a death, wasn't it?" I nodded. "Your marriage died at that point and ever since, you've been grieving." I was stunned for a moment, and then something clicked. I had never thought of it that way. I went away from that session accepting that my mar-

riage was dead and the person that I had been was dead, and that
now I was a new person, in a new life.

Madeline had to learn that her sadness could be a healthy and
finite response to loss, but that her awareness of this was impossible
as long as she continued to channel her grief into images of suicide.
Grieving needs direct expression, and as her therapist guided her
through it, she was able to reconnect more deeply to herself and
realize that grieving gives birth to choice. Madeline could mourn
the death of her marriage and create a new life.

Initial outpourings of grief are powerful, but grieving is not
something that happens only once. Grieving serves to humanize
one's pain (as opposed to the dehumanization and dissociation
which marks the suicidal trance); allowing oneself to grieve becomes a resource that people consistently turn to as they heal. Grief
may appear often during the return to life, and is sometimes accompanied by other emotions. In Ed's case, it was anger.

> *I still experience the grief. I still feel grief and anger that I gave in*
> *[to the pressure to attempt suicide]. It's not that my life stinks, but*
> *the situation—not being able to walk—does. When I feel it—and*
> *I'm pretty conscious of the stages I go through now—I'll stay in,*
> *take the phone off the hook, punch the wall, yell and swear at God,*
> *and just get it out. I don't take it out on anyone. Afterward, I feel*
> *better. I know I'm also fortunate, and I'm thankful for many*
> *aspects of my life. I mean, I'm glad I'm me, but there's always*
> *regret I had to learn it this way.*

LEARNING TO TRUST

> *I used to feel like I was tossed on the sea, being swished*
> *here and there. Eventually, I felt like the direction of my*
> *life began to come more from inside me. I got clearer. I*
> *felt like there was finally a way to do this. I can work with*

> *myself. I can change who I am. I can work with my*
> *dreams and learn about parts of myself. All this was a*
> *very new concept. (Mattie)*

Those who attempt suicide lose a dual sense of trust: they no longer trust themselves, and they find it difficult to trust anyone else. In the suicidal trance, people feel progressively dubious about their own sanity and also grow less likely to believe in the benevolence of the world at large. One woman, a therapist and mother of two adult daughters, said this:

> *In the trance, I lost the very thought processes necessary to create*
> *change. It was astounding to me that only after my trance broke*
> *did I realize that I needed to leave my husband, not kill myself and*
> *my children.*

Early in recovery, however, changes occur. Suspending doubt, breaking the suicidal context, and allowing one's grief to surface— all foster a new working relationship with one's emotional life and create the beginnings of confidence in one's own intuition and judgment. Here, trust and grieving seem inextricably linked. The act of grieving breaks the isolation and numbness of the trance. When long-standing sorrow surfaces, people realize that the pain they carry can be both recognized and assuaged. After this recognition, pain is seen, not as an indication of one's sickness, but as an understandable response to extreme circumstance. This is a powerful internal shift. People begin to view themselves differently. They begin to discard the nihilistic filter through which they have viewed the world, substituting faith, a bit of humor, and a sense of possibility in its stead. This allows for perhaps the most important and transformative stage of healing—learning to trust.

For Rennie it was the faint possibility that there was meaning in her painful journey that enabled her to end her heroin addiction.

Between these awful seizures, I would read. I was discovering that
things come our way when we most need them, and somebody had
given me this book. It was written by a heroin addict. It was called
Diary of a Drug Fiend! *I felt like these people in the book were*
where I was at and I almost felt like there was this connection
between us. In the book, people end up quitting heroin, and at the
end, basically what the book says is that the problem isn't heroin at
all. The problem is that you don't know what your "true will"—
your true purpose in life—is. It says, if you find that, you don't
need heroin.

Trusting oneself again takes time. For some, like Rennie, it is born
out of the intense desire to know "Why didn't I die?" Often, a person
discovers that a healthier self has been waiting to be born—that
these pains were labor pains, and not just errant suffering emanating from a sick mind. In this discovery lay the seeds, building blocks
of a healthier and less painful future.

I felt, "Whoa! This is really true." I mean, I didn't have a sense of
purpose yet, but I just intuitively grasped that all this had been
about trying to find it. I knew then that suicide and the drug stuff
wasn't going to be important for me anymore.

It is with these insights that people report having their first
feelings of success. They begin to invest a small amount of trust in
themselves. Whereas they had once felt their thoughts and feelings
to be their greatest liability, slowly—as if learning to walk again—
they develop balance, build confidence in their own inner counsel,
and experiment with both new avenues of expression and the
making of new decisions.

Learning to trust oneself enables the repair of another form of
trust as well. People are more willing to trust those who have been
attentive to them during this first delicate stage. They are ready to

believe that others may care, may understand their struggle, and may truly be able to help.

In allowing herself to become angry and to express feelings she had always kept inside, Mattie reached a critical point on her journey back to life. She was exhilarated with her newfound strength and was determined to discover more of it. A few months later, she had an experience that astounded her.

I changed to group therapy. I felt I really needed a safe place to feel the enormous feelings I felt inside. I needed a therapist who was not afraid of all that. In the first months of this group, everyone was exploding all over the place, but I held back. I would think to myself, "I'm just not an angry person." You know—total denial!

One day I said, "Okay, I'll try it." I truly thought, "I'll just kind of pretend." I started making sounds of being angry. That's what everyone else seemed to do. I was faking it, and then all of a sudden something snapped. Some wire must have hooked, because I started screaming. I wanted to rip the fucking room apart! It wasn't enough just to pound the pillows. I wanted to shred them. I wanted to break someone's fingers. That was the feeling. I just wanted to take someone's hand and bend it backwards and crunch all the bones. I didn't know it at the time, but it was my grandfather's hands. I wanted to make sure they didn't touch anybody ever again.

Psychotherapists debate the value of recognizing and expressing anger. Some consider emotional expression to be the very goal of therapy, while others accord it only secondary importance, regarding it as less significant than insight and understanding. For many who have recovered from suicidal pain, the awareness and expression of anger help to shatter the trance, once and for all. There are many, like Mattie, who feel that their anger helped them redirect their death wish outward. Rather than continually assaulting them-

selves with life-negating thoughts, they have begun to build an
awareness of the true objects of their anger.

> *I was completely shocked that that came out of me. I mean, I had*
> *just gone from mild-mannered Clark Kent to a murderess! It was*
> *also exciting. I really needed to know that I had that anger to*
> *protect me; that I had somebody in me who could kill if she needed*
> *to instead of killing myself. It just seemed like a much healthier*
> *way of being in the world. I mean, I'm still struggling with that—*
> *connecting with that part of me—but it definitely desensitized me*
> *toward being angry and having people be angry at me. I don't like*
> *it, but I don't fall apart.*

Trust forms in innumerable ways. Some people experience new
thoughts and feelings exploding into their consciousness like a
locomotive coming out of a dark tunnel. Some people find themselves listening to a small, soft voice within them. Others may sense
the presence of a deity, an angel, or God.

When Karl fled Kansas, inner wisdom seemed in short supply,
and God was the last thing on his mind.

> *I was in this room with this guy from the mob. I knew I was dead*
> *meat. I'd crossed them too many times. But this guy said, "I don't*
> *know why I'm doing this, but if you walk out, and don't turn*
> *around—keep on going and keep your mouth shut—I'll let*
> *you go."*

Karl considers this the third miracle in his life. Twice he had tried
to kill himself, with the most deadly means at his disposal, and
twice he survived. Now, the Mafia was letting him go. Furthermore,
the FBI told him that if he surrendered everything he owned, left
town, and sought rehabilitation, they'd back off as well. Karl had
lived the drug world, and he had friends who had been imprisoned
or killed. He knew an opportunity when he saw one, and he took it.

A day later, he arrived in Reno. A friend had told him of an experimental detox program, but Karl was hesitant and chose to lie low and try to kick the drugs himself. He was tired, confused, and still too frightened to feel relieved. Two weeks later, having unsuccessfully wrestled with his addictions on his own, Karl still felt paranoid and alone. Partly from desperation and partly from loneliness, he attended a church service. He couldn't remember the last time he had been in church, and he was dubious.

I walked in and I "read" the room—I had learned to do that, being in the business I was in—and I sat in the back. I always had to have my back to the wall. I noticed I felt safe there. It was the first time in a long while.

The preacher was the director of the detox program about which he'd heard, but he only half-listened to the sermon. Karl could never have anticipated what would happen next.

I wasn't really listening, until suddenly I heard the words, "Come out of the darkness; come out of your darkness and into the light." Simple stuff, but all of a sudden my whole life unveiled before me. All of the pain—the pain of alchohol, the pain of drugs, the anger, all the hurts as a child—all that I disliked in my life just flooded before me.

I stood up and walked to the front of the pews. Tears were streaming down my face—I was sobbing—and I got down on my knees. Something just broke inside me. I asked Jesus to take all the burdens, all the worries and troubles, and it really felt like I gave it all to him. I must have been there a few minutes—it's hard to tell—but when I got up I felt like I could breathe again. It felt like my world had completely changed. For the first time, I felt I had a future. Before that, I was just going through the motions.

It was a start, and although he didn't yet understand what had happened, Karl knew something had changed. For the first time in fifteen years, he felt love. Whatever happened that night, he knew he could trust what he had experienced. It was elusive but it was real, and it was powerful enough for Karl to enter detox.

> I started the program on Monday, and by Wednesday I felt no need for the drugs or the alcohol. Each Wednesday the group had a meeting called "Caring and Sharing," and people would get up and talk about themselves—where they'd come from, what they were into, how they felt. I couldn't believe it, but I walked up there and I told my story. Everything. I didn't leave anything out. I was weeping uncontrollably. After that, the craving for drugs and booze just left me. I didn't even feel withdrawal symptoms.

Three months later, Karl made the decision to "give his life to Jesus." Through long periods of contemplation and prayer, and under the auspices of a local church, he decided to pursue the ministry. He wasn't ready yet—he knew that—and it would take years of healing and maturation before he would function in that capacity, but he was ready to begin. He felt trust in himself and faith in his future for the first time in over a decade.

> I could feel love. I could feel God in my heart. It was the first time in a long time I could feel anything at all!

Perhaps the simplest gifts are the most powerful: moments of feeling where feeling had been absent; moments of peace where only violence had been known. For Karl, these moments were born from years of pain, meanness, struggle, and exploitation. They were born from a terrain so barren it was simply impossible for anything other than the strongest roots to take hold.

Karl committed two acts of trust. First, he trusted that God, in the infinite wisdom he hoped God would have, would help heal his pain and create order in his life. Second, in entering detox, he believed that his life, base as it had been, still had value and potential. These were first steps. He wasn't always certain, but he had charted his course and he would stay with it as long as he could.

LETTING GO OF DYING

Grieving and letting go of the single-minded fixation on suicide is like a spring rain. It marks the end of winter—the barrenness of suicide—and prepares the soil for planting. And yet, in the lives of those who recover, a struggle continues, despite vernal optimism and the stirrings of rebirth. As people begin the journey back to life, they may still struggle with the desire to die. Painful and destructive as the suicidal trance may have been, it was an ever-present companion. During times of stress, therefore—even during recovery—familiar suicidal thoughts and feelings still arise. As the context changes and people begin to experience happier and fuller lives, they react in one of two ways. Some decide irrevocably to never attempt suicide again; to them, this is a certainty, born from painful experience. For others, suicide loses its primary place as a response to pain more gradually, receding into the distance as more creative, healthy options arise. These people feel almost certain that they will never again attempt suicide and they are hard-pressed to describe a situation that would prompt it, but they will honestly admit that it still remains a possibility, even though an unlikely one.

Karen's children are a source of delight to her, as is her artwork. She feels her life to be rich and fulfilling. No longer a prisoner of the suicidal trance that stripped her of a sense of aliveness, Karen nevertheless sees the option of suicide as a token of freedom.

I wouldn't recommend suicide. There are so many other ways to wake up. I think it's good just to know you can leave if you want to—a back door, if the pain in life gets just so incredible. I risk more and I can tolerate more because I know I'm not trapped. I

know that I have an option to get out of that, but suicide is by no
means the only choice. I mean, I can go to India, Tibet, to the
North Pole, another state of consciousness, the woods, you know?

Recovery requires that people expand the range of their choices,
but it also requires the careful, patient rebuilding of their desire to
live. Psychologists monitor the early period of recovery carefully, for
it is delicate and may prove dangerous. As people begin to feel new
energy and strength, they may become disheartened by an early
setback and respond with another attempt. There has been too
much pain and too much heartache for people to choose life simply
for the sake of being alive. People must have a vision—an image—of
the future, and it must differ significantly from the past. They must
have a growing sense of possibility. Without it, their existence seems
perpetually suspended between living and dying.

After the episode, Cassie continued to feel confused. She had
successfully emerged from a painful divorce and custody battle, but
she often felt tired and depressed. She had received no counseling or
crisis intervention in the hospital following her suicide attempt. A
staff psychiatrist visited her just prior to her discharge, but he
seemed disinterested when talking with her. He dismissed her
attempt as a "midlife crisis" and walked out of the room. She still
needed help sorting through the confusing array of identities which
previous to her recovery had felt so separate.

It's really strange, and I'm sure it's not unique to me, but I've had a
lot of success in life as far as work [is concerned]. I've never had
trouble finding work. I often got the most coveted jobs in the school
systems where I've taught, even after the suicide attempt. So it felt
like a real dichotomy. How could you be successful and feel so
awful? I felt like a very successful failure.

Six months after her attempt, Cassie changed jobs, hoping for a
less stressful one. Her new boss, however, recognizing Cassie's

abilities, asked her for even more work than before. One morning, after a rigorous series of conferences and travels, she found herself back in a suicidal depression.

> *I had a fight with my boss. He was working me too hard, and making me go on that trip to Houston was the final straw. I was really angry, but I didn't yet know what to do with anger, so I directed it internally.*

Cassie could barely remember feeling so horrible. She felt too exhausted to make another suicide attempt, but she was still caught between the desire to live and the urge to die.

> *Monday morning I could not get out of bed. I was curled in a fetal position. I couldn't talk and I was incredibly depressed. I felt like a truly awful person. I felt like a failure. I had lots of suicidal feelings. I was so low, so depressed, and I just didn't even have enough will or energy to attempt. I couldn't do anything about it. It would have been redundant anyway. I was already dead. If I had been a little stronger, I know I'd have tried again.*

Cassie's fortunes began to change, however. She found a psychiatrist in Shreveport, the nearest city, and in one session she finally heard the words that dissolved her confusion and offered a way beyond the impasse.

> *He said, "This is why you are so unhappy. You are living somebody else's script—someone else's movie. Your mother wrote it, not you." It felt like this tremendous weight lifted off my shoulders. I thought, "You're right! I feel like a failure because I've been trying to live someone else's life!"*
>
> *You know, my mother was a teacher, and both her parents were teachers. Mother thought that was a respectable profession in the*

eyes of the community; that's what a woman should do, and that's
what I was supposed to do. When I was growing up, I'd tell her I
wanted to be a nurse or a doctor, and she would simply say, "No,
you don't," and so, of course, I didn't!

For the first time, there was hope, and Cassie pursued her recovery with a zeal she had never before felt. She was referred to a psychologist who helped her to identify the anger that she had always directed inward and to create more healthy avenues of expression. Cassie also desperately needed to rest, and she took a leave of absence to recuperate.

Throughout the early stages of her recovery, Cassie found that suicidal thoughts continued to exert their influence. Even while she was feeling a new sense of promise, she kept one refill of antidepressants ready just in case she wanted to give up during her sometimes arduous journey.

It was still a real struggle. I held on to that bottle as a way out. If
the pain or desperation got too bad, I would throw in the towel.
There was still this hopelessness; it was just less intense. It was in
the form of a question about whether I was worth *keeping alive—*
whether I had any value whatsoever. It was strange. Even though I
couldn't tell you why *I was so bad, I couldn't think of what was*
good.

Two years later, in the midst of very difficult circumstances, Cassie discovered to her surprise that her suicidal fever had broken. She had moved to Florida, and it seemed life was conspiring to send her a number of hardships all at the same time.

I was lying on the bed. I was exhausted. There was so much
pressure on me. There were severe money problems. The relation-
ship with my new husband was crumbling. The kids were extra-
demanding. Nothing was working out.

At the end of her resolve, Cassie discovered an indefatigable spirit.

> I had the thought, "Well, I could kill myself," and right after that, I thought, "Boy, is that ever unusual!" It seemed like a very strange and alien thought. I realized that something had really changed.

I asked Cassie to describe what caused this elemental change in her outlook. Thinking for a while, she replied, "I learned the rudiments of self-love." It took root as she felt the caring of two gifted therapists, and continued to grow through conversations with new friends, therapy groups, and deep personal investigation. Learning self-love stabilized her often turbulent recovery and opened her to novel ideas and experiences.

> I had this real sense that even though things were really bad, I wanted to be alive. Life's hard sometimes, but I wanted to continue living. I had learned to like myself, and I knew that if I felt that, then things couldn't always be that bad.

Befriending the world hadn't been easy. She had finally overcome feeling unimportant and ancillary. It had taken half her life. Befriending herself had been doubly challenging, but she had taken the first steps. She realized that her journey to health would bring new adventures, and for the first time, she really wanted to be alive to find out what was going to happen next.

Seven

===

Rebuilding the Self

Only as the trance dissolves can people begin to make the important shifts away from suicide and from images of a futile and meaningless future. It is then that the careful and painstaking work of rebuilding the wounded self can begin. And just as the stage of dissolving the trance contains substeps, so does rebuilding the self. This stage includes:

- Wrestling with and healing the difficulties of the past
- Taking responsibility for one's actions
- Investigating the question "Who am I?"
- Exploring oneself through creative work, and
- Cultivating an openness to unexpected and mysterious occurrences

HEALING THE PAST

There was enormous tension between me and Martin when I left. I was just feeling so angry—so hurt—that I

> *hit myself up and down my arms with a hairbrush. In*
> *therapy the next day, I didn't know why, but I felt so*
> *strongly that I wanted my therapist to see those bruises.*
> *(Chris)*

Healing the past represents a major stage of the recovery from suicidal pain. Many who attempt suicide have repressed significant portions of their history: emotions and images too painful to remember. Years may pass before one's personality becomes balanced and one's psyche allows buried memories into consciousness. Even when there has not been any extreme trauma, the destructive power of the suicidal trance can be so pervasive that memories, if not entirely repressed, may be somewhat occluded.

After a suicide attempt and well into recovery, there are often essential pieces of the person's experience that still need to be discovered, understood, and integrated. For most who have recovered well, psychotherapy of some sort has proven invaluable in reclaiming the past and charting a new direction for the future. Regardless of the form the healing takes, however, there comes a time when the past must be faced squarely and wounds must be addressed. Surprisingly for Chris, deep emotional pain, after nearly driving her to suicide, became her guide to healing the past.

> *I've studied about it now—read a lot about it—and I realize it's*
> *true for me. It's like the pain was so bad, that if I physically hurt*
> *myself in some way, it would wake me up, you know? It would*
> *bring me back to some kind of mental control; that the actual*
> *physical pain was better, or easier to deal with than the emotional*
> *pain.*
>
> *I talked a lot about it in therapy and what I discovered was that I*
> *wanted my therapist—someone—to know how deeply I was hurt.*
> *I don't think I had ever really experienced being the little-girl-me*
> *before. All of a sudden, I felt two years old, and I felt that old hurt.*

Chris pursued her healing assiduously. She looked forward to the individual- and group-therapy sessions, and in a short time investigated other options, such as art therapy and meditation. She was hungry to learn the fundamentals of interpersonal intimacy, and sought the company of people more skilled and more comfortable in it than she. Initially, her psychological inquiry focused on the present and recent past: her life now, her suicide attempt, and her marriage. Eventually, as she felt more comfortable in her everyday exchanges, she began to probe her childhood. But here Chris began to encounter difficulties, because essential components of her past still remained out of reach. There were gaps of recall and pieces that didn't fit. She was attempting to complete a puzzle without an idea of how many pieces there were. The strength of her emotions would surprise her, and sometimes her reactions would seem out of proportion. Child abuse had not yet become such a subject of interest as it is now, and both clients and professionals were often ignorant of its indicators. Chris lived with the odd sensation that her life was truly a mystery to her. She simply didn't know what she didn't know.

Nevertheless, Chris continued. She finished her BA and earned certification in art therapy. These activities, accompanied by years of psychotherapy, began to dislodge fragments of her memory, and she became an archaeologist of her own psyche, patiently uncovering forgotten events, connecting them with others, and revising her understanding of the past. She learned to balance the excitement of discovery against her fear of what lay below her awareness and her frustration of not knowing what it was. Reaching previously inaccessible regions of memory made her more sensitive to inner messages, and sometimes buried images would erupt unannounced into her consciousness, seemingly propelled by some outside force. This is what happened that evening when, superimposed on an old black-and-white TV, she saw the scenes of early childhood. Chris experienced that as the epiphany in her journey back to health.

I told you about the flashback of my father beating me, but I didn't tell you what was on the sitcom that triggered it. It was about this little kid from across the street whose grandmother died. He came in to talk to someone there in the TV living room, and then he broke into tears. The adult was asking him about his grandmother and giving him love and support for the fact that he felt so badly— that's what triggered it. I was that little child, but I never had that kind of response from an adult.

The flashbacks happened just like that a few more times. Each time there was more feeling that went with it, to the point where I would just hear about someone who died or watch anything like that and I'd have a reaction. The kids would go, "Oh, God. There goes Mom again. You can't let her watch these movies!"

The floodgates of memory had opened. There were more scenes of physical abuse with her father and some involving sexual abuse with other relatives. In each, she was able to see herself clearly, and in some mysterious way she could connect with the young child that she had been, offering understanding that had never been provided. Finally, Chris understood. These scenes explained the intense depressions and the seething rage she she'd always felt obliged to rein in when she sensed herself being mistreated.

––––––––––

In the years following her attempt, Mattie created a life that seemed full, rich, and happy. In many respects it was. But she had learned to hide her deepest feelings early in life, and the tendency was difficult to shake. No matter how esteemed she was by friends and colleagues, Mattie continued to carry the debilitating feelings of shame that had fueled her suicide attempt. Unbeknownst to her, this shame had its roots in a childhood of sexual abuse; but because the memories were still buried, the source of her shame remained obscured and instead was generalized to an obsession with body image. Thin and athletically built, Mattie secretly feared growing fat. At the same time, eating helped protect her from stronger emotions.

> *Eating created a trance—a state of being other than being in those horrible feelings. As long as I was eating, I would be sort of tranced out and not feel anything: filling myself up felt good. And then I would reach a point where I would panic. I'd come out of this eating trance and think, "Oh, my God! I've eaten all this food? I can't possibly do this without weighing 300 pounds!"*

To Mattie's delight, pregnancy seemed to cure her eating disorder. It was also the first time in her life she didn't feel shame. Happily, Mattie let herself grow and "take up space"—something she never had before allowed herself. The food binges and their consequent vomiting stopped.

> *I felt like I could live in my body. My daughter was growing right where—I didn't know it at the time—right where the incest happened. There was this wonderful life force growing there instead of come and yuck and horrible stuff.*

These years were joyous and full. Mattie was happily married and her daughter grew to be a bold and adventurous young girl. The bulimia had vanished, but there was still inner work to be done. That work was triggered by two events that finally uncovered the abuse that had driven her to a lifetime of shame and suicidal thoughts.

Therapists have observed that memories of abuse can surface when a person's child reaches the age that he or she was when violated. (The same has been found true of Holocaust survivors and their children.) Sometimes, at this point, memories break into consciousness in full scenes. At other times, a child's experience creates a sense of vulnerability in the parent.

When Mattie's daughter turned five, she was molested in her day-care center. Beneath the protective rage Mattie felt as a mother, she felt a shiver. Mattie quickly mobilized the community, forcefully initiating an investigation that led to the termination of the staff involved, but the events of the moment were too volatile for her to recognize what was happening inside her. She wouldn't realize what happened until some time later.

My daughter has been a teacher for me, indirectly. You know, her being a female child activated stuff for me. It was the final stage of my healing and it has involved all this remembering. What happened with my daughter seemed to open me to the next discovery.

As part of her continued training as a psychotherapist, Mattie would become acquainted with different kinds of therapy, trying them on herself and weaving pieces of them into her clinical work. She experimented with various group psychotherapies, studied the relatively new field of body-centered psychotherapy, and even sought the consultations of skilled massage therapists in the community.

For a number of months, Mattie had worked with a local body-worker named Pat. A registered nurse, a doctor of oriental medicine, and gifted massage therapist, Pat had been practicing for nearly twenty years in the United States and Asia. She had synthesized what she'd learned over the years and developed her own methods for healing problems of the body and the mind. Her work was gentle and unobtrusive, and maybe because of that, powerful memories were sometimes uncovered.

It was like going inside my body while having someone hold my hand. I didn't have to talk much, because she seemed to know what was going on. This one session, she was gently putting her hands on my abdomen and beginning to press a bit, like massage. Suddenly, she says, "It's too painful to go in there; you're not grounded enough. Let's come back up, rest for a moment."

For a while, whenever she would press on my belly below my navel, I would start shaking all over. I would get terrified. I knew I just couldn't write this off. I had to pay attention. Between her and my therapist, the memories became clearer. I saw, for the first time, why I wouldn't go near this body part, because that's where my grandfather used to rub his penis.

This was an enormously important insight for Mattie, and although disturbing, it brought understanding and a sense of finality. The body work and psychotherapy had helped her identify the perpetrator in her own life, and after her daughter's experience, she understood that what she had felt so ashamed about—what she felt were her private defects and flaws—was actually the internalization of an enormous cultural epidemic of child abuse.

The biggest turning point, in some ways, was being able to see that it's out there, not in me. One of my clients once said, "I thought the shit was inside of me. Now I know it's outside."

TAKING RESPONSIBILITY

In the beginning, one's sense of self is fragile, wounded, and immensely vulnerable. As people recover, they are able to surrender antiquated self-images and discover resources hidden beneath their suffering. One way or another, on the road back, they have to take responsibility for attempting suicide. After all, it has been a deeply disturbing event for others as well as themselves. But now, well into their recovery, the context for this admission has changed. People are now able to recognize that their past actions need not detract from their sense of self-worth. They begin to see that the suicide attempt was horrible, but they themselves aren't. It takes the skillful application of compassion to distinguish between accountability and self-castigation. Rather than further self-deprecation, this results in greater honesty and courage.

The assumption of personal responsibility is not a passive process. It doesn't happen because one is being lectured to. People who recover realize that an attitude of victimization and defeat, like old clothing that no longer fits, constrains them rather than comforts them. Old scenarios, rehearsed so many times, begin to seem outdated. At this point on the road back, people learn to create new and healthy opportunities for themselves and move beyond the pain. Taking responsibility signifies inner strength, developed as a consequence of trusting oneself and others.

Sometimes, with luck, the lessons are lightened with humor.

They had the on-call crisis counselor come in and talk to me. The first thing he said was, "Well, what did you do?" I told him I pulled my pickup into the garage and tried to gas myself. It was pretty hard to talk about it. He says, "What happened? Why didn't you do it?" I say, "My pickup died." He pauses a little, looking down, nodding, and then, "What kind of pickup you got?" I was shocked! I started to think this guy was a quack. I mean, here I am, barely able to breathe and he's asking me what kind of car I drive. But I tell him! I tell him I drive a Ford! And then he says, "Yep. That's what you get for buying a Ford."

At first I just glared at him. I thought, "What an asshole," and then we burst out laughing. It was pretty amazing. It was like he was saying, "That's life, and it's still going on and you're still part of it." You know, everybody else was upset and worried and caught up in the crisis, and he wasn't into that. He wasn't into the drama and the confusion. He was just focused. It made me feel real. It reaffirmed me and brought me back to reality, because it made me responsible for what I'd done. Everyone else was still seeing me as a victim, without any power, but he was relating to me as an adult. He was asking me to answer for myself. (Ian)

Taking responsibility is crucial to recovery. Coming at a critical point in one's healing, taking responsibility means acknowledging, to oneself and to others, the damage that has been done. People must face honestly the interpersonal consequences of having almost killed themselves. Ian learned to distinguish the subtle differences between being responsible *to* others for the effect on them of his actions, and being responsible *for* them. One of Ian's lessons in personal accountability involved the near loss of an important relationship.

There's this pharmacist I work with. Night shifts, and we got really close. Her best friend got killed in a car accident and it was the first person she had been close with who had died. We started spending more time together after that. I still remember her face when she saw me after my attempt. There was so much pain. She looked at me and said, "You were in that much pain?" I said, "Yes." And she asked, "Why didn't you talk to me?"

It was really hard. First her friend died, and now she almost lost me. I didn't have an answer, but I knew I had to be there and face her. I felt accountable. In part, I did cause her pain. It was hard being there, but I didn't offer any excuses. No bullshit. I also didn't try to take care of her. I knew I was gonna lose the closeness I had with her. It's been six months, and we are just now beginning to really talk again.

These were Ian's growing pains, and they were sobering. But however difficult his interpersonal relationships became, Ian learned he could face them and emerge stronger. He no longer feared someone else's judgment, and, in fact, he learned that it could become the starting point for an honest dialogue.

Early in her recovery, Ruth had times when the honesty of others was almost too much to bear. She was seeing a therapist who refused to coddle her. He demanded that she recognize the harm she had done to herself and others.

He would say to me, "You're a murderer! You don't try to kill someone else, but you try to kill yourself!" It felt scathing sometimes. I'd protest, but he'd look at me and say, "Smells like bullshit to me." It was hard, but I knew he cared. He helped me realize how sick I was. He took it very seriously, so I had to.

The message was sobering, but being required to admit the severity of her depression seemed to animate Ruth's recovery. Her next therapist, too, was firm, and in addition, required from her a formal commitment to live and apply herself to the therapy. She asked Ruth to be accountable and this activated resources that had lain dormant within her.

My next therapist and I bonded emotionally right away. Then she got breast cancer. She decided that she only wanted to work with people who were really motivated and serious. She was choosing life—to battle her cancer—and she demanded that I choose life and stick with that choice.

She really put her foot down, and I felt that if I wanted to stay with her, I was gonna have to work. I made a commitment to live for three years. No matter what, I won't do anything suicidal. After three years, I'll see. I've begun to take my diabetes medication regularly. I've joined a gym and I work out three times a week. I'm getting nutritional help and I've gone back to Narcotics Anonymous meetings. I feel great. I'm pretty amazed with myself!

When suicide attempts occur within a family context, the process of taking responsibility often becomes heart-rending and complex.

Chris could see that her daughter was struggling. She seemed anxious and was having trouble being intimate with friends. Although it was many years after the suicide attempt, Chris had an intuition that her daughter's memory of it was at the root of her distress. Chris wasn't looking forward to it, but she felt it was time to talk to her daughter and tell the entire story of the event that she had witnessed as a two-and-a-half-year old.

> She still remembered me running out the door and her screaming after me. That was pretty traumatic for her—both the attempt and then when I was gone for a couple of days in the hospital and she didn't understand. I sat her down to talk. I knew she was having trouble being close—with her friends and with me. She was afraid that if she got close, people would cause her pain. I said to her, "I really screwed up. I know I caused you a lot of pain."

These were challenging moments. Chris keenly felt her responsibility as a mother and the importance of finally telling her daughter what really happened, but the task seemed herculean.

> I had to swallow my pride. It was very humbling. I hadn't wanted to talk about it, so I also had to let go of my fear and hesitation. Until that day, none of us really spoke about it. I said, "I want to tell you where all that pain came from."

> She broke into tears and shook. It was hard, but she was really focused on me. She really wanted to hear the whole thing. Afterwards, she was more relaxed than she'd been in a long time. Over the next few months, she began to get a lot closer to me, and then a lot closer to others.

Catherine's attempt to suffocate herself in the garage successfully communicated the seriousness of her plea to her cocaine-addicted husband, but it was deeply disturbing to everyone involved, especially her ten-year-old daughter. Here, she describes the process of taking increasing levels of responsibility for her actions.

> My daughter said, "How could you shaft me like that." She was angry and scared. She felt she wasn't important to me if I could do such a thing. We talked about it a lot. At first, I was in denial. I said, "I didn't shaft you. I decided that you would live with your aunt." Well, that didn't go over very well! I still couldn't take full responsibility for it, you know—really be open to how it affected her.

> I thought about it, counseled on it, and eventually I got clearer. I apologized to her and explained that I know that no one could replace her mother and I understood how it made her feel unimportant. I felt pretty guilty after that for a while. I felt extremely bad for putting her in that position. For a long time, I think she didn't want me to believe she understood, because she was still angry and she didn't want me to feel okay about it all, yet.

Taking responsibility contradicts the suicidal trance. In the trance, one feels powerless and has little awareness of other people's thoughts and feelings. In this later stage of recovery, people take the initiative to understand and acknowledge the effects of their actions on others.

> So we continued to talk about it in bits and pieces. We still do. In a strange way, the attempt has given us an opportunity that we might not have had—to talk about not only this but a lot of other things, freely. She's fifteen now, and we are continually reaffirming how important we are to each other now. She's going through a lot, as most teenagers do, but we have this wonderful communication. She feels she can tell me anything.

Catherine had begun bridging back to her daughter shortly after the attempt, but that was only part of her work. Her attempt arose from her fury toward her husband, and although the event was a powerful wake-up call for them both, they would still need many hours of conversation and therapy, to save their marriage. For Catherine, taking responsibility also took the forms of deep contemplation, forgiveness, and developing compassion.

I was still angry at him after the attempt. He was frightened—of being left, of my being so unstable, of the power of my aggression— and that I was able to go through with it. He was so frightened, in fact, that he wasn't really able to be there with me afterwards. So then I was scared that I'd be alone and that I wouldn't have someone close to me after the attempt. That scared the shit out of me!

It took us a long time to regain that closeness. We worked a lot in therapy, and spent many hours focusing and meditating on forgiveness and compassion for each other and ourselves. It seemed like as I forgave myself—developed more compassion and love for myself—I could listen to him more. And he did that with me, too. That's how it started.

Tim's life was filled with people who cared for him. They stayed close throughout his ordeal. They spent hours each day in the hospital, and remained loyal even through the most difficult periods, when Tim's hands were bandaged and immobile and he was surly and uncommunicative. The time came, however, after months of their ministrations, when he had to be there for them. The crisis was over, and there had been much talk. Now Tim had to listen.

It involved my fiancée, my best friend, and his wife. We were all seeing our own therapists at this point, and we began seeing a therapist together. It was the combination of these things that began to reestablish the foundation of my life. One day, it was their turn to be brutally honest. It got pretty intense in the room.

They said, "It wasn't okay what you did! We're not gonna accept this right away. This is gonna take time for us to deal with. You know, you did something really awful. It was not a nice thing to do. This sucks, and if you think it's been okay for us, you're out of your mind! We're gonna hang around—we're gonna be here and we love you—but we're angry too." I had been getting a lot of the caring part, and now this was the tough part. My fiancée told me that if I ever did this again, she was done—end of relationship.

This was the most difficult encounter since the death of his parents. Tim could feel himself wanting to wriggle away and avoid their candor. Yet, in listening, in keeping his seat through the hard parts, Tim discovered new resources inside.

I had many reactions inside. On one level, it pissed me off. But I was also scared. On another level, I was really touched. They really had hung in there for me, and now they cared enough to be really honest. That was the beginning of slowly getting committed to living, and even thinking of taking care of others. It was also the start of not just being totally consumed by myself, my life, my experience, so I could be there with my fiancée.

Tim let himself feel their suffering, and he found himself caring for them. He discovered that he could extend beyond his pain, and he felt ready to let go of the trauma of the past twenty-eight years. It wasn't automatic, and years of reflection would still be necessary, but that decision altered the course of his life.

WHO AM I?

Rebuilding the self requires a sustained committment to investigate the precursors of the attempt and to heal the wounds of the past. It also requires taking responsibility for the pain one has caused oneself and others. But for those who recover most successfully, the journey extends beyond the actual attempt and its repercussions and into the meaning of one's life and one's sense of purpose.

Spiritual traditions throughout the world contemplate the question "Who am I?" In Judaism, this question addresses the responsibility of being chosen by God. Christians identify with Jesus's sacrifice and attempt to follow his example in their daily lives. Hindus undertake spiritual practice to experience Atman, the divine self within, while Buddhists argue against the existence of a real or central self altogether, and aspire to a state beyond all personal identification—the state of emptiness.

It is part of human nature that during and just following times of heartache, disappointment, and loss, we ask, "Why is this happening to me? What does it mean? In what kind of world could this happen?" Life is always accompanied by suffering, and suffering heightens the urgency of our search for meaning. Inquiries into the meaning of life are universal, but those who have attempted suicide seek the answers with special intensity. In confronting death, theirs has been a most rigorous spiritual practice—an unceasing meditation on life and death. Now, on the road back, they ponder the question "Now that this has happened, who am I?" In these early stages of recovery, the answers form the foundation of their journey toward understanding.

With each new step—each success and each setback—people amend their understanding of who they are. They update their files. The question "Who am I?" is a familiar one. At its worst, during the withdrawal and trance phases, it was part of a closed loop, a recursive set of life-negating interrogations. The answers were few, and all of them pointed to suicide. During the recovery, however, the answers become more varied and plentiful. They serve to build confidence and faith in oneself.

Ed was furious after his fall. He viewed himself as nothing but the sum total of his broken bones, and the self-loathing and fury he experienced knew no bounds. In time, however, he began to define his identity more broadly, and included in it his creativity, his ability to educate others, and his indomitable spirit. Karl had asked for release from his "poor, pitiful life." He felt subhuman. Eventually, however, he would discover that even *his* soul could find redemption as a child in God's family.

When people who have attempted suicide decide to live, the question "Who am I?" provides a reflection of their progress and a direction for the future. Since the answers can be gathered only "in the field"—engaged in life—they offer a consistent feedback after each experience along the way.

Life became smoother for Catherine. Her husband had successfully quit cocaine, and was supporting the family by teaching at a local high school. The children were older and healthy and needed less attention. Catherine found herself wondering who she was apart from her family.

> *It's been a process of questioning over time. I began by asking myself, "Who am I, other than a wife and mother?" I had a friend who was dying of AIDS, and one night I had spent twelve hours with him. I felt so much well-being inside of me. I felt so much love, so much compassion and creativity.*
>
> *I started thinking, "I am someone who is very capable of giving and being able to handle situations like this. I'm really good here." To me, there is a mystery to life and death that compels me, and showing love and understanding in those situations is so important. This illness really needs that right now.*

Ian remembers the exact moment when his sense of identity changed, dramatically and irrevocably. It was a surprisingly simple event, happening on a first date that wasn't going so well. Ian had felt the attraction to his new friend. It was strong and familiar, and he was looking for some warmth and comfort after the previous harrowing months. They went to a furniture outlet to browse through carpeting for his new living room, but something seemed odd. Ian felt as if there were two different people inside him. He could feel his old self wanting to please—wanting to agree with every suggestion his friend offered. At the same time, he was appalled at his friend's taste. Cautiously at first, Ian would reiterate his preferences. After all, it was *his* house. He could feel himself getting tense: there seemed to be a less familiar self inside him that was becoming irritated. Soon, his small preferences grew larger; minor differences between them became major points of argument. Ian could feel the part of him that wanted to relent and create peace at any cost, but he couldn't shake another part that, regardless of how inconsequential the whole episode really was, would not give in.

> *As we were walking out of the store, he said to me, "God, you can be such a bitch!" I just looked at him. I thought to myself, "This is someone whom I don't even know. Before, I'd probably fall in love with him!" Now, the attraction was gone. He said, "Maybe looking at carpet was a bad idea," and I said, "No. It was a really good idea! It worked out really well!" I think he left very confused.*

> *I began to have a sense of myself. I wanted to get into another relationship, but I didn't want another one where I was pleasing somebody else and not getting anything back. I don't want a relationship like I had, where I am consistently unhappy.*

Success in recovery begins with little experiments and small decisions. These, in turn, lead to major changes. Ian stopped perceiving every event as a confirmation of his inadequacy, and began to substitute a newfound curiosity about the world in place of the aversion with which he had always regarded it. Life became an able teacher, and he its avid student. Ian's story illustrates significant ways in which those who were suicidal discover who they are as they heal.

> *Yeah, it's a sense of identity—a sense that I matter, that my life is my life, my experience is my experience—and if someone wants to be a part of it, I welcome any relationship that is mutual.*

Ian began to shed his need to please. In doing so, he discovered the anger beneath. He had experienced a number of betrayals, and some of them were inexcusable. His lover Kevin had been HIV-positive and concealed this from him. Kevin had been asymptomatic, so throughout the entire three-year relationship Ian had no reason to suspect his illness. Their physician also refrained from telling Ian. A few months after the attempt, Ian confronted his doctor.

> *I told him I'd been putting things together. I told him, "As a member of the hospital staff, I can go through the records and check, but I suspect you knew about it all along." He tried to weasel a bit, but I continued to be angry.*

Ian finally claimed his right to be a respected member of the human community. He experienced a new clarity in his thinking and a strength of will he had never felt before. The episode with his physician proved just the beginning.

> *The anger got stronger after that. I started getting angry at my whole life, for never feeling acknowledged—always the emphasis on the negative, on what I didn't do for someone else. At that point, I decided that everyone treated me badly!*

> *Suddenly I saw what was being done and how it was being done. I understood where the control was and how I was manipulated through my life, how I was disempowered, how the power through my relationships always lay with the other person. I saw how I was kept a victim, and how I kept myself a victim. At that point, I decided to change.*

Ian's answer to the question "Who am I?" had dramatically changed him. He became assertive on his own behalf. He demanded to be dealt with honestly, and he learned to exercise his right to be heard. Finally, he abandoned his victim posture. His mood lightened and he experienced a newfound freedom. For the first time, Ian began to feel whole.

CREATIVITY

The artist produces for the liberation of his soul.

SOMERSET MAUGHAM

Healing the past, taking responsibility, and pondering the question "Who am I?" form the building blocks for healing a self that has been debilitated by suicidal pain. As recovery continues, people increase their sensitivity to healthy impulses from within. For many, the creative process proves to be a tool for further internal investigation, as well as a source of great satisfaction. During an earlier stage, when in a suicidal trance, a person can use the creative process to intensify the trance and reinforce the sense of futility. The works of poets such as Anne Sexton and Sylvia Plath and of visual artists such as Diane Arbus express the agony and isolation of the trance. During recovery, however, the creative process can play a significant role in the flowering of a new life. It can serve as a guide in finding repressed memories, as a reminder of little-used strengths and abilities, and a bridge from the solitude of the trance into the world of personal relationships. In most creative acts, it is not clear whether people choose to create art or whether the muse "chooses" them. Often people say of their creations, "It seemed to have a life of its own," or, "It wasn't something I planned." In each instance, however, those recovering chose to remain open-minded and attentive to what was developing inside them. A simple choice was made to surrender to a process little understood because it contained transformative power.

Jason spent what little free time he had in the afternoons and evenings painting large portraits of punk and heavy-metal musicians. Joan Jett and Motley Crue were favorites. He worked with black paint and thick brushes, and like Jason himself, the portraits were passionate and rough-hewn. The likenesses weren't as important as what they represented: life on the edge, and the bold and courageous expression of one's innermost drives, raw and undiluted.

> *I just started doing it. Some days it was trash. It was an outlet for me—a pressure release. I had to make a statement—get it off my chest. It would let out all this anxiety out that I was feeling. At the end of a painting, or a poem in my journal, I'd just close the book and let it go. Sometimes people would talk about it with me. So I guess it expanded my outlets for communication, too.*

Whether in poetry, dance, or painting, creativity provides a beacon for guidance and a route back inside. It is a way to reconnect and to experience one's inner life as being capable of beauty and wonder rather than only pain. Some fashioned careers from their hours of artistic concentration, but without exception the process of creating has been far more important than the artistic product itself.

In addition to her math training, Karen was also a choreographer at the time of her suicide attempt. She had regularly produced performances and danced in them as well. Years later, however, she chose painting as a way to weave together her inner life, which had become so fragmented. The process of painting was new to her, and often Karen found herself perplexed.

> *I'd sit back and say, "Shit, I wonder why I'm painting that?" I would paint beautiful flowers that were wilted, and I would have stone castles with chunks fallen out of them, roads that would go nowhere, and a bicycle that was twisted and broken.*

While almost everyone else in Karen's mural class was painting pristine landscapes and perfect flowers, she was learning the skill of listening to herself. Sometimes images would virtually flash onto the canvas before she recognized them. She painted on impulse, only later attempting to understand what she had produced.

> *Sometimes it would happen before I would know what was going on. It felt like something coming through that I didn't have access to in other ways, and it was profoundly healing, both to do it and to be guided by it.*

The world of people still seemed dangerous. Karen would circumscribe her movements and limit her contacts. Creativity, however, provided her a protected space of unlimited dimension. Working on murals that would take months to complete, she could step into an alternate reality where she could move freely until she felt safe.

> *Some people would say to me, "Don't you go absolutely crazy spending all those thousands of hours on those pieces? You know, I could never do that. I'd go mad." For me, it was more of a healing, meditative state that I wanted to create, and one way was through making large pieces. I could be in it for months and months.*

As she moved deeper into the woods, her work became more intricate. She left the mural form for tapestry, and added quilting and soft sculpture to her wall hangings. Sometimes the images would be fantastic; at other times, the creative process revealed wounded and hidden parts of her personality. Karen didn't know for certain, but she sensed that some parts of her were healing.

> *It was a weird recovery process. I'd look at a blank wall for long periods of time, just waiting to see what would come. Just watching the white—and then I could start seeing. Something was mate-*

rializing, like in a sci-fi movie. Sometimes it was boring stuff, like seeing my mother sitting there in her housecoat drinking a cup of coffee and eating a half piece of toast. Other times there were these little pictures—faceless people peeking out. Wounded, without features, looking at me. I just wasn't able to paint a face. It baffled the hell out of me at the time!

Tim had been an athlete in southern California. He was comfortable running down a pop fly or leading a fast break on the basketball court. He liked listening to Motown's rhythm and blues, and followed the rise of the Beatles, but his body had never experienced anything like folk dancing and his heart had never before been stirred as it was by the music from eastern Europe.

Upon landing in Humboldt County, he made friends with a newly formed dance troupe called the Humboldt Folk Dance Factory. Their "statement of purpose" contained only two words: "design frenzy." They would learn dances from around the globe, teach them to fellow townspeople, and dance all night. Tim's bounty became twofold: a community of enthusiastic and creative people and the discovery of Balkan music. Almost immediately, Tim felt at home.

The music struck such a chord in me. I mean, it was really different at first from athletics, but within six months I had learned over 500 dances. Everything from Greece, Bulgaria, Turkey, and Macedonia. In fact, I started listening to music from all over the world, but still nothing resonated like these.

There were times, hearing the first strains of a gypsy violin, that his chest would expand reflexively, as if it were attempting to embrace the entire world. Not satisfied with simply listening to the music, Tim studied the clarinet as well, in order to experience the sounds from the inside. Music accompanied Tim throughout his journey of recovery. It had predated his suicide attempt, and was there to welcome him as he returned. With each year, its meaning for him deepened: it spoke to him of his life.

This music is passion and pain. From the very beginning, it expressed to me both ecstasy and deep suffering—this dual sensitivity. It just spoke the truth to me, and it was expressing my deepest experience of being alive—both ends. "Life is joy; life is short."

OPENING TO THE UNEXPECTED

There is one elementary Truth—the ignorance of which kills countless ideas and splendid plans: The moment one definitely commits oneself, then Providence moves, too. All sorts of things occur to help one that would never otherwise have occurred.

GOETHE

It was a Saturday night and it was gonna be the first time I sang publicly since I was a small child. I never could hold a note. My voice was so bad that the congregation was warned in advance. (Karl)

During the recovery from attempted suicide there may be critical incidents in which something unexpected occurs: odd coincidences, puzzling encounters, events that stretch our sense of possibility. The creative process offers experiences of the unexpected, when information previously buried makes its way into one's consciousness; but the unexpected may also emerge in other contexts, and when it does, the decision one must make is to remain open and uncommitted to any particular outcome. This is a time to be receptive, rather than active or decisive.

Bigger is not better here. It seems to make no difference whether these incidents are dramatic or subtle. All are truly felt to be meetings with Goethe's "Providence." Often the best response people can manage when facing the unexpected is to get out of the way, allow the incident to happen, and reflect on its meaning later.

Only months after Karl entered detox, he felt called to continue his recovery through prayer and testimony. He was developing confidence in himself and trust in God, but nothing had prepared him for what happened on his first Christian retreat.

> *We had traveled a long way, and we held hands after getting out of the vans. There are so many traffic accidents that we were giving thanks for arriving all right. Something was different. It was in the air. Electric. We all felt it, and we were weeping and singing praises.*

Pastor Warren, the minister of the congregation, had received musical training years before joining the church. He enjoyed composing new melodies for old hymns and traditionals, and teaching them to the congregation. He discovered that music was a special form of prayer, and that it could move people, deeply and powerfully.

Karl chose Pastor Warren for his mentor. He felt a rare kindness and understanding from him, and was intrigued with his unorthodox approach to the Gospel. The pastor welcomed drug addicts and alcoholics in recovery, ex-gang members and runaways to his congregation, and certain nights of the year they all gathered for a special service called Testimony. It was an evening of contemplation, prayer, and music, and often a few members of the congregation would approach the stage, speak about their lives, and sing.

Before the events began, Pastor Warren felt concerned about how his new tone-deaf student would fare onstage. Often, such performances were as much a leap of faith for the pastor as for the members to be featured, and on this night, despite years of performance experience, Pastor Warren felt palpably nervous:

When it was Karl's turn, I told the congregation that testimonies are important for their content and heart. It doesn't matter how good a voice you have, but what's behind it. I worked with him, tried to teach him, but he could never really find the key! I warned the group that what happened next might not be pleasing to the ear.

Karl remembers the next moments photographically. Never in his wildest imagination could he have foreseen such an experience.

I was gonna sing the old spiritual "O Ship of Zion." I got up onstage. I was nervous, too. When I opened my mouth, I felt sucked out of my body. I don't know how else to describe it. It's like I was there, but also watching it happen. Then I started singing, and I hit every note. It was beautiful! It felt like I could sing anything! I remember seeing everyone's jaw just drop, especially Pastor Warren's!

There was nothing to do but let the event play itself out. The stage was his, and there was majesty in the feeling. Surrendering to what he felt was a greater force, Karl felt love, joy, and a deep inner strength. He also felt a presence.

That's when Jesus zapped me. It was him singing. Just before I left the stage, I heard a voice whispering: "Now this is why I saved you all those times. I had a calling for you here. I want you to tell people that no matter how bad things are, there's hope. I want you to tell them that."

The experience of surprise is dramatically different from the character of the trance. By its very nature, the trance prevents anything new from breaking through. One's perception has been so compressed, into a narrow, self-defeating loop of thought and feeling, that one is unable to receive anything new, despite the urgent need for it. Unexpected occurrences like Karl's were once dismissed as fabrications of unbalanced minds, but today mental health professionals are beginning to acknowledge not only that they are legitimate, but that they play an important role as "turning points" or "wake-up calls" in people's lives.

Unexpected occurrences vary infinitely in their form. Chris had an experience that involved physical injury and a mystical journey.

This was a number of years after the attempt. I had remarried, and my husband and I decided to move to San Francisco, where we'd both go to graduate school. We had two children, so it was a major move we were contemplating. I was looking forward to it, but it was difficult saying good-bye to our lives up there. Most difficult, I think, was that I had to sell my horse. She was pretty old but real gentle and responsive. I was sad to say good-bye. One afternoon I was giving a demo ride to this family who was thinking about buying her for their daughter. I guess I wasn't paying attention. I saddled her quickly—I didn't even have shoes on— and rode out into the pasture. Suddenly the horse shied. I think she smelled a bear, and she reared and twisted, and when I toppled off, my head hit a stone. I was knocked unconscious.

Chris awoke about an hour later, but during that time something happened. While comatose, she had experienced a rich and extraordinary scene. In one stroke, it cemented her commitment to life.

I saw myself hurtling through bright light, falling down a tunnel. I landed in a beautiful meadow, with incredibly colorful flowers and trees and a band of people on horseback. The leader walked over to me and leaned forward, slowly and gently. Then he asked me, "Are you ready?"

I realized that he was asking me if I was ready to die, and I knew then that I wasn't. Even as it was happening, I felt the absurdity of

all those years wanting to die, and now that I was given the
opportunity, I wasn't gonna take it! I hadn't quite committed
myself to living on the earth yet, but that's what I wanted. It may
seem crazy, but it was very real to me. My body was in incredible
pain the weeks after that, but what I remember the most was that I
had truly, definitively decided to live.

At this point in recovery, events like these seem to serve a dual purpose. Firstly, they offer a test, challenging the unsuspecting recipient to be surprised. They require the willingness to entertain the unknown, rather than reduce all events to the familiar suicidal conclusion. Secondly, serendipitous events such as these ask us to broaden our perspective on reality and entertain new points of view. This change can widen our idea of what is possible and lead to deeper levels of understanding and healing.

Karl's surprise proved warm and blessed. Chris's included visual beauty and a sense of clarity. But not all unexpected occurrences are pleasant. After a long day of work, years after her attempt, Mattie was leaving her office. It was summer, and the daylight filtered through the trees on the street. Suddenly, she was attacked. A man had assaulted her from behind.

It was in broad daylight. He viciously attacked me. He tried to rip
my clothes off. I broke free and ran across the street, back into my
office building. He chased me inside and two co-workers and I
barricaded the back door while he was on the other side, trying to
push it open. We called the police and he ran away.

They caught him later, but there was something about what
happened that woke me up. The memories of my grandfather's
abuse hadn't come back yet, but I just knew inside that there was
something I would have to deal with. I decided I wasn't gonna rest
until I figured out what it was.

Mattie chose to attribute a deeper meaning to a traumatic event. It became a source of reflection and direction in her quest for understanding.

Less dramatic events also have power. After arriving in Florida, Cassie began working with a female therapist—her first. She seemed to be a woman of great caring and considerable personal power. Cassie had experienced power from a woman before— her mother—but never in combination with such kindness and insight. In this particular incident, her therapist's help seemed so ordinary that for a time, Cassie didn't realize the gift she had been given.

> *She saw me individually, but also saw my partner and me together from time to time. She suggested that he get this book* Positive Magic, *and read it. Well, he bought it, but just kind of passed it to me. I don't think he even glanced at it. I'm sure that years later he was very sorry, because that book changed my life and I was no longer the same person he originally moved in with.*

Cassie continued to struggle. She was a highly competent professional but had little self-esteem. The insights she gleaned in therapy were all helpful, but she continued to be burdened. Her hopelessness sometimes blinded her to resources that could open her mind. In this case, one lay right on her bookshelf.

> *I let the book sit for a long time, and he would get on me about it. I thought it would be kind of vacuous. When I finally got around to it, I hadn't read more than a few pages when I thought, "Oh, my gosh. Somebody has put in writing what I've always believed!" You know, I spent years as a child arguing with the church, to myself and out loud. No one ever listened, or they scolded me for thinking such things. All of a sudden it had a name, and I knew I was not the only person in the world that felt this way.*

This was the message that I always wanted to hear. It was real simple, but it said it the way I needed to hear it. It said that my life was in my hands, and I had the choice as to whether or not I wanted to take that ball and run with it or let myself believe that I was there at the whim of everything that came by. It said, "I am my highest self and all I need is within me." It told me that I had control over my life and if I didn't like something, I had the power to change it. My therapists had directed me to the door, but it was this book that handed me the key!

Eight

Reaching Out

All real living is meeting.

MARTIN BUBER

By this point in recovery, significant changes are underway. Curiosity and excitement begin to replace hopelessness. Multiple possibilities now present themselves. There have been some difficult choices, leaps of faith, and unexpected occurrences on the road to recovery, and at each juncture the decision to live has been reinforced a bit more. The people understand that a world that was once limited and lacking promise now offers many opportunities for a rewarding life.

Recoveries from attempted suicides require enormous courage and strength of will. Those who haven't contemplated or attempted suicide may find it difficult to imagine how withering the never-ending chorus of death-promoting thoughts and feelings can be, and what effort it takes to overcome them. And yet no recovery occurs in isolation. A portrait of the road back is never complete without chronicling the contributions of others, who offer clarity, compassion, and love. Since suicide takes place amid crushing isolation, it is only reasonable to expect that some of the greatest healing moments occur when others break through.

Roberta had contemplated suicide for many years, but was stopped shortly before her attempt. She came from a well-known family in Peru who had fled to the United States to escape political persecution. As years passed, the family scattered. Roberta found herself in an abusive and suffocating marriage, with two daughters and a future that seemed devoid of promise.

> *I had been planning suicide for a year or two. Working out the details—how I would do it and when. I couldn't see leaving my daughters behind in the wake of their mother's suicide, so I was going to take them with me. It was a difficult decision, but, in the state I was in I thought it was the best thing. I planned it for this particular Saturday morning. For the past few months, I had felt like a robot, just in a trance, and I was really feeling that way on that Friday.*

Roberta had arranged her suicide meticulously, but there was ambivalence beneath her resolution, and unconsciously she intimated her intentions to a colleague. Luckily, he guessed the meaning of her signals and broke through her trance.

> *My office partner and I were walking down this street downtown, going to lunch. I thought I was concealing it pretty well, but I must've said something suggestive—something about "not being around." He stopped right there, took my shoulders in his hands, and looked me right in the eyes. He said, "If you kill yourself, I promise you that every day I will visit your grave and shit on it!" I was stunned. I just stared at him, and then we burst out laughing. A minute later, I broke into tears and crumpled to the sidewalk. We held each other and cried and talked for the next two hours, just sitting there.*

Reaching Out is a stage of healing that spans the entire recovery period, from the first post-attempt moments through the years beyond. People report life-changing interactions that shake the foundations of the trance and important relationships that help defuse self-destructive impulses. While rebuilding one's relationship with oneself, relationships with the outside world must also be rebuilt. The suicidal trance has stunted one's ability to reach out, and learning to relate with others honestly is essential. Reaching out requires people to learn new social skills in three ways:

- Asking for help
- Being seen, and
- Recognizing support

These form the cornerstones of lasting, healthy relationships.

ASKING FOR HELP

The suicide attempt itself is a communication. For some it is a farewell, and for others it is a last despairing cry for help. In either case, it is a message that expects no meaningful response. Direct communication with others has long since proven impossible or ineffective and there seems to be no other way to express such suffering except through a suicide attempt.

On the road back, it is essential that people learn to request help from others, directly and consistently. For many, the next call for help often comes just following the attempt itself. After swallowing a wide assortment and a large quantity of pills, Karen, lying on the couch, discovered that she wanted to live. As she began to feel numb and cold, she noticed that other ideas began to enter her mind. She could leave town and live. She needn't kill the body that already felt so dead. Perhaps there were other options. She called her family, and spent the next few days in intensive care.

The day after her attempt, Chris knew she couldn't be alone, and asked her friend for shelter and company. Rennie, realizing she would probably attempt again or be killed on the back streets of Mannheim, called on her family for help. "I told them, My life is completely unmanageable. I need help in getting out of here." They pooled their finances and her brother flew with her to the United States so that she could begin again.

Asking for help is a key step on the journey back to life for a number of important reasons. As an interpersonal gesture, it continues to dissolve the isolation of the trance. The constraint that prevented people from speaking about their pain or finding comfort and aid has lifted somewhat, allowing them to reach out. Requesting help also seems to mobilize one's energies toward healing. In asking others for assistance, people become more actively engaged in the process of their own repair.

The day after her attempt was thwarted, Deborah consented to have breakfast with her friend, the physician who had interrupted her attempt. She was alarmed at how numb she had felt the night before. She didn't know what to do next and needed his help. Although he wasn't a psychiatrist, his medical training warned him that a follow-up of some kind was necessary.

> He was very gentle in his inquiries. He was nonjudgmental, saying things like, "This does happen. People do feel this way, and you can get past it. I care about you." At the end, I agreed to find somebody to talk to about it. I felt a lot better after talking with him.

Ian's first direct call for help also occurred just after the suicide attempt. Groggy, he got out of the truck, left the garage, and wobbled to the bedroom. He was already hours late for his shift at the hospital, and there were messages on his machine. Then he did what he had never allowed himself—he called a friend. With one call, he broke years of secrecy and a few weeks of virtual isolation.

See, until then, I had withdrawn and I had pulled away from everyone. I told myself, "I don't want to be around anyone," and that added impetus to the whole idea of killing myself.

But, something had changed. Ian's attempt was real. As a medical professional, he had a sense of the damage he had inflicted on himself. His grief was also real. The isolation and loneliness felt undeniably painful, and for the first time he would risk the possibility of imposing on someone and of being judged, and ask for help.

Peg and I were close, but I never talked about how much pain there was. I didn't want to push myself on her. I didn't want to burden everyone with what was going on with me. [After the attempt] I wanted to talk. And I wanted somebody to tell me that it was okay, 'cause at that point I still wasn't able to tell myself anything. I felt such an unqualified sense of support from her. She came over, and I lay on the bed and just cried. God, it's making me cry now. Gratitude.

Asking for help is a skill. As people practice it, they become more sensitive to the kind of help they need and more realistic about the kind of help they are likely to receive. As their requests grow more focused, the possibility of satisfaction increases. One's confidence is tentative at first, and may proceed in fits and starts, but eventually it develops.

After Robert tried to hang himself, he entered a series of group homes. Although he felt the benefits of the staff's discipline and care, he knew that a more enduring problem remained unaddressed. His first requests for help lacked clarity and were self-destructive. With experience, he learned more direct and satisfying ways.

At first, I ran away from the group home. I had worked on a lot of my issues and I think it was a cry for help, saying, "Look. I've been here for almost two years and I haven't worked on my drug problem." After a few weeks on the street, I went back and started working really hard on it. I told everybody what I needed and got a lot of support. I started going to AA every night and I talked about my drinking in every meeting.

BEING SEEN

After asking for help, the next step is to be seen. This means allowing increasing levels of intimacy; allowing others to understand one's confusion, and even feel the pain that has generated the attempt. Being seen means one has to be transparent to "significant others," after being cloaked in secrecy for so long. For those who have suffered extreme family dysfunction or chronic alienation, this may be the first time they permitted others such proximity. For many others, it has simply been a long time. In any case, being seen represents significant movement toward healing, and is critical to building real personal relationships.

I think what comes to mind is not words so much; it's being seen by people—the moments when I'd feel really seen. It started in therapy, and then, as I let it happen more, I felt it with close friends. (Mattie)

Mattie's women's group provided the opportunity to take risks she previously thought impossible. For the first time in her memory, she allowed the more hidden parts of herself to be noticed. On such occasions, instead of changing the subject or redirecting the focus, she remained quiet and simply watched what happened.

There would be these moments, you know, where someone would say something or look at me and it would make me just leap! I was scared, but I wanted it. It was when I felt like they saw beneath the

entertainer, the funny one—when they saw the sad kid inside and
felt drawn to that part, and touched it in some way.

The women would act as a mirror, reflecting not only the socially acceptable aspects of her personality but the more tender and fragile parts as well. Mattie was beginning to learn the difference between humility and shame, and gradually grew more forthright in revealing herself.

You see, it was my belief that nobody wanted to be around this kid
because she's so hurt. So, when anyone ever expressed interest in
that part, I'd just melt. It made me feel hopeful, too, that these
parts of me could be integrated. Each year, I've become braver, to
let people see me rather than hide those parts.

Rennie virtually threw open the doors to being seen, and in doing so received the first direct acknowledgments of her worth. She knew nothing about therapists, but inadvertently landed in the office of one when in fact she thought she was seeing a chiropractor.

My sciatic stuff was still acting up, so that's why I went. Well, he
says, "I'm not actually a chiropractor. I practice Reichian therapy,
and yes, that does involve the body." It turned out he did a whole
string of things, and suddenly I was in therapy! I thought therapy
was the most exciting thing that ever happened in my life. I would
go into a session and get caught up in this whirlwind of emotion,
and I would come out and everything would look different. All
sorts of stuff would bubble up from inside.

He was the first person ever to tell me that there was something
really valuable inside me. The first time he said that, I thought,
"Huh? Are you talking about me?" I went through a lot of hard
times afterwards, but from that point, I had this faith that life was
definitely getting better.

Some of most powerful descriptions of being seen are the simplest: unadorned sentiments spoken directly by someone who cares to tell the truth as he or she sees it. Faith attempted suicide by slashing her wrists. She was nineteen. Six years earlier, her father had died suddenly, leaving her mother with five children and a fledgling business. The family was too stunned to grieve. Tensions ran high. Faith became the acting-out adolescent toward whom all the family pain, frustration, and anger were focused, and by the time she was a late teenager, she was floundering in a chronic unresolved conflict with her mother. Although she survived her physical injuries, it seemed only a matter of time before she would attempt suicide again. Her mother sent her to therapy, but refused to attend with her. Little was accomplished. A few months later she met a new friend. He was older and had seen a little more of the world.

> We'd been having this long talk. You know, these intense talks you have when you're a teenager. I didn't know what to do, and I told him I felt crazy. He just looked at me and said, "You're not crazy. Your family is." I've never forgotten that: it was such a relief. You know, therapy hadn't worked; nothing else was happening except I was dying there. I left shortly thereafter. I'm forty-eight now. Looking back, it was one of the most important conversations I ever had.

These are examples of the passive-receptive dimension of being seen, but there is an active one as well. It involves re-creating social networks capable of honest exchange and forging relationships with people who are willing to venture into territory beyond conventional discourse. The active dimension of being seen requires a choice—a willingness to express a range of thoughts and feelings significantly deeper and more genuine than the previous ones. The rewards include relationships offering responsibility and freedom, warmth and humor, give and take. As Ian finally recognized, there are often people nearby who are willing or have been waiting for precisely this kind of connection.

Ian had spent some time with a highly skilled counselor the year before his suicide attempt, but had never truly communicated the depths of his suffering. Caught between his need for help and the desire to please, he had soft-pedaled his confusion, and fooled both himself and his therapist into believing he was in better shape than he was.

> *I hadn't really gone as far as I thought, but I wanted to make her feel like she was doing her job—like she was helping me. And so it was very difficult to face her and say, "Hey, you know, I led you on. I wasn't as well as I tried to make you think."*

> *Once I did that, I was a lot more honest and open with her. That's when the real healing could start. I was afraid she would judge me about what I had done. I expected her to get angry or say that everything we talked about was just bullshit. I expected a big confrontation, but it didn't happen. But, you know, it's like I confronted me, and in doing that, I opened up, and we really started therapy.*

When people find new confidants and create relationships that can function at greater levels of intimacy, they sometimes choose to end alliances that do not support the next stages of growth. Ed progressively distanced himself from friends who couldn't understand his creative pursuits and his homosexuality, and Rennie severed contacts with friends in the drug world. Mattie left her boyfriend and their circle of friends. Although she hadn't recovered the memories of abuse yet, she reasoned that the isolation in which she was caught only strengthened the likelihood that she would kill herself. Recognizing what was absent, she made a bold decision.

I created exactly what I was missing. I knew [the isolation] put me
at risk for suicide, so I got this juicy group of women around me
that I could live with and talk to and cry and laugh with and be
mad at men with! We gave ourselves a lot of permission to feel good
that we were a bunch of women living alone. Now, friends and
community are two of the most important things in my life.

RECOGNIZING SUPPORT

The ability to recognize potential sources of support is a major
breakthrough. Suicidal trances lasting many years virtually prohibit
interpersonal exchange. When one views one's life as a long, desperate, and solitary struggle, confidence withers that anyone else cares,
or that anyone would even want to. Recognizing and utilizing
support becomes not only a skill to be developed, but an enormous
act of faith.

As Robert's recovery progressed, he exercised greater insight in
his use of group support. He had decided to confront his alcoholism
publicly, and this act of boldness galvanized his recovery. He felt a
momentum he had never before experienced; and the more diligent
he became, the more confident he grew. He turned to the staff of his
group home for support and they responded with encouragement.
Robert discovered he had allies. The more responsibly he acted, the
more freedom they allowed him. This was a truly novel experience
for him. It seemed that everyone was working together for his
success. He had never even entertained the notion that this was
possible.

There were a lot of people on the staff who were really pulling for
me. I mean, it felt like everybody loved me! They were proud of
me! Then it was like I was one of their favorites because I had
turned it around. They were always saying, "That's really great.
Nice going." I had really overcome the self-destructive behaviors
and all of it.

Years had passed since Teresa landed back in Prescott. Life had gotten easier, but not by much. Without a family to lobby for her interests, her guidance counselors at school dissuaded her from her primary aspirations—becoming a physician or a nurse. They saw her as a wayward child, for whom such pressures would be too great. She studied cosmetology, and in the next ten years, she proceeded to work full-time, have two children, and consecutively marry two abusive and addicted husbands. There were many fights, and she continued to consider suicide. Teresa was now an intelligent, highly capable woman who was still driven by the unrequited need to have someone notice her pain. She was locked in a desperate loop of violent marriages, and she reasoned that her only recourse for herself and her children was to leave.

> *One night, I drank an entire gallon of wine and I was having seizures on the floor. I didn't really want to die; I just wanted my husband to know the pain I was in. I wanted him to know I was alive. I thought, well, if I did die, then maybe it would be significant and then my kids would never go through what I had. Well, when I woke up, I decided, "That's enough." I took the kids and left.*

In deciding where to go, Teresa took the first step toward recognizing the need for support. Just as when she boarded the bus for Prescott years ago, Teresa had little idea of what lay ahead of her.

> *It was very scary. One evening, I went to the Women's Shelter. Nobody would know where I was, and I needed rest from the abuse and the fighting. It was just as scary as leaving my mom. I was calm outwardly, but underneath I was petrified. That's when the biggest portion of my recovery came.*

Teresa was starting over. Her decisions would be short-term ones for a while. She would take one step, assess the results, take another step, assess the results, and then take another.

The people there were very supportive and caring. It took about three weeks, and then one morning, I found myself thinking, "My God, I really like myself!" I realized that it was okay with just me noticing me. That was enough.

I realized two important things: that I keep picking people who aren't the least bit interested in anyone else, just themselves; and that I always thought I had to do something drastic to be noticed. I started thinking, "Maybe around different people I wouldn't have to do that!"

At some point on the road back, people often feel compelled to face once again their family, their friends or their colleagues. Sometimes, the act of reentering an earlier context yields surprises.

It was late and the floor of the hospital was virtually empty. The last thing Ian wanted was to spend the night working with Stan. They never really spoke, and Ian had avoided him since his attempt, choosing to work shifts with colleagues who seemed less opinionated. Stan was in his fifties, reserved, conservative, and straight as an arrow. He wasn't a great conversationalist, but he would offer his opinion on a subject freely and deliver it as though it came from God. Although no words had been spoken, Ian had always imagined Stan's judgment of him would be negative, first for being gay and now for the suicide attempt.

We were just sitting there, you know—light conversation, keeping everything topical. All of a sudden, he says, "I want to thank you for coming back to work. I know this is hard for you right now. It would be really difficult for me to come back and face all these people knowing that they knew. I want you to know that not everybody knows."

I was shocked that this person was opening up to me and being caring. It really touched me. Then he said, "None of us are very far away from that. All of us have that option. All of us have felt like giving up. You're not alone in this."

It felt like he really cared. And suddenly, I realized that there were a lot of people there who cared. Maybe they didn't know how to show it or express it, but they were really there.

Nine

Allowing Others In

People arrive at this stage of recovery through generous portions of faith and hard work, and by cultivating the ability to remain open during periods of confusion. After years of rejecting help or not knowing how to let help in, or after living in an environment lacking compassion and support, people on the road back learn to reach out toward others. In doing so, they continue to dissolve both the trance and its accompanying doubt. As the willingness to choose life is tested again and again, each test provides new opportunities to deepen one's relationships with others.

Allowing others in involves letting oneself be strengthened and healed by healthy personal relationships: relationships of understanding and guidance, warmth and acceptance, respect and perspective. Allowing others in means experiencing from others what was missing or unavailable earlier in life during the devastating precursors to the suicide attempt: during traumatic loss, extreme family dysfunction, and chronic alienation. It was in the absence of empathic responses to hardship that the suicidal trance grew. Recovery is the time to experience what one missed long ago.

Allowing others in involves a "willful receptivity": a conscious decision to permit others intimate access and to allow oneself to be nourished by their caring. An extension of reaching out, this stage serves to consolidate the newly acquired skills of learning to ask for help, allowing oneself to be seen, and recognizing sources of support. It is not possible to change the past, but in receiving the experiences that were missing during the darkest hours of confusion and pain, people may significantly change their relationship to the past and to the painful events that shaped it.

Personal accounts of recovery are replete with surprising exchanges and extraordinary relationships with others. Some involve clinicians and crisis workers who are skilled and insightful. A great many involve nonprofessionals who happen to be present, for one reason or another, and are willing to offer something genuine and truthful. Regardless of their training or background, these people respond with a blend of compassion, honesty, and common sense.

We have already witnessed some of these interactions: the dry and insightful wit of Ian's crisis counselor as he inquired about the truck and the unexpected vote of support from his co-worker; the psychiatrist who told Cassie that she was following her mother's script; the admitting internist who offered Chris his trust and empowered her to begin life anew.

It is instructive to look more closely at these exchanges. What makes them so healing? What forms do these "missing experiences" take that help to move a person toward self-discovery and peace of mind? There are four major types:

- Mirroring
- Seeing a bigger picture
- Experiencing the humanness of others, and
- Extending to family

In the earlier stages of recovery—breaking the trance, rebuilding the self, and reaching out—one plays an active role, but the healing power of missing experiences lies simply in one's willingness to receive and savor them. The major task at this stage, therefore, is to allow oneself to open and be nourished.

MIRRORING

He said, "Madeline, I'm not gonna try to make you fit in with what the world thinks you should be or do. I'm gonna help you discover what you want to be and how to achieve it." Now that was truly amazing. (Madeline)

In the study of infant-parent relationships, mirroring refers to an interaction in which the parent communicates to a child—through words, tone of voice, and gesture—how delightful and beautiful the child is. It can also refer to exchanges in which the parent communicates to the child an understanding of the child's pain, whatever the cause: an upset stomach, an incident such as falling off a bed, or being startled by a noise. In those moments of "mini-shock," when an adult is present to offer comfort, the child learns that its pain is understandable and containable, and that its safety can be reestablished. Consistent mirroring results in a deep empathy between parent and child and a growing confidence within the child that she or he is prized and protected. Eventually the child will be able to rely on the mirroring, internalized, even when the parent is absent.

The concept of mirroring is useful in studying the descent into and the recovery from the suicidal trance because this type of empathic communication was missing while the trance was developing. The expression by others of understanding and support (and possibly protection) either was absent or couldn't be received. Later, as people progress through recovery, there still exists a strong need to know that there are at least some persons who understand the suffering they have experienced. And just as mirroring provides a sense of comfort for a small child, messages of compassion and insight and expressions of respect and confidence will convey to one

who is suicidal a faith in his or her basic goodness, assurances that
the pain is finite, and confidence that healing is possible.

> *I was very scared at first, but I was also intrigued with him. He
> didn't want to be sexual or be in any particular kind of relation-
> ship. I would have bolted, I couldn't have handled that. But after a
> while I felt there was no danger in this person. He was noninvasive,
> nonthreatening. And he could communicate the way I do. You
> know, with most people, you send out a signal and they don't
> receive it. He could receive it and then send it back. It was a little
> startling in the beginning. (Karen)*

Karen looked forward to her meetings with Tomás. They would
pass long stretches of time together without speaking, both of them
writing poems, reading, or gazing over the land. Their connection,
with its quiet understanding, was different from any she'd known.
Each moment that passed without exploitation or deceit was a
moment that strengthened her still tenuous hope that life might be
better.

> *He was one of the few people on the planet I felt safe with. I met
> him when I was living way back on the land. He was a monk, a
> scholar, a poet—multiple references! Fire in the ice. I thought,
> "My God, I haven't run into anybody like this before." It made
> living on the planet feel a little more normal.*
>
> *We were sharing the same state of being in the world but not of
> it—he because of his training and me because the line to func-
> tional reality had been snipped and I was just left with the
> spiritual. Because of that, there were things I wanted to learn from
> him, and things he wanted to learn from me.*

People who play significant and positive roles in the recovery of
others communicate a deep and abiding sense of respect. Mirroring

is an expression of such respect. It conveys compassion for
one's suffering, and a willingness to acknowledge the validity
of each person's particular way of returning to life. These "significant others" are able to distinguish the acts of suicidal violence
from the person inside, whatever his history or the severity of
his confusion. Whether they are highly trained psychologists or
merely friends, fellow patients, or waiters at the local greasy spoon,
such people manage to maintain a genuinely high regard for someone recovering, regardless of circumstances or life-style. For the
recipients of their attention, this is a powerful and often a novel
experience. In recounting their stories of recovery, many acknowledge that for a time, that respect was enough to sustain them. When
it was hard to feel good about oneself, one could go on if someone
else did.

When Ruth was a teenager, she had spent time at an uptown youth
center. Valerie was a supervisor and counselor there, and they
immediately liked each other. In some ways, they grew up together,
though separated in years by more than a decade. Valerie taught Ruth
the rudiments of counseling when she took a job there, and later
became a clinical psychologist while Ruth completed medical school.
Their relationship continues today, twenty years after it began.

*From the beginning, she was much more than a supervisor. She
was a role model as a professional black woman. Smart. Attractive.
She taught me a lot about that. Most of all, she had confidence in
me. She saw how much pain I was in, but she was firm too. She told
me that I could do things, no matter how I felt. She would look at
me and say, "You can do that. You can do anything you want if you
put your mind to it." You know, feelings are not facts.*

*She also taught me about getting along with people I didn't like
and not just curse them out and leave. She respected me enough to
demand more of me professionally and in turn she offered more of
herself. Also, we had fun working together!*

During the time Teresa lived at the women's shelter, she enjoyed both formal and informal contact with the staff. She was assigned a therapist, but there were many others who would stop and talk during the day just to see how she was faring. With time, Teresa began to feel the effects of the respect and positive regard she was receiving.

My first initial feeling was, "I'm not weird. If I was weird, they wouldn't be talking to me and acting like they cared. I must be okay!"

I began to feel important. I don't think I had had that feeling since kindergarten. You know, when I was little, I could affirm myself. I never had any problem believing anything I thought was valid and reasonable, but then all the years from nine on I never believed in anything I thought and neither did anyone else. I remember feeling affirmed as the shelter took me right back to that safe spot in my playhouse where I was once confident and okay.

As time went on, I'd hear them say to me, over and over, until it began to sink in, "You're perfectly fine, and a wonderful person, and your thinking is clear about such and such. We have a lot of confidence in you." It felt real, and over time, I would call on it whenever I was feeling hopeless or like giving up.

Jason's tenure as a ward of the state was about to come to an end. Early this year he would turn eighteen, and he was anticipating his emancipation from the group home. He was more than ready to join his friends in New Mexico, and it felt that time just couldn't move fast enough. Just before he left, he received a surprise. Each year, the board of directors of the group home, in conjunction with the school system and local business people, gave an award to someone who turned his or her life around—a "comeback" award. To his astonishment, Jason was selected. In receiving the award, Jason was acknowledged for the difficulties he had overcome and the perseverance with which he applied himself. He was no longer suicidal; he had stopped using drugs; he had completed his high school education; and as a bonus, he was considered a budding painter on the local art scene. These sentiments were appreciated by Jason, but it was what was said when he was presented the award that meant the most to him.

> *You are recognized not only because of your courage, but because you have cultivated and preserved your own unique and creative style of charting your way in the world. In your own way, you have enriched the lives of others. We respect who you are and who you have become and we want to express our confidence in you as you continue into the future.*

At some point in the journey, people describe meeting someone who understands that perhaps the greatest gift for one who has felt so inadequate and peripheral is the investment of confidence and faith. This is also a type of mirroring. It comes in the form of enthusiastic expressions of support and in the quiet communication of trust that accompany teaching and mentoring. Sometimes it is done directly and purposefully, as if to fill a tank that has long been empty. Robert's team of supervisors would consistently cheer him when he was doing well or when he had negotiated another hurdle. They were warm in their praise and affectionate in their tone.

> *They were always pulling for me. I felt really loved by everyone. They treated me like I was their favorite, and kept on telling me how big an accomplishment it was to turn around my drinking and self-destructive behaviors. The way they were, it was promotion, not pressure.*

His supervisors also required that Robert be responsible for his actions. This communicated two important messages: that they were confident that he was able to exercise discrimination and restraint, and that he was worth the close attention and scrutiny they provided. Both messages were clearly appreciated by Robert.

They were strict. They expected a lot from me, but they were ready to give six, seven, eight chances. They'd never give up on you. There was a lot of support. They also let me work at my own pace. So I learned, when things get a little crazy, how to stop them from snowballing. Now I can talk about it first. Admit I screwed up. I don't have to bottom out to start over.

The investment of confidence helps us to tap hidden resources. Receiving such trust and faith enables us to believe in ourselves. We develop deeper trust in our perceptions and reasoning abilities, and then develop a greater sense of our own competence. With this kind of mirroring, we are able to understand our own styles of learning—how we learn best. Some people grasp concepts quickly but need help in applying them. Some are overly quick to take action and need to slow down a bit to reflect.

Catherine was angry and frustrated. In some ways, her second suicide attempt was a throwback to earlier days—days when the rage was so strong and when she felt so undervalued that there was no way for her to express her feelings other than self-destruction. This time, however, she knew the moment she was placed in the hospital just where to get the understanding she needed. She also knew it wouldn't be easy.

I was in the behavioral sciences wing for about two weeks following the attempt. I was assigned a psychiatrist, and I didn't like him at all. He had a real aggressive nature, and he wanted to give me medication. I told him I didn't want the drugs. He didn't help me. He was definitely a "You have to go along with the program or you're not doing it right" kind of person.

Catherine wouldn't be thwarted. From the hospital, she called a man who was well known in town. He was the director of a local pain clinic, and a meditation teacher. Catherine was white, born and raised in the southwest; Patrick was an African-American born on the islands off South Carolina. Her background was strictly Roman Catholic, and he had taken vows as a Buddhist. But her hunger for guidance was strong, and it rendered their individual differences irrelevant. Their relationship was forged on the anvils of confidence, mutual respect, and hard work.

Catherine would call him daily from the hospital, agitated and exasperated. She wanted to be discharged, but by law she had to remain there. Patrick's voice was steady, his outlook hopeful; he expressed faith in her resourcefulness. He began to teach her how to help herself.

> *He taught me some things that I still use. He taught me how to work with all the nervousness and irritation inside. He taught me some breathing exercises, over the phone. Some things to imagine before I went to sleep. I practiced them and it worked! He challenged me to stop smoking cigarettes and was merciless! Some days in the hospital, I'd be crying. I would tell him, "Patrick, I just want to get out of here!" He'd say, "Use this place as a temple. Try to learn as much as you can from being there."*

SEEING A BIGGER PICTURE

> *I needed to hear that there are other options besides killing myself. (Deborah)*

People who have been most helpful to those in recovery have demonstrated the ability to be intimately involved without becoming unbalanced in the drama of the attempt. They maintain perspective, and continually endeavor to relate to the person rather than the events surrounding him or her. This in itself constitutes a form of the missing experience.

At breakfast the morning after her attempt, Deborah needed a bigger picture—a portrait of the future that didn't include killing herself. Simply and directly, her friend tried as best he could to help her.

> He said that I was important to him and he wanted to remain my friend, and he said, "The only way you're gonna do that is alive— both of us alive, in the same time and place." He said, "These are the ways I can help, and these are the ways I know help other people. It's not over."

These kind words had enormous impact. Deborah's perspective had been truncated so drastically that she could see no further than the present moment. She no longer felt like killing herself, but she still feared what the future might hold. If not a full portrait, her friend offered at least the outlines of a future which contained the possibility for healing and at least one good relationship.

> Like if you're going down a creek and you're in the boat and you can't see what's up ahead. But if you were able to float up like a bird, suddenly you would have this view and you'd get to see that the river actually turns a whole bunch. There are some rapids, but calm spots too; up there's a cliff; and there's the background. All of a sudden, there's this view that you've got which is available to you, that isn't when you're down inside the boat. That's what he gave me that morning when we talked.

The best helpers also seem able to maintain a long-range view. Perhaps from years of experience, they can see the "big picture"; and they understand that the heart will mend and that true self-worth ripens slowly.

Soon after kicking heroin, Rennie stopped drinking. Next, she

wanted to stop smoking cigarettes. She began to relish each challenge. She developed a method for each of these adventures. First,
she would rally support—tell people who cared what she was
attempting to do—and then she would throw herself into the task.
Later they would all talk about it. She was learning what worked best
for her, and her confidence soared.

Rennie had come a long way. She had developed a flexibility of
mind and was able to learn from an increasing variety of situations.
Along the way, she found mentors with a wide range of styles. Peter
was one. During her unavoidable disappointments, he was encouraging, yet firm. During her ecstatic successes, he kept her feet on the
ground. He played the pole to her tetherball, as she traveled the
spirals of her recovery.

> Peter was always there for me, but in a challenging way. He was
> my sponsor in AA, and we had the most incredible relationship. He
> didn't make it easy. There was nothing he wanted from me, and he
> was always painfully honest. I completely trusted him. Sometimes,
> when I was clingy—when I wanted someone to hold onto—he
> would pull the rug out from under me and say, "Wait a minute.
> You can do this by yourself." It never felt like he was abandoning
> me. He was always there for me, but he wouldn't do things for me.

The relationship that Rennie and Peter created was governed by
mutual trust and exacting truthfulness. Rennie provided the desire
for freedom and Peter provocatively offered encouragement and
insight. Over time and with Peter's help, Rennie grew to enjoy the
challenge of discovering herself.

> One thing that really turned my head around was when I quit
> smoking. I went through some really nasty times, almost as bad as
> with the heroin. I felt like I was this infant left out in the snow by
> myself and I was just wailing and wailing. One time it got really
> bad and I called Peter.

He was away, so it took a few days for him to get back to me.
He called just after listening to my many messages. He said,
"What happened? What happened?" I described how I was feel-
ing. I said, "Oh, God! I thought this was the end," and I described
how I thought I was gonna die, and how I was wailing, and how
difficult. Well, he just let me finish talking and then he asked,
"Well, did you enjoy it?" I was shocked! But then I thought about
it and said, "Well, I guess in a strange way, I did!" That was a
big lesson—that a lot of times, even when I think I'm not, I'm
enjoying it!

EXPERIENCING THE HUMANNESS
OF OTHERS

People who are returning to life are often touched by the honesty
and humanness of others. Perhaps nothing is more important,
therefore, when relating to survivors of suicide attempts than allowing one's humanness to be a significant part of the exchange. This
provides the survivor an experience that was missing before and
during the suicidal episode—an authentic interpersonal exchange.
By the time the suicidal trance develops, one's world has become
virtually devoid of intimate connection. As the distress intensifies,
people often experience greater caution and discomfort from others
rather than a genuine connection. Those who understand this and
have allowed their humanness to guide them often provide the most
positive influences on people who are recovering.

Madeline's experience illustrates this. For years she had been
searching for someone to appreciate how devastated she felt after
ending a marriage that had borne four children and that had been
her vehicle for political action for almost half a century. She felt
friends expected her to "get over it" quickly, and some of the therapists who had been recommended also grew exasperated with the
tenacity of her pain. Eventually, as we've heard, she found a therapist
who asked her to describe her separation in detail, and she finally

was able to plumb the depths of her loss, grieve for the end of her
marriage, and move on.

I was curious as to why she trusted this particular therapist more
than the others she had seen. After so many disappointments, why
did she choose him? Her reply spoke directly to her appreciation of
his humanness and his ability to weave it into his therapeutic style.

> *Octavio and I hit it off right away. I had to have a feeling of real*
> *interaction from a therapist. I needed to see his humanity. He told*
> *me about his early life in Chile. He was straightforward and*
> *honest. He even told me that he had been arrested and tortured*
> *there. He told me that one day he sat down and asked himself,*
> *"What do I want to do with the rest of my life? There may not be*
> *much more of it." He was talking about himself, but I knew he was*
> *talking to me as well.*

Often, people *discover* themselves to be an important part of
another's recovery. It wasn't a job they had contracted for, or an
official assignment. The connection may arise from deep filial
devotion, from strong friendship, or more simply from one's compassion for others. But even if one is highly trained, there is no
prescription for how to be human. In ways infinitely varied, people
share their stories, display their eccentricities, and permit their
emotions to be seen and felt. However this is accomplished, people
choose to let go of traditional roles or conventional expectations and
allow themselves to become visible. The results, as Teresa describes,
are often unexpectedly effective.

> *I remember talking to the social worker there, Lois. I said some*
> *horrible things to her about my abuse, and I expected her to do*
> *what everybody did—close down, get a chalk-white face, and just*
> *get me out of there as soon as possible. But she cried! She cried, and*
> *had expressions on her face that I had never seen looking at me*

before. She never took her eyes off me, and her face showed the pain. I mean her face actually showed the effect of what I was saying!

Mattie had never known anybody like Aaron. She was in the middle of an argument with a former boyfriend when he called. Aaron had just arrived in town from New York, and was entering the graduate program in which Mattie was a student. He had some questions.

I was annoyed. "Why is he bothering me now?" I got off the phone pretty quickly, but as I hung up I had this thought, "This is the man I am going to marry, sure as the day I was born"—and I hadn't even seen him yet!

Her previous boyfriend had blond hair and blue eyes, and he was tall and broad-shouldered, so in many ways, except relationally, he was the man of her dreams. She was startled, therefore, upon her first sight of Aaron.

I thought, "How can I be with this person?" He's shorter than I am, darker and heavier. After some weeks, he told me he would like to pursue the relationship further. He was awkward and embarrassed and kind of formal about it. He was someone who was tender and sweet and attentive to me—who really liked me. I think I was so hungry for that that I was smart enough to hang in there even though another part of me was pushing him away.

A number of critical incidents sealed their improbable relationship and provided Mattie with partnership during her long journey of recovery. Mattie had become pregnant. She planned a trip to Seattle—the basement of the airport, specifically—where people flew to have abortions. She intended to go alone, but Aaron refused to let her. He was adamant.

I didn't know who the father was. The two possibilities disavowed having anything to do with it, and Aaron just took over. He was wonderful. I was having real trouble letting him do that. I was secretly having fantasies of bleeding to death by the side of the road. I kept trying to push him away, and he kept sticking, like Super Glue.

Long-term relationships provide an opportunity to grow and change. They can help suspend one's desire to die, and help re-create one's relationship to life. They are not always easy, as Mattie learned, but the rewards are worth it. Through his clear thinking and foresight, Aaron challenged her to grow.

Later on in the relationship, he was like an anchor. He was so grounded, and so into wanting genuine relating, that he became a symbol to me that it was okay to be here—to be alive. He was thoughtful, too—thinking about what would help the relation-ship. When he would get mad at me, I would freak out. I was totally terrified of people being mad at me. He would just be normal mad—it was pretty common in his family—but I'd freak. One day he said, "We can't have a relationship unless you learn to express your anger and deal with mine." It was kind and clear.

Mattie accepted the challenge to transcend her fears, and grew stronger. In time she realized her dream of a healthy and mutually respectful relationship, and eventually began to challenge Aaron.

I think there are definitely places that I couldn't have gone without this relationship, hard as it was sometimes. The last test was, after I had him up on a pedestal for so long, we went through the stage of me bringing him down, about ten feet under! It was hard for him, but he stayed and we made it through. I'm not sure I would ever have made it without him.

EXTENDING TO FAMILY

Receiving the "missing experience" allows people to feel nourished and emboldened in ways that were impossible during their withdrawal and their suicidal trances. They become more open to expressions of respect and confidence, develop broader perspectives, and are able to accept the gift of other people's humanity. A final achievement often noted involves the creation of a healthy relationship with one's family, redressing what was wrong in the past, and charting a more positive future. Sometimes the new family relationship includes the birth of a child.

> *[With] my newborn, I felt worthy, because I had this God-given miracle, this child to work with in my life. I had a chance to see through her eyes. It opened me up to an innocence that I couldn't see before. That's what started opening doors. (Catherine)*

The birth of a child changes lives. It allows us to reexperience an innocence long past and to feel unconditional love. It is a mistake, however, to assume that parenthood mends everything that is broken and creates clarity where confusion has reigned. Nevertheless, for some of those who appear in this book, raising a child has added significance to their future and given them added motivation to deal with the past.

Having a suicidal history adds a unique dimension to a person's role as a parent. The decision to end one's life meant that there would never be anyone to follow. A decision was made, as Mark wrote, "to put a period at the end of a run-on sentence." Now, the person chooses life not only for himself or herself, but for another human being.

Giving birth to her daughter allowed Mattie to feel for the first time that she had "landed on the planet." She gave birth to a sense of belonging as well as to a child. For the first time, she felt free of shame, and was able to master her potentially fatal eating disorder. Similarly, Karen, upon giving birth, decided to "connect with at least one person on the planet—my child!" It would take time for her to bridge to others, as well as an enormous leap of faith, but the relationship with her son gave her a new perspective.

For people who were already parents, the decision to die, knowing their children would be left with the riddle of their parents' suicides, made them overwhelmingly conflicted. Some reasoned that their children would be left in better hands. Some believed that their children would barely miss them.

Chris could not describe without tears the pain of hearing her daughter scream after her the dark night of her suicide attempt. She will feel that pain for the rest of her life—a wound reminding her of how unworthy she felt and what she almost lost. She came within a hair's breadth of losing not only her life but her daughter as well. For some years during her road back, Chris nurtured that child's life gently, as one would cradle an egg about to hatch. Her daughter became her cause and her primary focus of concern, until a broader vision could take hold.

For Catherine, parenting also proved to be an enormously rich source of inspiration during her road back.

> I wanted that child to have a better chance at life than I did. Being able to see the world through that child's eyes—how innocent, how clean, how warm, how happy. It was refreshing. I realized that I could create that for her and for myself, and having a few mess-ups on the way was gonna be okay. We might get off the track, but we'll get back on.

> I started praying, talking to God, meditating, and listening in earnest after that. My child became a new motivation for figuring out what was healthy for me. I read a lot, learned things through people like Patrick, and learned to watch people—I watch what they do. Now I really look to see who seems happy and who's not.

Ten

Giving Back

The recovery process is necessarily deeply introspective and self-focused. Those recovering have rescued their lives from near disaster. They have replaced crushing hopelessness and unbearable pain with confidence, personal and professional success, and, in many cases, optimism. Such accomplishments are a testament to the resilience of the human spirit and an affirmation of what collective efforts can achieve.

There is a final step in successful recovery, however, that completes the cycle of healing. This occurs when people emerge from the emphasis on their own struggles, and devote time and energy to the problems of others. The act of "giving back" is an offering to others of what one has learned along the way. It serves to integrate the lessons learned and insights gleaned during the road back.

An overwhelming proportion of those interviewed for this study are now devoting their lives to some form of community service. Some are doing medical or mental health work; some are utilizing art of various forms to benefit others. They work intensively with individuals or with groups, or they attempt to affect public policy and educate the general population. Some are physicians or nurses; many are now therapists. Some have become writers of theatrical or technical works. Many volunteer their time at suicide-prevention centers, feeling that they are singularly well equipped to understand the darkness that surrounds suicide.

Vic now lives in northern California. Four or five afternoons a week, he takes a phone shift at the local suicide prevention center.

> *I didn't know if I was going to able to help. Not until that first call, when somebody said, "You don't know what the hell I'm talking about," and I could say, "Yes I do, 'cause I've lived it." Sometimes I can be feeling pretty depressed, and as soon as I get the first phone call, I can feel myself lifting up.*

> *For me, it's kind of like my therapy, too. It's a two-way communication the way I do it. They talk and I talk. You know, they want to hear about other people's lives. They want to hear a voice that knows. Sometimes I just feel really good. I think, "What I did back five years ago can be turned around to help somebody so maybe they don't have to go through it."*

Rennie is completing her degree in Chinese medicine. Through acupuncture and the application of herbs, she is successfully treating people who want to end their drug addictions. Robert is in training as an emergency medical technician, and Karen has received a master's degree in counseling. Her great love involves working with artists whose creativity is blocked.

Mattie is a psychotherapist and clinical supervisor with many years of experience. She has specialized in working with women who have been abused, and is highly regarded for her skills as a group therapist. She echoes what many have stated: that at some point in the recovery, personal healing is furthered through a broader focus and a commitment to others.

I'm alive not only to heal myself, but to help other women heal as well. It's been important for me to learn to see the bigger picture, and I'm trying to help others do the same. It's easier then to be hopeful or excited about even the "bad" things that happen, when you know it's just part of a larger process.

Ed has created an educational corporation, Alive to Thrive, which produces materials designed specifically to reach children, teenagers, and people who are drug-addicted or suicidal. More recently his work has expanded to include the disabled. He is completing another book of essays and poems, and as time passes, he sees his work less as suicide prevention and more as life enhancement. His choices illustrate how "giving back" is both an offering of his hard-won expertise to others and an experience of further healing for himself, as he earns appreciation and respect. Recently, Ed was asked by the Federal Bureau of Investigation to speak at an "advanced crisis negotiation seminar." Following his participation, he received this letter:

I would like to thank you for the outstanding presentation. Your open and frank discussion of suicide and depression, both on a personal and professional level, was deeply moving for the class. These seasoned and experienced police officers from around the U.S. and abroad found your presentation to be extremely meaningful. On a personal note, I cannot thank you enough for your dedication and willingness to share your knowledge and wisdom with all of us.

Some altruistic ventures, like Ed's, are large undertakings. Other acts of service are smaller but no less significant. Teresa has been a practicing nurse for the past ten years. She has studied a number of medical specialties and enjoys a wealth of work experience. On certain days, quietly, she performs a little ritual.

Sometimes when I look at the charts, I read about these ladies—
what they do, what's happened to them, the difficulty they're in—
and I think, "God, you know, I could be there today if I hadn't been
so lucky." I go down to the unit and talk to them. I want them to
know that there's strength in them: you can hear it in their voices. I
want them to know that we all have that drive in us to make it.

For many, the act of giving is intimately linked to a sense of
spirituality. Karl has devoted his life to his street ministry, address-
ing a deep and abiding social conscience. He is a priest of the
disenfranchised, and that work leaves him feeling richer than he
could ever have imagined years ago.

Altruism forms the bedrock of Catherine's spiritual practice.
Through her volunteer work, she has realized the relationship
between helping others and healing herself.

It opens my heart. It keeps it soft. You do things for people. You act
in a certain way, in the spirit of Jesus or the Buddha, or whoever.
When I spend time with people suffering from AIDS, I don't claim
to understand homosexuality, but all I can see is a needy human
being, and if I get too caught up in myself and worried about this
and that, then I'm not good here. I can be such a shit to myself, you
know? So the better I feel about myself, the more open I am to
seeing the goodness in other things, even AIDS.

Eleven

Now

A suicide attempt leaves its mark. Like the wound Jacob received when he wrestled with the angel of God, it is deep and lasting. Recovery is the process wherein that wound is acknowledged and accepted: one allows oneself to be humbled and transformed by it, and one makes a choice to give up the war. People have chosen to leave the suicide trance and its distorted perceptions, and open themselves to the world in its entirety—good and bad, highs and lows. These choices can finally end one's commitment to the act of suicide, and transmute the wound into a guide and teacher. Instead of being a torturous or crippling reminder, the wound may become a symbol of a spiritual encounter—one that has changed a life forever and will never be forgotten.

We have come a long way in this book. We have explored the precipitous descent into suicide, investigated the desperate moments of the suicide attempt, and witnessed the difficult and often heroic return to life. People have made critical decisions—life-and-death decisions—and they've had to choose not once, but many times on the road back.

I have chosen to interview people who for the most part now lead lives that they find rich, meaningful, and satisfying. My purpose was not only to chart their recovery past the possibility of attempting suicide again, but to follow their progress to its apex. From their stories we can begin to understand how lives can be reborn like the mythical Phoenix, rising from its own ashes.

There are still important questions to ask, however: Have there been significant shifts in one's relationship to the world? Have there been major changes at the deepest levels of self? In previous chapters, we have examined personal experiences of the suicide attempt in great detail. This chapter provides a final opportunity to review and summarize. Here, we can pull back from the details and identify the broad strokes—the major shifts that have consolidated hard-won gains.

"Giving Back" is one of these major shifts—people reorienting from an almost absolute focus on oneself to an altruistic commitment to helping others. In doing so, people have applied what they've learned, expanded their sense of personal identity, and realized the connection between their personal growth and the social welfare of others.

There are four additional dimensions in which such major shifts take place. Progress along each of these pathways is essential to the successful recovery from suicidal pain. This includes the movement

- From powerlessness to authorship
- From loss of faith to a working relationship with the spiritual
- From being feeling "stuck" to becoming "unstuck," and
- From a lack of belonging to a sense of place

At some point the journey of recovery and the ongoing process of growth become indistinguishable. One's identity as a survivor of a suicide attempt fades and is replaced by an image of oneself as someone who continues to grow and struggle like everyone else, learning how best to work with oneself in ways that lead to happiness and fulfillment. There is no end to this process, and people who have traveled the perilous road back from suicide understand this perhaps better than most. Their growth is their lifeline. Like all humans, they can become enmired in old thoughts and old patterns, but they have developed strategies for freeing themselves of these. And although there is no sharp dividing line between recovering and recovered, their relationship with themselves and with the world has fundamentally changed.

FROM POWERLESSNESS TO AUTHORSHIP

The darkest moments of the suicidal trance occur just before and during the attempt. Whether they bring a cacophony of raging thoughts and feelings or a deathly stillness, they are pervaded by a sense of powerlessness—impotence to alter the downward course of a life besieged by unbearable pain and suffering, with seemingly no hope of relief from within or without.

One of the most significant shifts that occurs during the road back is the birth of "authorship": the ability to act, which is engendered by the will to live. Central to the rediscovery of one's aliveness is the growing belief that it is possible to make choices that affect one's destiny. Like dawn in a forest, the light may enter slowly and quietly, but it raises one's spirit and is rarely forgotten. "Authorship" means the capability of making choices, and the recognition that the ability to choose one's destiny lies within oneself. For those who recover, it is this connection with their inner oracle that becomes paramount. As Teresa describes it:

> I hear that strong person inside telling me what to do, and most of the time I listen. Sometimes I don't and I suffer the consequences, but at least I consciously know what choice I've made.

Sharon, whose mother attempted suicide every two years, began to realize that her destiny was in her own hands. Her models when she was growing up were confusing. On better days, her mother was a powerful and decisive woman, but at other times she felt deeply victimized by her pain and was self-destructive. For much of her own adulthood, Sharon felt doubtful that her fate would be any different.

> *I finally understood clearly that I could continue down this road, or I could realize that my choices in life—are my choices. I developed this feeling of love for myself, through therapy and good friendships, and I said, "Look, we've gone this far down the path; let's not make it any worse than it has been."*

> *You know, we don't know how much time we have left, so if you don't know, then you better be doing what you want to be doing. I've now given myself tremendous permission. I've decided not to go back to my job—to what I was doing. It's a lot of money to give up, but I was so unhappy. At this point, if I want to stay in bed all day, or sit and read a good book—eat ice cream—I give myself permission. I mean stuff I thought I'd do in retirement. But we may not get to retirement.*

Rennie awoke from her last attempt with a certainty that she had to end her drug addiction. Unless she did, she felt she could never understand the meaning and purpose of her life. She credits that decision, and the courage to kick heroin, with generating the momentum that carried her through the difficult periods. Cassie was told she was living someone else's idea of what life should be, and the seeds of her own "authorship" were planted.

Robert had tried every form of truancy, just about every drug available to him, and most kinds of liquor produced in the United States. He had spent time in juvenile detention, in an inpatient treatment facility, a residential group home, and on the streets. There was barely a life-style he hadn't tried. After all the help—all the experiences—he had to reckon with himself.

I said to myself, "I'm tired of this life-style. I'm tired of giving in to my negative side." I wanted to accomplish something—to be somebody. I didn't want to be homeless on the streets or a high school dropout living in some little shack with a wife and three kids and starving. I didn't want that. I wanted to be successful.

The decision to assume authorship of one's life often emerges from considerable pain. The journey of recovery often entails having exhausted the limited options we thought were given us, and discovering that there are near-limitless possibilities from which we can choose. Those who understand this have learned both the freedom involved in choice-making and the power of authorship.

The first decision Ed had to make was to live. A full and creative life, however, would require more.

It's not enough to say, "Don't commit suicide," or "Don't take drugs." You've also got to ask, "What do you have that's better? What's gonna turn me on to life?" Carpe diem! Seize the day! You have to make your life extraordinary—if it's music, if it's art, if it's philosophy, if it's sports, whatever. Put your energy into something that you believe in, and then share it. Don't keep it all to yourself!

FROM LOSS OF FAITH TO
SPIRITUAL GROUND

My parents are fundamentalist Christians and Aaron comes from a line of orthodox rabbis! So I just have a horror of anything that smacks of religion. I don't even like the word spirituality!

But for want of a better word, there's some "thing" beyond me, or maybe it's that part of me—some sort of oneness, wholeness, connectedness that we're part of. It keeps me interested and it keeps me going—the mysteries of life. (Mattie)

Many people who have survived not only the attempt to kill themselves but also the arduous process of recovery, have turned toward religion or spiritual practice in an effort to understand where they've been and where they are going. Most have felt so forsaken in the world they knew that they feel it imperative not only to assert their desire to live but to seek a new understanding of the world and how it works. Many have spoken of their need for a more harmonious life and also a search for meaning—a sense of purpose beyond mere survival. Most spiritual practices emphasize charity toward others as well as religious contemplation, and many who have attempted suicide find that this duality has a relationship to their recovery.

Now I believe that people come into this world with a purpose. It's a spiritual practice and a way of living on the planet. My lesson was to learn to like myself, and my purpose is "joy through service." My pleasure is from doing it, not from getting back. (Cassie)

Catherine began to attend church again. Her meditation teacher helped her to blend her strong religious tradition with practical matters of the present. She began to read voraciously, from the Gospels to the Mystics, the Buddhists to the Gnostics. She is creating an active spiritual practice for herself, rich in diversity.

I go to church every Sunday. I like to keep a spiritual ritual going and to keep it alive for me. I don't agree with a lot of things that the Catholic church says, but I feel most comfortable with it because it was the way I was raised. Even as a child, I had a lot of faith in praying to God. My faith and practice has deepened a lot since all this.

I've also gone to meditation classes. Now I meditate on compassion, understanding, love for myself. It doesn't happen overnight.

Sometimes I'd sit hour after hour and it would be cold and dark
again in there, and then the next moment, it would change and I'd
be just floating. I feel I have tools now. Faith and tools. Now I think
God is everything—the good and the bad.

Some, like Catherine, have returned to earlier religious affiliations
but have made significant changes based on their suicidal experiences. Others, no less devout, chart their own spiritual paths. Their
practices may be less formal, but are no less significant.

Tim chooses each day to open his heart as wide as possible. In
addition to dance and music, he has become trained in rehabilitation psychology. He is now pursuing a graduate degree in counseling, learning to work more effectively with a wide range of the more
severe psychological problems. He is a far cry from the young man
who only years ago nearly succumbed to unbearable rage and pain.

You know, my vision had been to go away to the mountains and
die. Now, even if there were a Black Plague or a Holocaust, I would
live it to the point that I died, you know? I would try to be as
conscious and loving as I could in the moment.

One of the really profound moments I had in the past few years
was when I saw La Bohème. *I realized as I was sitting there that*
God wants me to embrace all this stuff—everything—and as I do
that, my heart grows, my spirit grows. Sitting there that night, I
had such a feeling of expansion. I cried like a baby.

Chris had always felt some presence—some form of energy or
warmth—close by. It was there upon getting into bed after taking
the pills, and she felt it near when she lay under the bridge and saw
the beauty of the full moon. But during the confusion of her suicide
attempt she misunderstood it to be a confirmation of her choice to
die.

That presence has now become a cornerstone of Chris's spiritual practice. Her experience suggests to her that it is possible to achieve a state of being that is pure and undivided, and she aspires to attain it consistently. She has devoted herself to studying texts from a wide selection of spiritual traditions, and she spends time each day in meditation.

> *Sometimes when I'm meditating, I'll feel it, that sense of presence—absolutely right, completely whole. For a few moments, I'll feel really held, really blessed.*

Ruth can't yet name the force that she has experienced, but she is aware that it is part of her recovery and accords it respect.

> *There's a power that's bigger than myself that has kept me alive this long, despite how severe my suicide attempts were. I seem to be connected to it and it's connected to me, and if I let myself surrender to it, then there's so much more that can happen. I've realized that I can't and don't control everything. Something's brought me this far, and if I just shut up and let it happen, I'll be directed.*

Sharon doesn't have a name for the higher force she has experienced, either. It doesn't seem to be identified with any religion or institution, and that's fine with her. After years of struggle, she has discovered that spiritual attainment does not depend on esoteric practices, nor on temples, nor other conventional places of worship. Sharon has discovered spiritual reverie in ordinary things.

> *It's made me see that you can take pleasure in the smallest of things. The touch of your skin. A scent from somewhere. Just reading a book. Some really major things have shifted for me, but it all started with the realization that there could be small pleasures in life as it is.*

FROM BEING STUCK TO
BECOMING UNSTUCK

*I had this dream. The last scene was a field of sunflowers
nodding in the sunshine and someone saying to me, "Life
has no form but life itself." I didn't know what it meant
at the time, but it felt like she was telling me the real stuff.
It was about cycles, and patience. (Chris)*

*In fact, every time it occurs, I say, "What is this, a test?"
(Cassie)*

The process of healing is never linear. Progress toward happiness
is accompanied by setbacks, hesitations, moments of losing one's
balance, and even by the gravitational pull back toward suicide.
There are very few who, having attempted suicide, fail to entertain
the idea of it again. In fact, for those who have recovered their will to
live, health is not the absence of suicidal thoughts, but a markedly
different attitude toward them.

Roberta, the Peruvian woman who almost killed both herself and
her children, discussed this in a letter:

*[Recovery] has to now respectfully include that a phenomenon
such as suicidal trance can occur. It has to acknowledge that others
may or may not be there for us. You have to extend beyond the veils
that cloud most people's sight. There is some unspeakable under-
belly of life that you have visited and have come out alive. It is a
long road, and recovery is trusting that life holds all possibilities
when before, it seemed to hold none.*

Whereas previously, suicidal thoughts and images occupied the
center of one's consciousness, now they simply take their places in a

stream of diverse sensations and images. One notices them, perhaps investigates them a bit, and then lets them go.

When I get in that stuck place, I completely lose track of the fact that 95 percent of the rest of my life is fine. While I'm in that, it feels like that's all there is. Now I remind myself to give it ten minutes. "Just wait, and if you're patient, it will change." You don't know how or into what, but it will change, and so let's see. (Chris)

Suicidal thoughts and the adversity that generates them become a traveling companion on the journey of growth and awareness. Thoughts that once nearly destroyed an already fragile psyche now serve to warn that old patterns are being triggered and need attention. Ian found it difficult to summon the centrifugal force necessary to escape his predisposition toward self-sacrifice. Time and time again he would avoid conflict by adopting a pleasing demeanor, but would be seething inside. The results were costly to him, for it felt as if he were trespassing over his own soul.

It's still very seductive to get back into that—very difficult. Last week Kevin, my "ex," was admitted to the hospital, on my floor. I work on the oncology floor, where they put a lot of HIV patients. By Friday night, he was spiking a temperature of 105. I still care a lot about him, but it also brought back the feelings of being alone—worthless—because there's Kevin with his partner, and I didn't have somebody to care for.

It used to be my job to take care of him! I started to pester the nurses and doctors to get really involved in how he was doing from hour to hour, making suggestions. At some point, I finally got it. I understood what I was doing. I realized I was buying back into this again. I said to myself, "Wait a minute! These nurses are competent professionals. They do this all the time. I know because I work with them!" And I pulled back.

*Hopefully, I'll be able to recognize the trigger even earlier. Some-
day, I may be able to catch it before it occurs!*

Ian is describing what many have identified as critical to their
recovery. A crucial point on the road back is the time when a sense
of proportion returns. Events that previously signaled the end of
all hope now become only moderate disappointments. They are
unpleasant, perhaps, but survivable. Feelings that at one time
seemed to crush the spirit now serve as reminders that one can
respond in other than suicidal ways. When Ian allowed himself to
feel the grief that he had held in since he was a child, he discovered
the capacity to reevaluate the importance of his relationships to his
life as a whole.

*At that point, the relationship stopped becoming the focus of my
life. It became just a relationship, as opposed to my whole reason
for being. I could grieve for it, because it became a real loss at that
point, not symbolic of everything.*

Years have passed, and Teresa has now permitted herself limited
contact with her mother. She feels it's important for her and her
children, but it is rarely satisfying. Teresa finds her mother unable to
focus long enough or deeply enough to sustain meaningful conversation, and although Teresa sometimes feels the desire to spill her
heart and describe in detail the journey she has made, she knows her
story would fall on unreceptive ears. This is disappointing, and
occasionally it reminds her of the isolation that was so painful to her
as an adolescent. Over time, however, Teresa has detected a change
within herself. Her mother is no longer the center of her world nor
the source of her redemption. Through years of therapy and study,
trial and error, Teresa has created a rich network of support and
understanding. She has internalized the respect and the positive
regard others have shown toward her, and her mother's failings are
rendered more or less harmless.

I'm finally letting myself realize that she doesn't have the capability to relate because she's never left that zone where she feels comfortable. She doesn't talk about what's real and she hides a lot, but I've wanted to attempt to have a functional relationship with her.

The hate—the hate I felt for her—began to consume me. It can eat at you more than at the other person. I don't hate her anymore. I mostly feel a lot of sorrow and compassion. It was a big thing when I discovered that I really don't have to like my mother as a person. I love her, but I don't care to be around her all that much. I get understanding and recognition elsewhere.

Developing a sense of proportion enables people to negotiate the circuitous and sometimes painful road back to life. Although in the past they rarely enjoyed the emotional latitude to roll with life's punches, they are more skillfully able to do that now. Little upsets remain so, and bigger ones are met with a sense of challenge, purpose, or, if nothing more, a sense of humor. Perhaps no one has expressed her newly found sense of proportion more robustly than Sharon: "I mean, life is life, and your emotions are only emotions, so let's get on with it!"

FROM A LACK OF BELONGING TO A SENSE OF PLACE

I was on a meditation retreat. It was in silence, the entire ten days. I would wake up in the morning and hear the birds chirping outside. As I listened, I started laughing. The notes that the birds sang seemed to fit right into a song by a new group called The Digable Planets. I've listened to that song on my Walkman while doing aerobics. It sounded like the birds were singing the chorus: "It's good to be here. It's good to be here." (Faith)

The experience of belonging can be defined in many ways. It refers to the experience of feeling "grounded"—connected to ourselves, to our bodies. It describes our affiliation with the rest of humankind, and the space we occupy as a living beings on the planet. Belonging also refers to a sense of place, of being "at home," greater and deeper than in any particular location. It is a tangible feeling of being connected. Everyone shares in the search for rootedness throughout one's lifetime, but perhaps no one experiences this search as intensely as one who has attempted or contemplated suicide.

It is difficult, if not impossible, to experience a sense of belonging and at the same time feel suicidal. The experience of the suicidal trance and its precursors is so extreme that most often such a deep sense of connection is severed. In the recovery from suicidal despair, however, one of the most profound shifts is from disconnection and alienation to a sense of belonging. People who once felt separate from humankind and profoundly different from others are now cultivating a sense of connectedness, to carefully selected social networks and even to the earth itself.

Karen needed virtual seclusion in order to reconnect to the world. The abuse she had suffered left her deeply mistrustful of others, and she felt her only choice was to begin again deep in the wilderness. Isolating herself on the land offered the opportunity to start over and discover her most elemental relationship to life. As she grew to feel stronger and her sense of connection with the land deepened, she slowly was able to allow others into that life.

Chris would take long walks in the countryside where she lived. For quite some time, only that place felt safe and nourishing. It was her lifeline; it was home. When she was away, she would long to return. As her healing progressed, however, she noticed that she had internalized her sense of place. It was with her regardless of where she was or what she was doing.

I felt like that was the only place I could live. I couldn't stand to be away. After a few years, though, I noticed that when I wasn't there, I could close my eyes and I could see myself walking on the land. I could feel the air, smell the trees, feel the paths under my feet. I was connected to it. It was inside of me.

Recently, geography is less important to me. It's less important to be "there." It's even less important for me to have a home. I feel like I have home inside me now.

There are two steps to reestablishing (or creating for the first time) a deep and enduring sense of belonging. The first is what we have called "breaking context." It was necessary to leave—physically or psychologically—the social context in which one's trance developed. The second step involves broadening the scope of one's belonging. This step reflects a progression from inner to outer. It starts with the awakening of one's senses, and the feeling of being connected to one's body. It continues to develop through special relationships: with therapists, "significant others," friends, and mentors. One's connection then expands to the broader community of humankind; and some, like Karen and Chris, find their place in the ecological community of all living beings. For when we pull the camera back to obtain a wider view, we can see that the quest for belonging extends beyond the limited world of one's original family—beyond the social context that gave rise to the trance—toward greater humankind. These leaps take time, and as Roberta describes, arise from very simple beginnings.

For me, the first sense of connection happened with my body. It was a physical sensation of actually living in my own skin. It shocked me, because I wasn't aware I was out of living out of it!

Then I started noticing colors, and feeling the sun and the air on my body. All my senses were coming alive. You know, I was poised for flight for so long—always ready to leave—that I never noticed

these things. My first sense of connection again was with the
physicalness of the world.

Belonging also arises from the perception that one is important
to others, and that one may have a specific role to play in their lives.
The losses and abuses Ruth suffered gave rise to a profound doubt
that this was true for her. Compounding her pain, she always
assumed how little her presence meant.

In the course of deciding to live—making that commitment—the
people in my life began taking on more importance. I realized how
important I was to my remaining family, my cousins. They're nine
and fourteen. It would be devastating to them if I wasn't here.

Ruth also discovered that part of belonging is learning the art of
creating community. It was a skill she hadn't exercised for twenty
years, and its disuse was reinforced by the belief that no one would
care to join her. During her recovery, she committed herself to
reaching out to colleagues. In a sense, the actual results were
secondary to the fact that she was taking the initiative, for in
asserting her desire for friendship she was claiming her place in the
human family. To her delight, people responded in kind.

I started putting effort into other relationships. I made a commit-
ment to be in touch with people three times a week. At first it was
an experiment. I discovered that when I reached out, people began
reaching back. I was astonished that when I was sick people would
call or bring me things. I never felt like I mattered before. Now, I
have a life!

In the course of recovery, some people experience a sense of
belonging whose boundaries expand beyond the personal. The
possibility that others too have experienced devastating pain is
recognized, not simply as an abstract concept but accompanied by

real compassion. One realizes that suffering is an inevitable part of
being alive, and differences in its form and intensity seem irrelevant.
Paradoxically, people begin to feel more closely connected to humankind through compassion for the same pain that once made
them feel so separate. One woman describes this experience as
kinship:

> I started thinking that possibly my pain is no greater than that of
> millions of other people. It occurred to me that I might not be the
> only one who has felt so much pain. At that moment, I started
> feeling a sense of kinship—that we've all suffered and that we're all
> connected in that way. That was when my walls began coming
> down. I could really feel people again: their pain, their love, their
> anger—all of it.

The feeling of belonging may extend even beyond the interpersonal theater, into trusting the journey of life, its ups and downs, and
regardless of how unfathomable. After years of feeling profoundly
separate from other people and from life itself, some begin to feel
themselves held and cradled by a greater force, confident that even if
fate isn't always benevolent, it is not to be feared.

Madeline finally allowed herself to grieve and say good-bye to her
failed marriage, but it left her cautious. Her trust in human relationships and in life had been compromised, and she was wary of
extending herself and being hurt. It was as if the world was flat, and
one false move would send her falling forever, and out of reach. At
seventy-four years of age, she didn't expect much of her life to
change. To her surprise, an unlikely encounter left her feeling quite
different.

> I was shocked, frankly! He is a bishop from Ghana, studying in
> America for a while. It was love at second sight! We met at a
> political function, introduced by old friends, and then he called
> and invited me to visit and meet his ten-year-old daughter. I'm

not really looking for a spouse, but I'm very surprised and happy. I never thought this would happen to me. We may be going to Ghana very shortly.

Madeline decided to take another risk. She is allowing herself joy and a sense of adventure. She is willingly entering new territory. Madeline is choosing to trust the enigmatic and serendipitous unfolding of life rather than retreat in fear, and regardless of how the relationship with her new friend evolves, this choice declares her trust in and connectedness to life.

It's scary, moving into the unknown like this. It may work out and it may not. There are definitely some obstacles. He's a black Methodist and I'm an old white Quaker! He's got a ten-year-old daughter, although I love her already. He's got his church and community in Africa, and although I'd be willing to go, who knows if they'd be willing to take me.

But you know, regardless of how this works out—and I'll probably be disappointed if it doesn't—I feel a lot of joy and happiness again. I'm not afraid to feel that. And I feel it not only toward him, but toward my children and friends. Toward life. I don't know where this will end up, but I know I have other options, and I won't go through what I did before.

For those who have attempted or seriously contemplated suicide, the distance traveled, and the leaps of faith in allowing oneself to feel excitement and joy, are almost beyond comprehension. Our greatest lessons may be learned through pain, but they are best integrated through feelings of pleasure and well-being. The willingness to be alive on the planet—to be truly present—means we are ready for what life has to offer: pain and loss, to be sure, but also a full measure of joy, belonging, and fulfillment. In the return to life this willingness will dissolve what remains of the suicidal trance. And although there will always be an awareness of the trance and a profound respect for its power, something else has grown larger and taken root more deeply. The willingness to feel joy again may indeed be the strongest declaration that one has returned to life.

My journey to feel the joy of life was one that began to grab my interest. One day I was wondering, "What's the bridge to that?" when I suddenly realized that actually, I was the bridge. After all the work, it was in enjoying myself again that I began to feel a self big enough to help me step out of death hovering over my shoulder. (Roberta)

Epilogue:

Suicide Revisited

Attempting the physical part of the suicide, I don't think was useful. I mean, I could have died! (Rennie)

Waking Up, Alive was researched and written with the assumption that the most important questions about suicide can best be answered by people who have come as close as possible to the actual, lethal act and who have recovered. I've continually resisted turning to familiar theoretical positions concerning suicide, in favor of the real-life experiences and thoughtful reflections of those who once felt its grip, believing that the most important elements of the suicidal experience would emerge in the chronicles regardless of differences in the particular circumstances. The success of this work therefore rests on its ability to describe the many-layered experiences of those who have attempted suicide or seriously contemplated it and who have recovered.

At the close of each interview, I posed the same question to all the people I talked to: "Given the growth in your life—the happiness which you never expected to feel and the sense of purpose that had always eluded you—and given that this growth has happened after your attempt, would you recommend attempting suicide as a response to pain—as a solution?"

Most took some time to contemplate their response. They wanted to be clear, and they had many years to reflect on. Their suicide attempts represented the absolute bottom, the nadir of lives that had plummeted out of control; and yet it couldn't be denied that it was only after their suicide attempts that they were able, or willing, or ready, to begin the process of healing. For many, the attempt itself had shattered the suicidal trance. Once that was accomplished, it seemed they could allow the years of suppressed pain to emerge and build the skills necessary to negotiate their way to health. This gave rise to disturbing questions: Could it be that attempting suicide provides a catalyst that other experiences simply cannot? Is it necessary for people to descend so precipitously in order to arrest their fall?

This study sets forth the truth as experienced by those who had been there. I was especially interested to hear from those whose suicide attempts were the most severe. Not surprisingly, the answers were anything but uniform.

Chris has recently negotiated her second divorce. The marriages were similar in her choice of partners and in her tendency to submerge her own needs and desires. Chris had learned much in the years between marriages, and her second, although ending in divorce, felt much healthier than the first. Nevertheless, she suffered familiar feelings of despair and futility. And yet, rather quickly, with the support of friends, colleagues, and most of all, her now teenage children, she began to rebuild her life. Our first meeting took place on the morning when she and her second husband decided to separate; our final conversations occurred over a year and a half later. This period was one of the most painful since the time of her suicide attempt, and I was curious to hear her reply to my question.

Attempting suicide was a damn hard way to go. It's very destruc-
tive and painful. I wouldn't want anyone to succeed, you know?
No I don't recommend it at all. I know there are situations that are
really painful—emotional pain and physical pain. I would still try
to learn how to live through it, learn how to be with it in a different
way and gain from it what it is that there is to gain, rather than
attempting suicide. I recommend that to clients of mine as well.
Maybe that's heartless and cold, but after my experiences, I really
do feel that way.

Chris conveyed a certainty born of difficult experience. She was no
stranger to pain, but she emerged believing in its educational
properties. She was cautious not to proselytize, but now she strongly
feels that every instance of adversity contains the potential for growth.

Karen considered my question for some time. It seemed as
though she was scanning the many parameters involved in a co-
herent response. A visual artist, she answered with images. They
embraced her views not only on suicide but on what could possibly
have helped to break the trance in which she had been trapped.

If someone said to me, "You know what? It feels dead to you
because this reality just isn't alive. It makes sense that you'd be
going crazy. Let's go into the woods. Let's go to Kenya. Let's go
someplace different. Let's change reality. We can do it! You don't
have to die. We can kill this reality and then do something else.
You're just feeling bad right now and you don't see it, like a mouse
in a maze." You know, behind door number one there was abuse.
Door number two was boredom. Door three, freeways and chaos.
If that's all you see, then you say, "That's it, I should be dead." You
know, if someone said, "There's life beyond that. Let's make a
deal!"—You know, there are so many other ways to wake up.

Most people I asked now reject suicide as an escape from unbearable pain. Those who have recovered have entered a world vastly

different from the one they tried to leave. Their recovery wasn't simply a matter of becoming strong enough to handle the cold world that they had known, but of exercising their ability to reshape it into a different world—one of compassion and caring. Before the trance was broken, none of them were able to foresee their capacity to accomplish this.

When we last spoke, Tim had just returned from a four-week tour of Eastern Europe. His dance troupe traveled through Hungary, Turkey, Bulgaria, and even war-torn Croatia, in the former Yugoslavia. They performed their dances, learned new ones at small village parties that lasted late into the night, and continued to explore the lands whose music he loved so much. He found himself being a liaison between his troupe and local artists, and experienced a new strength within himself.

> It was a very important demonstration of how far I've come—how resilient I am now. I was the one who reached out to people, even though I didn't speak the language. If there was misunderstanding or conflict, people called on me. The last night, we performed at a refugee camp in Hungary. There was this couple, they were in their sixties. They came to see us dance. After the show, they danced with us until four o'clock in the morning, just to show us their heritage—the beauty amid the horror. Man, could they dance!
>
> All this is possible now. You know, I tried to kill myself 'cause the suffering was so far beyond my ability to manage. In the loss of my sanity, I didn't want to live anymore. I understand it, and have a lot of compassion for myself, but I wouldn't choose attempting again. I wouldn't recommend it. There are just too many other possibilities.

Robert felt the same way. Perhaps because of his youth and his limited experience, or the sense of pride he felt in his recovery, he is more severe than some in his judgment of the suicide option.

I'd never recommend it. It's just running away, because every time,
what really helped was counseling, having someone there for you
basically. I mean, if you have problems, there's lot of ways to deal
with them. For me, there's always something I haven't thought of,
some tricky maneuver that the counselor will know. It's when you
stuff your feelings and don't deal with them that they get worse.
They always get bigger. Sometimes they get violent.

There's always help. It doesn't have to be a psychiatrist. It could
be a friend. And it doesn't take much. I mean, if someone said to
me, "I know you're having a hard time with your parents, but I
care about you—come stay at my place for a few weeks and work
things out," I'm pretty sure I would have said okay.

The answer to my question was more complex for some. Although I have intentionally decided to leave the question of rational
suicide for later research, it naturally and understandably arises
here. Madeline responded with a political conviction: "Ultimately,
people have the right to decide about their lives and their death. It's
their choice, and it's really hard to judge from the outside." She
acknowledges that she has contemplated suicide as a possible response to failing health or loss of her faculties.

My father apparently had Alzheimer's. He had it for years. I
wouldn't want to put anyone through that. In that sense, if I have
any say, and my children all have instructions about what I
want—whether they'll do it or not, I don't know—I would want to
end my life.

But I would also say to anyone going through what I was caught
in, "Don't try to hide it. Be open about it and try to get help from
your friends." And I would tell the friends, "Don't ignore it. Don't
brush it under the rug. Let them talk about it."

Almost fifteen years after his attempt, Mark was paralyzed from
the waist down in a fall while on vacation with his fiancée. The event

did not revive past inclinations toward suicide. Instead, it galvanized
his resolve to continue on.

> I once thought, as I was going to the school of hard knocks, that
> graduation would be my suicide. That was always looming ahead
> of me and that was what I had as my clear goal. I guess I passed
> that graduation, and now I'm on my post-doctorate degree. I now
> know that suicide's not what my goal is.

Mark continues to teach at the college. In addition, he has
become an authority on nutrition, and in particular, on vegetarian-
ism. He has written several books and pamphlets, and is invited to
speak at conferences throughout the United States.

> My major motivation for being a vegetarian was ethical—not
> wanting to kill animals. I feel that no one has the right to take any
> life but one's own. And so, if the only life you have the right to take
> is your own, then I might as well take advantage of that one life.

An in-depth knowledge of nutrition and its relation to a healthy
life-style is Mark's offering to humankind, and he's thrilled when
lecture halls are full and people become inspired by what he tells
them. His life at the present time is rich and fulfilling, and he offers
his expertise happily for all who want to hear, flavoring it with his
humor and wit. But the pursuit of optimal health plays a sobering
role in his life as well. When Mark imagines the future of his body,
serious questions arise.

> Right now, I'm still very healthy. I don't get pressure sores, or the
> UTIs [urinary-tract infections] that everybody gets who's para-
> plegic. None of the complications. Right now, I am the healthiest
> paraplegic alive! There is definitely the possibility, though, that
> after some years, ten or fifteen maybe, my kidneys will begin to
> break down with the increased pressure.

But when that day comes, I've decided not to go on dialysis, and I know I don't want tons of pharmaceuticals. Ever since I took all those aspirin, I've never taken drugs again, except for the week in the hospital after the fall. If a major health crisis comes, I think it will be time for me to end my life. My father was recently in the hospital, near death. I was thinking, "What a terrible place to die, in a hospital room." I'd prefer to die in the woods. That is my decision. I'm at peace with it.

For some, like Ian, the suicide attempt functioned as a wake-up call. In the absence of his willingness to seek help and support, Ian's attempt launched a flare too bright to ignore. Ian wrestles to reconcile the positive outcome with such a self-destructive method.

I don't recommend it. I mean, I don't want anybody to try and take their own life, but I feel that for me, if I hadn't have done that, I couldn't have gotten to where I am now. There was such a strong sense of power and control over my own life during the attempt. It was the birth of that. If that's what it takes, I hope others are as unsuccessful as I was. I hope they bought a Ford!

When last heard from, Jason was in New Mexico, forging a new relationship with his family, playing music with friends, and continuing to learn the art of video documentary that he had studied at the group home. Before he left, I asked him this question. As always, Jason was ready to offer both his personal reflections and some sociological insights. Consistently I've been impressed by the willingness of Jason and other teenagers to offer their unedited opinions about this difficult subject.

Suicide is such a taboo thing, in terms of talking about it. It shouldn't be. It should be brought out in the open. Then people can acknowledge and say, "Yeah, sometimes I feel like that." But they don't, because if they say anything they fear, "I'm gonna be labeled crazy." But many of us teenagers are not afraid to talk about it. You gotta talk about it, because it's a reality. You know, it's the silent ones that go off and do it.

I wish people could hear this. I know it's a freaky little story, but damn, I wish I had had someone to say these things to me. It would've given me new insight. It might not have changed everything, but—. As for me, I don't have too many qualms about dying. I figure death will take me when it takes me. Any day is a good day to die. But no day is a good one to take your life.

Although all the recoveries chronicled here are unique and remarkable, Ruth's is especially so. She has come so far from apparently so little. When we first met, she was having a hard time and was still quite depressed. The breakthroughs described above happened shortly thereafter, and when we next spoke, almost a year later, Ruth had graduated from her residency program in psychiatry and was now an attending physician. She works at a city methadone division and acts as its medical liaison with area hospitals. She supervises younger medical interns and residents and offers psychotherapy to individuals and couples. She also conducts seminars to ob-gyn residents on their attitudes and behaviors toward drug-addicted mothers and their families. When we recently spoke, I was more than a little surprised to hear how much life there was in her voice.

"It's no longer an option," Ruth answered, almost before I could finish posing the question.

My other attempts used to terrorize everyone else. My last attempt really terrified me! This was very scary. In making the commitment to live for the next three years, no matter what, I realize that I can keep focusing on how awful I feel, or I can give life a chance. I've been looking out the back window for so long.

Ruth had pursued her care with great perseverance. Intelligent and insightful, she arrived at the point where she knew all the reasons for her torment. The time had come for her to make a courageous decision. Regardless of the difficulty, she would not attempt again. The results were startling. Freed from the obsession of suicide, her mind could now entertain the many other possibilities before her. Each possibility, in turn, gave rise to others, many of which Ruth never imagined. She has become an inspired young physician with a deep social conscience, and her world contains people with whom she can openly share her love and caring. After much hard work and heartache, Ruth has finally given birth to the future.

I have never been this at peace with myself. When I feel depressed sometimes, late at night, and ask myself, "Why am I living?", I answer, "'Cause you can't kill yourself." Then I tell myself, "You'll feel different tomorrow . . . feelings don't last." And it's true! The choice to commit suicide just isn't attractive anymore.

Just look at how my life has changed so far, and this is just the first year of my promise. I know terrible things could happen in the future, but in a way, I want to see it. I want to see all of it now. I'm truly looking forward to what happens next.

Selected Bibliography for
Personal Healing and
General Interest

Alexander, Victoria. *Words I Never Thought to Speak: Stories of Life in the Wake of Suicide* (Lexington Books/Maxwell Macmillan: New York, 1991)

Alvarez, A., *The Savage God: A Study of Suicide* (Random House: New York, 1971)

Bass, E., and Davis, L., *The Courage to Heal: A Guide for Women Survivors of Sexual Abuse* (Harper & Row Publishers: New York, 1988)

Colt, George, H., *The Enigma of Suicide* (Summit Books: New York, 1991)

Conroy, David L., *Out of the Nightmare: Recovery from Depression and Suicidal Pain* (New Liberty Press: New York, 1991)

Dunne, E., Dunne-Maxim, K., and McIntosh, J. (eds.), *Suicide and Its Aftermath* (W. W. Norton: New York 1987)

Gallagher, Ed., *Will I Live Another Day Before I Die? Thoughts on Suicide and Life* (Foundation of Thanatology: New York, 1989)

Godwin, Gail, *A Southern Family* (Morrow: New York, 1987)

Grollman, E. A., *Suicide: Prevention, Intervention, Postvention* (Beacon Press: Boston, 1988)

Joan, Polly, *Preventing Teenage Suicide: The Living Alternative Handbook* (Human Sciences Press: New York, 1986)

Kushner, Howard I., *American Suicide: A Psychocultural Exploration* (Rutgers University Press: New Brunswick, NJ, 1991)

Lester, D., *Questions and Answers About Suicide* (Thomas: Springfield, Illinois, 1987)

Levine, Stephen, *A Gradual Awakening* (Anchor Press/Doubleday: New York, 1979)

Lifton, Robert Jay, *The Broken Connection* (Simon & Schuster: New York, 1979)

———, *The Future of Immortality and Other Essays for a Nuclear Age* (Basic Books: New York, 1987)

Moffat, Mary Jane, Ed., *In the Midst of Winter: Selections from the Literature of Mourning* (Vintage Books/Random House: New York, 1992)

Muller, Wayne, *Legacy of the Heart: The Spiritual Advantages of a Painful Childhood* (Simon & Schuster: New York, 1992)

Osgood, N., *Suicide in Later Life: Recognizing the Warning Signs* (Lexington Books: New York, 1992)

Richman, J., *Preventing Elderly Suicide: Overcoming Personal Despair, Professional Neglect, and Social Bias* (Springer Publishing: New York, 1993)

Styron, William, *Darkness Visible* (Vintage Books/Random House: New York, 1990)

Selected Clinical Bibliography

Berman, A. L., and Jobes, D. A., *Adolescent Suicide: Assessment and Intervention* (American Psychological Association: Washington D.C., 1991)

Evans, G., and Faberow, N., *The Encyclopedia of Suicide* (Facts on File: New York, 1988)

Freud, S., "Mourning and Melancholia," in *A General Selection from the Works of Sigmund Freud* (Doubleday/Anchor: New York, 1957). Originally published in 1917.

Hillman, James, *Suicide and the Soul* (Spring Publications: Dallas, Texas, 1976)

Leenaars, A., Maris, R., McIntosh, J., and Richman, J. (Eds.), *Suicide and the Older Adult* (Guilford Press: New York, 1992)

Leenaars, A., (Ed.), *Suicidology: Essays in Honor of Edwin S. Schneidman* (J. Aronson: Northvale, New Jersey, 1993)

Lester, D., *Psychotherapy for Suicidal Clients* (Thomas: Springfield, Illinois, 1991)

Maltsberger, J., *Suicide Risk: The Formulation of Clinical Judgment* (NYU Press: New York, 1986)

Maris, R., Berman, A. L., Maltsberger, J. T., and Yufit, R. (Eds.), *Assessment and Prediction of Suicide* (Guilford Press: New York, 1992)

Pfeffer, Cynthia, *The Suicidal Child* (Guilford Press: New York, 1986)

Richman, J., *Family Therapy for Suicidal People* (Springer: New York, 1986)

Schneidman, Edwin S., *Definition of Suicide* (John Wiley & Sons: New York, 1985)

————, *Suicide as Psychache: A Clinical Approach to Self-Destructive Behavior* (Aronson: Northvale, New Jersey, 1993)

Stillon, J. M., McDowell, E. E., and May, J. H., *Suicide Across the Life-Span: Premature Exits* (Hemisphere Publishing Corp: New York, 1989)

Suicide and Life-Threatening Behavior, Journal of the American Association of Suicidology, (Guilford Press: New York, 1970–).

Some Facts About
Suicide in the USA

Facts Based on Official Statistics

- Currently there are slightly more than 30,000 suicides annually (83 suicides per day; or 1 suicide every 17 minutes), with 12 of every 100,000 Americans killing themselves.
- Suicide rates in the USA can best be characterized as mostly stable over time with a slight tendency toward an increase.
- Rates of suicide are highest in the western regions, with the Mountain States highest.
- Suicide is the eighth leading cause of death.
- Males commit suicide at rates and numbers of suicides three to four times those of females.
- Firearms are currently the most often utilized method of suicide by essentially all groups (e.g., males, females, young, old, white, nonwhite) and the rates are increasing.
- Suicide rates have traditionally decreased in times of wars and increased in times of economic crises.
- Spring and Mondays consistently rank highest in the number of suicides.
- Suicide rates are highest among the divorced and widowed and lowest among the married.
- Rates of suicide are highest among the older adult population above age 65.
- Elderly adults have rates of suicide more than 50% higher than the nation as a whole and the young (age 15–24).

- Youth (15–24 years of age) suicide rates increased more than 200% from the 1950s to the late 1970s. Following the late 1970s the rates for youth have remained stable or slightly lower, although current rates are also approximately 200% higher than in the 1950s.
- Suicide ranks third as a cause of death among young (15–24-year-old) Americans, behind accidents and homicide.
- White suicide rates are approximately twice those of nonwhites as a whole.
- Native Americans (American Indians) are the racial/ethnic group with the highest suicide rates overall, but great tribal group differences exist.
- Blacks and Hispanics exhibit lower risk of suicide than in the moderate (middle) range when ranked among the other reporting nations of the world.

Facts Based on Research Findings

- Although there are no official statistics on attempted (i.e., nonfatal actions) suicide, it is generally estimated that there are at least 8 to 20 attempts for each death by suicide.
- Risk of attempted suicide is greatest among females and the young. Females have generally been found to make 3 to 4 times as many attempts as males. Estimate of the ratio of young attempted suicides to suicidal deaths have generally ranged between 100 to 1 and 200 to 1.
- Mental health diagnoses are generally associated with higher risk of suicide. Groups/diagnoses at particular risk are the depressed, schizophrenics, alcoholics, and those with panic disorder.
- Feelings of hopelessness (e.g., "there are no solutions to my problem") are found to be more predictive of suicide risk than diagnoses of depression per se.
- The socially isolated are generally found to be at high risk for suicide.
- The vast majority of those who are suicidal display clues and warning signs.

Other Issues

- One conservative estimate is that at least 3.5 million Americans today are survivors of a loved one's suicide.

For more information, please contact:
American Association of Suicidology
2459 South Ash
Denver, CO 80222
303-692-0985

Resources

Alive to Thrive, 60 Union Avenue #2BB, New Rochelle, New York 10801, 914-576-0355. Consulting to educational institutes, public and private schools, and law enforcement agencies about suicide prevention, substance abuse prevention, disability awareness, and self-esteem.

American Association of Suicidology, 2459 South Ash, Denver, CO 80222, 303-692-0985. A national informational resource for literature, media, conferences, community suicide-prevention centers, and support groups.

There are local support groups, prevention and education centers in most towns and cities throughout the United States and Europe. Consult your telephone directory or call the American Association of Suicidology.

Index